HUMAN RIGHTS STANDARD FOR RIGHT TO HEALTH

About the Author

Aruna Kumar Malik, is currently working as a Assistant Professor of Political Science, Gujarat National Law University, Gandhinagar. He is also associated with several research Institutions and Universities in India and abroad.

Human Rights Standard for Right to Health

Aruna Kumar Malik

CONCEPT PUBLISHING COMPANY PVT. LTD.
NEW DELHI-110 059

ISBN-13 : 978-81-8069-854-5

First Published 2012

Published and Printed by

Concept Publishing Company Pvt. Ltd.
A/15-16, Commercial Block, Mohan Garden
New Delhi-110059 (India)
T: 25351460, 25351794, *F*: 091-11-25357109
E: publishing@conceptpub.com W: www.conceptpub.com
Editorial Office: H-13, Bali Nagar, New Delhi-110 015, India.

Cataloging in Publication Data--*Courtesy:* D.K. Agencies (P) Ltd. <docinfo@dkagencies.com>

Malik, Aruna Kumar.
Human rights standard for right to health / Aruna Kumar Malik.
p. cm.
Includes bibliographical references (p.) and index.
ISBN 9788180698545

1. Right to health—India—Balasore (District) 2. Medical economics—India Balasore (District) I. Title.

DDC 362.10954133 23

Preface

According to a standard definition, human rights are those rights one has by virtue of being human. This definition suggests that human rights belong to every human being in every human society: all human beings have them, equally and in equal measure. Implied in one's humanity, human rights are generally presented as being inalienable and imprescriptible—they cannot be transferred, forfeited, or waived. Many people, especially but not exclusively in the West, believe that human rights exist irrespective of social recognition, although they often acknowledge that the plurality of religious traditions and value systems from which they can be derived make their foundation controversial. For those who believe in human rights, the problem of their source is rarely considered an obstacle to asserting them. From their point of view, what is important is that human rights are evident.

This book starts with examine and analyze the effectiveness of the processes, the role of different factors within those processes, and also seeks to identify possible new avenues in standard setting. It is also an attempt to understand the processes involved in standard setting and draws lessons through the examination of different standards and their contexts. It also looks at fresh thinking of human rights experts who seek to initiate or advocate for new human rights standards and thinking or approach of officials engaged in intergovernmental and governmental organizations. The overall pursuit is to examine the process of relevance of standard setting in the heights discourse with specific focus on right to health. Therefore, human rights should be imperative in delivery of care and implementation of public-health programmes.

Three main relations between health and human rights exist: the positive and negative effects on health of promotion, neglect, or violation of human rights; the effect of health on the delivery of human rights; and the effects of public-health policies and programmes on human rights. Despite the advances in the study and advocacy of health and human rights, we still do not fully understand the nature of these relationships, how they interact, or their value to medicine and public-health practice. In this article we address the public health aspects of these relations, and highlight where further research and action are needed.

A brief history of health and human rights

Since the Nuremberg trials and the creation of the UN more than 50 years ago, interest in the association between health and human rights has grown. Until the beginning of the AIDS epidemic in the 1980s and the end of the Cold War, these two issues evolved along parallel but distinctly separate tracks, perhaps as a consequence of the state-centric (i.e, greater political concern for general state and public interests than for specific individuals or communities) view of the world that prevailed in the second half of the 20th century. However, governments have a responsibility both to deliver essential health and social services and to enable people and their families to achieve better health by respecting human rights.

The idea of health and human rights as a subject of study is fairly new, and we need to recognise the different ways in which advances in health and human rights can be achieved. Human rights feature in many different ways in the health work of international non-governmental organisations, governments, civil society groups, and individuals. These ways can be broadly categorized as advocacy, application of legal standards, and programming (including service delivery). Some stakeholders use one approach; others use a combination in their work. We use standard setting as the main theme to show the effectiveness of right to health approach, although examples in neglected diseases, or other serious health issues could effectively serve as illustrations.

The process of standard setting at the international level suggests complexity, negotiation, and consensus building. It also calls into play competing national interests, cultures, and ideologies. As if these aspects were not enough, more difficult matters of the asymmetry of power, the ability to participate effectively in the process, and the capacity to own both the process and the product come into play. Unpacking process, therefore, is a tricky and pivotal question. For it is quite often the case that control over the process makes the final outcome predictable and, sometimes, moot. Where complex and competing players exist, the process becomes as essential as the product itself. Thus, questions must be asked about fairness, transparency, ownership, democracy, and participation in any probing discussion of process.

The present book consists of seven chapters. The first chapter includes purpose of the study, ranging from statement of the problem, selection of field site, review of literature, review of health policies in post-independent India, rationale, objectives, methods of analysis, sources of the data, chapter schemes of the thesis, limitations of the study.

The second chapter starts with an introductory note on setting human rights standards which includes the importance of the study. This introductory note introduces various facets of the study. It deals with an understanding health from human rights perspective, which covers the theoretical and philosophical foundations of the book. It broadly captures standard setting philosophy and its origin of the study, which gives the base to the present work.

The third chapter deals with the concepts, scope, definition and the sources of international human rights law, international treaties, customary international law, implementing the international right to health.

The fourth chapter covers the human rights standards in health: Indian scenario, delivery of health services in the public sector, organizational structure of the public health delivery system, goal-setting and strategic interventions, an overview of the evolution of the health system in India and peoples' perceptions and responses to right to health. It also covers health as human right in India: constitutional and legal dimensions, constitutional mandate to the state, health as right to life, states' obligation to preserve life, role of courts in realization of right to health and peoples' perceptions and their responses towards right to health.

The fifth chapter deals with the health care delivery in Orissa, genesis of health sector reforms in Orissa, Orissa health system development and public-private partnership, process of decentralization, formation of district health committee and district overview. It also captures cases which stand as testimony to provide evidence that health as human rights.

The sixth chapter captures the basic information of the Balasore district in Orissa in the form of profile of the district. It includes statistical data and hospital administration, institutional arrangement, which is reference point to enter into rights discourse.

The last chapter attempts to provide summary. It covers reclaiming health an unfolding struggle for right to health. It also includes some suggestive measures for the better access to health for weaker sections of the society.

Aruna Kumar Malik

Acknowledgements

This form of formal acknowledgements should not be regarded merely as a thanks note, it is the best portrayal I could attempt of my respect and love for those few who have been indispensable in accomplishing this work. In the course of writing this book, I received assistance, advice and encouragement from a variety of sources.

It is true that words are not always capable and powerful carriers of the subtleties and manner of emotions, but if the feeling is true the intensity is felt on the other end. I place on record my everlasting gratitude and reverence to Prof. G. Haragopal and Prof. G. Sudarshanam for their guidance, support and encouragement. Without their accessibility and academic stimulation they generated, to this book would not have taken this shape. Their richness, as academicians and as human beings has not only left an indomitable influence on my understanding of human rights but also has influenced me to strive for a meaningful life. I claim with pride that I cannot think of a better activist at this stage.

I also thank Mr. Debendra Kumar Malik (APD, DRDA, Balasore), and Prabodha Kumar Malik for their inspiration and suggestions. While doing research in Bedipur Hospital, on the health system of Orissa, I was fortunate in having the talented assistance from persons like Ashes, Prabodha.

Indira Gandhi Memorial Library and Computer Centre, University of Hyderabad, CESS Library, NIRD Library, IGIDR Library system proved an extraordinary source of knowledgeable and research oriented books, journals and other documents which are related to my topic.

Other individuals also contributed to this work with their valuable suggestions and constructive criticism. I thank them all. I should also like to note the generous financial assistance provided by the University of Hyderabad through University Fellowship Scheme. This fellowship supported me to do in-depth and intensive study on this topic.

Ultimately, however, it was not professional or institutional assistance, but rather the support, encouragement and patience of my family that contributed most to this enterprise. I express my gratitude to my parents who constantly encouraged me to go for higher education though they are illiterate. While I sit for reading my brothers are constant source of inspiration because they have taken it as a challenge to give me higher education which they could not have. I do not have words to express my feelings to them who have dedicated their entire life for their younger brother which is truly important in the world. My uncle and brother-in-law and also the members of my family served as a sounding board and critic of many of these pages and to them I offer my thanks for accepting in good spirit the many intuitions into our lives caused by this work.

Typing service somehow manageable to produce a virtually flawless product, meet the deadline and remain thoroughly pleasant.

Any shortcoming found in this book is completely mine.

Contents

List of Tables

Glossary

Body Mass Index (BMI) is the ratio of weight (in kg) to height (in metre) squared, i.e. weight/(height).

Case Fatality Rate (CFR) for a particular disease is the number of deaths due to that disease as per cent of total number of persons affected by it, for a given period of time, usually computed for a period of one year.

Coefficient of Variation (CV) is a measure of relative variability and is expressed as the ratio of standard deviation of a variable to its mean value multiplied by 100.

Crude Birth Rate (CBR) is the number of births per 1000 population. The CBR for a single year is usually calculated as the number of live births during a year divided by the estimated mid-year population and multiplied by 1000.

Chronic Energy Deficiency (CED) is defined in terms of the value of Body Mass Index (see above). A person is said to be having CED if his/her Body Mass Index is less than 16 kg/m^2, that is, weight (in kg) per unit height (in metre) squared.

Crude Death Rate (CDR) is the number of deaths per 1000 population. The CDR for a single year is calculated as the number of deaths during that year divided by the estimated mid-year population and multiplied by 1000.

Education Deprivation Index (EDI) is the sum of percentage of out-of-school children in the 6–14 years age group and adult illiteracy in 15+ age group population.

Gross Enrolment Ratio (GER) is the population of a particular age group enrolled in schools as per cent of total population in that age group. When there is no adjustment for overage and underage population enrolled in a particular age group, it is referred to as GER, while it is called as net enrolment ratio (NER) when overage and underage population are excluded.

Infant Mortality Rate (IMR) is the number of deaths of infants under one year of age for every 1000 live births, usually computed for a period of one year.

Life Expectancy at Birth (LEB) is the number of years expected to be lived at the time of birth, given the current mortality trends.

Maternal Mortality Rate (MMR) is the number of deaths of women during pregnancy or childbirth per 1,00,000 live births.

Neonatal Mortality Rate (NNMR) is the number of deaths of infants before 28 days of life per 1000 live births, usually computed for a period of one year.

Perinatal Mortality Rate (PNMR) is the number of infant deaths during the first week since birth (as well as still births and foetal deaths beyond 28 weeks of pregnancy) per 1000 live births, usually computed for a period of one year.

Poverty Gap (PG) is defined as the per cent difference between the poverty line (see below) income/consumption expenditure and the average income/consumption expenditure of those below the poverty line. Thus, it measures the depth and intensity of poverty.

Poverty Line (PL) is normatively defined as the level of monthly per capita consumption required to enable a minimum calorie intake (usually expressed as per capita per day) by an individual to lead a normal life.

Poverty Ratio (PR) is the per cent of population below the poverty line (see above), for a point in time. This is also referred to as the Head Count Ratio.

Sex Ratio is the number of females per thousand males.

Slide Positive Rate is the number of malaria positive blood samples as per cent of total number of blood samples examined.

Squared Poverty Gap (SPG) is a measure of the severity of poverty as it takes into account, in addition to the poverty gap (see above), the distribution of the poor below the poverty line around the average income/expenditure of the poor.

Undernutrition is defined in terms of the value of Body Mass Index (see above). A person is said to be undernourished if his/her BMI is less than 18 kg/m^2.

Hard Law is composed of conventions, covenants and protocols that are binding on states which have ratified, accepted or acceded to them.

Soft Law includes declarations, principles, plans of action and guidelines. It is often said that these documents are not legally binding because states have not formally agreed to be bound by the provisions they contain. Nevertheless, they can have considerable political and legal weight.

Abbreviations

ADMO	Additional District Medical Officer (Public Health)
AIDS	Acquired Immune Deficiency Syndrome
AH	Area Hospital
ANC	Ante Natal Care
ANM	Auxiliary Nurse Midwife
ARV	Anti Rabies Vaccine
AWW	Anganwadi Worker
BEOC	Basic Emergency Obstetric Care
BMW	Bio Medical Waste
CDMO	Chief District Medical Officer
CEOC	Comprehensive Emergency Obstetric Care
CHC	Community Health Centre
CME	Continuing Medical Education
CPR	Contraceptive Prevalence Rate/Couple Protection Rate
D & C	Rules—Drugs and Cosmetics Rules
DCG	Drug Controller General
DDC	Drug Distribution Centre
DFID	Department For International Development (United Kingdom)
DIMIS	Drug Inventory Management Information Systems
DMET	Director of Medical Education and Training
EDL	Essential Drug List
EOC	Emergency Obstetric Care

FLE	Family Life Education
FP	Family Planning
FRU	First Referral Unit
GMP	Good Manufacturing Practice
GoI	Government of India
GoO	Government of Orissa
GSDP	Gross State Domestic Product
HIV	Human Immunodeficiency Virus
HMIS	Health Management Information System
HRD	Human Resource Development
ibid.	Ion beam induced deposition
IAP	Indian Association of Paediatricians
ICDS	Integrated Child Development Scheme
ICMR	Indian Council of Medical Research
ICPD	International Conference on Population and Development
IEC	Information, Education and Communication
IMA	Indian Medical Association
IMR	Infant Mortality Rate
IQ	Intelligence Quotient
ISDN	Integrated Services Digital Network
ISM & H	Indian Systems of Medicine and Homeopathy
LBW	Low Birth Weight
MCI	Medical Council of India
MDSS	Multi Disease Surveillance System
MIS	Management Information System
MMR	Maternal Mortality Ratio
MO	Medical Officer
MoHFW	Ministry of Health and Family Welfare
MPHS (M)	Multi-purpose Health Supervisor – Male
MTP	Medical Termination of Pregnancy
NFHS	National Family Health Survey
NGOs	Non-Governmental Organizations

NPP	National Population Policy
NSQ	Not of Standard Quality
NSSO	National Sample Survey Organization
OFA	Obstetric First Aid
OHFWRP	Orissa Health and Family Welfare Reform Project
OHSDP	Orissa Health Systems Development Project
Op.cit.	Opus citatum/opere citato
OOP	Out of Pocket (expenditure)
OPD	Out Patient Department
IPD	In Patient Department
OVHA	Orissa Health Sector Development Project
PFA Act	Prevention of Food Adulteration Act
PG	Post Graduate
PHC	Primary Health Centre
PHC	Primary Health Care
PHC (N)	Primary Health Centre (New)
PF	Plasmodium Falciparum
PLA	Participatory Learning Exercise
PMU	Project Management Unit
PRI	Panchayati Raj Institution
PSPU	Policy and Strategic Planning Unit
PT	Presumptive Treatment
PWD	Public Works Department
R & D	Research and Development
RCH	Reproductive and Child Health Programme
RDD	Rural Development Department
RTI	Reproductive Tract Infection
RWSS	Rural Water Supply and Sanitation Department
SDMU	State Drug Medicinal Unit
SDPHC	Sector (Single Doctor) Primary Health Centre
SDTRL	State Drug Testing and Research Laboratory

SHG	Self Help Group
SIHFW	State Institute of Health and Family Welfare
SRS	Sample Registration Scheme
STD	Sexually Transmitted Disease
STG	Standard Treatment Guidelines
STI	Sexually Transmitted Infection
TB	Tuberculosis
TBA	Traditional Birth Attendant
TFA	Target Free Approach
TT	Tetanus Toxoid
UG	Undergraduate
UNDP	United Nations Development Programme
UNFPA	United Nations Family Planning Association
UNICEF	United Nations International Children's Emergency Fund
W & CD	Women and Child Development Department
WHO	World Health Organization
WMT	Waste Management Team
ZSS	Zilla Swasthya Samitee

1

Scope and Methodology

Introduction

Health is a critical investment for human resource development and poverty alleviation in India. Public policy for health has been based on an implicit assumption of health care as a basic right which people should not be denied access to as they are not able to pay. Yet, the resources provided by the Government to achieve better health status through the provision of high priority primary health care services for the vast majority of Indians has been inadequate. Goals have been achieved only to a limited extent, despite the fact that India spends both the private and public sector at higher percentage of its GDP on health care in comparison to other Asian countries that have achieved greater improvements in the health status of its peoples. If we see current level of public health expenditure in India, especially spending on preventive and promotive primary health care services, is inadequate and has not kept pace with the growing demands being made upon the system. If the Government is to achieve its stated objectives, which are reasonable and achievable, reorienting priorities within the health sector is critical. The challenge is twofold in nature that a strategy needs to be developed which would encourage the private sector to contribute more mobilization of resources to take preventive measures and promote health care services and the second challenge is that the public sector needs more investment and also it needs to regulate and monitor private care provision.

Status of Health Standards in India: Review of Literature

The health services of India affect the lives of some 800 million people in one of the world's poorest countries. This alone would make it a worthy subject for study, but surprisingly there are no good accounts of the Indian health system and human rights in the literature on comparative health systems or on human rights health systems of individual states or regions. Far less is known about health care provision and human right in India.

The present research is explorative in nature. Not many research studies have been undertaken on assessing human rights and health status in Orissa state from the perspective of the standards. This is also to see the ground realities to judge the dimensions that the standard setting exercise has been debating for more than six decades. The recent studies done in Orissa and all-over India have been reviewed in this part of the research work.

N.D. Kamble in his work "Rural Health"[1] has explored the fact that the health service provided by the state machinery in rural areas is very low compared to the standards in urban areas. He has also supported his research work with statistical data which authenticate his claim that out of the total number of primary health centres or clinics provided to a district by the state, less than 37 per cent are found in rural areas and among the available primary health centres more than 70 per cent are dysfunctional due to lack of facility like electricity, supply of medical peripherals as also the absence of doctors and the support staff. He also states that the type of treatment received by the rural masses is dependent upon their socio-economic status.

His research on morbidity and mortality rate in rural areas is also interesting, which he has supported through data. He states that while the morbidity rate in rural areas is many times higher than the urban, the mortality rate due to lack of proper knowledge and medical attention is at least double compared to the mortality rate in urban areas.

Another study on rural health by Stuart Gillespie, this is a case study of malnutrition and ill-health among South Indian tribals.[2] He claims that mortality rate in tribal areas are influenced by two facts: malnutrition and inaccessibility to medical facility.

Abhijit Banerjee, Angus Deaton, Esther Duflo (Feb. 28-March 5, 2004) study on *"Health Care Delivery in Rural Rajasthan"*, (EPW) point out that the delivery of health care and health status is very low, largely poor population of the region. The study shows that the quality of public service is extremely poor and that unqualified private providers account for the bulk of health care provision. The low quality of public facilities has also had an adverse influence on the people's health. In an environment where people's expectations of health care providers seem to be generally low; the state has to take up the task of being the provider or regulator.

T.K. Roy, Sumati Kulkarni, Y. Vaidehi, in a survey on *"Social Inequalities in Health and Nutrition in Selected States"*(Feb. 14-20, 2004 EPW) collected information on variety of aspects relating to fertility, family planning practice, mortality, utilization of maternal and child health care services, nutrition and health. Apart from this, it also gives data on basic socio-economic characteristics of household. Analysis of differential between four major groups in Indian society, presented in this work, brought out effect of social stratification on utilization of health care programmes and nutritional status. It clearly brings out that differentials between SCs, STs, OBCs, and 'others' category; health is far from any standards that we discussed earlier. Orissa health status shows very high inequality in socio-economic variable and Assam shows the least inequality.

Assam, West Bengal and Orissa, are at different stages of socio-economic development and demographic transition. The situation is relatively better in West Bengal. Orissa has done better in fertility reduction than many other states, but it is one of the poorest states in India on the criterion of mortality, particularly infant and child mortality which is substantially high in this state.

Purna Chandra Upadhyaya, in his Article "Poverty and Health Conditions of the Nats of Mirzapur" points out that the sickness makes poor when they are unable to meet their needs. The health seeking behaviour of the Nats (Nats is a community) is interesting because there are still many traditional healers in the community and these traditional healers have practiced traditional healing system over a long time. Yet the Nats like many others do seek help from modern medical system as well, especially when they feel that traditional methods are not proving effective in curing the ailments. At that moment they feel to go to modern hospital but these modern hospitals in terms of facilities are far from satisfactory.

The health care facilities are provided in each of the block of Mirzapur district, but there are only four hospitals, dispensaries of PHC per 1,00,000 population. The number of beds does not exceed more than 10 per 1,00,000 population and it is as low as 2.2 beds per 1,00,000 population. It does not need any more evidence about the availability and accessibility of doctors, nurses, medicines, etc. in government run health institutions.

Walsh and Warren (1979) explain that the new economic and political climate finally led health policy-makers to reassess the comprehensive PHC strategy. It began gaining ground that the PHC strategy was too idealistic and given the financial and practical constraints, government would be better advised to select and target diseases on the basis of prevalence, morbidity, mortality and feasibility of including efficacy and cost. This new approach, which came to be defining as selective primary health care, its state responsibility to take care of them those who are sick and old aged and to give them timely help in terms of medical treatment and free service.

The study conducted by V.B. Annigeri on "District health accounts: An empirical investigation" (2003, May 12-13), shows in different perspectives like funding agencies on health sector, public and private partnership hospitals, households income levels, structure of the health administration. Even he takes a look at the profile of household's survey. About 13 per cent of households belong to scheduled caste and 5 per cent of households belong to scheduled tribe. Other backward communities constitute about 33 per cent; a majority of the households have extremely low income per month. For example, about 40 per cent of the households are earning less than Rs. 1,400 per month and 28 per cent income between Rs. 1,400 to 2,500, which affects to meet their health expenditure. When they are suffering any kinds of diseases, they borrow money from other, which harm them in future; moneylender takes more interest and exploits suffering people. In this regard governmental hospitals need to take initiative for curing the disease and to access primary health centre with an efficient doctor and also other medical staff.

Another study was conducted by Vimal Balasubrahmanyan. Her work on "Women and Burden of Child Health"[3] reflects some of the common norms of the society. Studies have shown that various societal constraints, inaccessibility of health clinics, inconvenient clinic timings and indifference or just absence of health personnel have resulted in low immunization levels even when mothers have been aware of the need for it. She points out that health policy is not realized on ground level. It is violating the human rights in general and right to health in particular.

The interesting study jointly carried out by UNICEF and WHO argued that "owing to the high cost of sophisticated equipment and other requirements, it tends to benefit minority of the population, a substantial share of limited resources……curative services and more generally, personal services, tend to receive undue emphasis….. In many developing countries over half the national health budget is spent on health care in urban areas, but it does not bring out the picture of rural areas."[4]

The study conducted by R. Cassen (1978) in his work "India: population, economy, society"[5], argued that 'India's health system shares several features of the pattern of health services in other developing countries (including) a large share of health budgets devoted to major hospitals in urban centres and a consequent relative neglect of the rural health infrastructure.'

Amartya Sen, in his article "Objectivity, Health and Policy", shows the relationship between income and access to health care, and showed a worsening of inequalities to access in health care. Sen also suggests that the need for objectivity in health assessment, he brought out two significant distinct exercises: (a) in critically appraising the health status of the people and (b) in scrutinizing policy issues in promoting good health. The demands of objectivity are quite exacting in both the exercises. He also highlighted that the first problem, that of objectivity in appraising health status. This appraisal can run into problems with the subjectivity of perceptions. In his work he discussed two rather distinct aspects of the need for objectivity in assessing health status and policy. First, as far as health conditions are concerned, self-perception proves to be a rather unreliable guide to the prevalence of illness and ill health, but, at the same time, provides important clues to the persistence of these deprivations. Second, on the question of policy assessment, it is important to go beyond simple 'pro' and 'anti' attitudes about the respective roles of markets and of governments actions.

Other aspects of health services have been vigorously attacked by Indian commentators; indeed, it is hard to find anyone with a good word to say about them. Only government and official publications dwell on the positive side of the medical history since 1947. One critical source summarizes the strengths of the Indian health system as follows: "It is obvious that there are several achievements to our credit, such as reduction in mortality rates or increase in expectancy of life at birth; the expansion of medical research and education; the expansion of health care services including especially the establishment of the primary health centres; the excellence of our specialized institutions; the control of communicable diseases like smallpox, cholera, plague and malaria; the provision of MCH services on a large scale; the initiation of a family planning programme; and the investment of far larger funds than at any time in the past."[6]

It then argues that the weaknesses of the system are greater still. However, as with many of the critical discussions the report does not develop a theoretical account of the mismatch between health needs and health services. The criticisms are specified in the following terms:

(a) Health services are not integrated with wider economic and social development;
(b) Virtually no impact has been made on basic aspects of disease prevention and health maintenance, such as nutrition and environmental sanitation;
(c) The most vulnerable social groups remain largely excluded from health services, whether vulnerability is indicated by poverty, age, sex, geographical isolation, or other factors such as occupation which increases the level of disease and illness.
(d) Health education is virtually non-existent; and
(e) The goal of participatory involvement remains a chimera.

In the words of the joint Indian Council for Medical Research-Indian Council for Social Science Research study "the imported and inappropriate model of health services is top-heavy, overcentralized, heavily curative in its approach, urban and elite oriented, costly and dependency creating. The serious shortcomings of the model cannot be cured by small tinkering or well-meant reforms."[7]

In developing its strategy and action plan to address inequalities and promote health and human rights, the state intends to focus more clearly upon the difficulties experienced by service users, patients, and included groups in terms of accessing health and health services. The reviews reflect different dimensions of human rights and health conditions of the people and their present status in terms of health service in the state. Some of the works represent the health care accessibility, affordability, quality, which are remote to the rural area. There are a number of constraints and hurdles which need to be addressed through human rights approach to reach the people. To know these problems and constraints one has to review the policies in general and health policies in particular.

Review of Health Policies in Post-Independent India

The context of health-policy making after 1947 is set by two major influences—the report of the Health Survey and

Development Committee, known by the name of its chair, Sir Joseph Bhore, and the activities of the Central Council of Health. The Bhore Committee went into the problem deeply and published four-volume report[8] which, in the tradition of British Committee reports, gave a detailed analysis of available data, evidence of expert witnesses, and recommendations. However, alternative proposals were also emanating from the Congress Party itself. Congress established a National Planning Committee (NPC) in 1938, under Nehru's prompting. Nehru's socialism was essentially Fabian and involved national planning for a mixed economy, but his more radical ideas were dimmed in the intense politicking of the first years after independence and his interest in the National Planning Commission was almost lost. The committee report on public health was shorter, less well argued and unorganized, and drew on far less detailed analysis of the existing situation than the Bhore Committee Report. Without support of secretariat or any political power within the Congress Party, the measures disappeared with very few traces. Thus, the Bhore report provided the framework for health strategy and continued to be an important part of the debate on health standards and strategy in India.

In many areas the two reports overlap and show their common reliance on a perspective on rural health which had been developed under the League of Nations Health Organisation and implemented in different degrees in Yugoslavia and Nationalist China. Both looked toward a socialized system of health services in which public health provisions dominate and eventually replace private medical practice. It is important to note that Bhore's phrasing was very similar to the Beveridge report, which foreshadowed the National Health Service in the United Kingdom that "no individual should be unable to secure adequate medical care because of inability to pay for it."[9] This statement is similar to Article 21 of the Constitution of India, when we refer to this article notes than we find it quite similar to the Bhore Committee Report which has subscribed this idea from the Beveridge report.

On the other side is overthrowing of colonial rule and rising aspirations of the liberated people, the establishment of democratic forms of government in some newly independent countries, the initiation of the cold war, and the formation of Non-Alignment Movement (NAM)—all these have been the major factors in impelling the new leaderships in these countries and the newly-formed international organisations to pay attention to their problems. International organisations, such as World Health Organisation (WHO) and the United Nations Children's Fund (UNICEF), along with bilateral agencies, came forward to help and improve the health status of the people in the needy countries.

The availability of the so-called silver bullets tempted these organisations to launch special 'vertical' or 'categorical' programmes against some major scourges such as malaria (DDT and synthetic antimalarials), tuberculosis (BCG vaccination), leprosy (dapsone), filariasis (hetrazan), and trachoma (aureomycin). It took them quite some time to realise that these vertical programmes were not only very expensive but also failed to provide the expected results. These programmes also hindered the growth of integrated health services. This led them first advocating the integration of health services, and then going to individual countries to promote country health planning and later, attempts to popularize country health programming. In the mid-1970s, WHO associated with the World Bank to link its activities with poverty reduction programmes. A World Health Assembly Resolution in 1977 (WHO, 1985), aiming for a programme of 'Health for All' through PHC by 2000, set the stage for the 1978 Alma Ata Conference.

In order to understand its relevance, it is necessary to dwell on the principles laid down in the Declaration and analyse them in the context of present changing realities. The Constitution of India has recognized the 'Right to Health' within the ambit of the 'Right to Life'. The inherent implication in its broad definition of health is the duty of the state to ensure that right to all its citizens. The Declaration clearly lays down the collective responsibility of governments to address inter- and intra-country inequalities as well as to ensure health as their basic human right. It overtly recognizes that the status of health in a country is subject to international policies and politics.

The 'philosophy' looks redundant in face of the fact that developed countries selectively advocate, adopt and propagate policies, international as well as national at the cost of a compromised status of the sovereignty of many countries. Yet, the philosophy only reinforces its own relevance today simply because the need for a pro-poor development strategy becomes even more indispensable in the face of the discriminatory nature of policies of various international institutions of governance. There is more at stake for the developing countries than ever before.

The Declaration advocated peoples' participation in planning and implementation. At the international level, the World Health Organisation and the United Nations Children's Fund gave countries an international platform to discuss the health of their people. Today, the World Bank dictates health sector policies and programmes, often ignoring the most neglected areas and states.

Primary Health Care (PHC) has been identified as the key strategy to ensure 'Health for All' by 2000. There are a number of key elements of the strategy and its target. First, it is a social target. Thus, HFA has been given the status of a merit good. At the same time, the Declaration advocates health as a part of development. This is of critical importance since it recognizes health as a primer to development. India, contrary to many voices, has also recognized this which is evident from policy documents. For instance, the National Population Policy begins thus: "The overriding objective of economic and social development is to improve the quality of lives that people lead, to enhance their well-being, and to provide them with opportunities and choices to become productive assets in society."[10]

However, at the same time, it is also true that not much of this gets translated into priorities visible from action. This, in turn, is evident from the declining budgetary allocations for health (and other social sectors) and the irrational or inadequate utilization of available resources as well as areas for which external aid and loans are taken—a clear reflection of priorities. What exists today is a fructification of priorities. A planned development pattern is not supplemented by a planned investment pattern. This scenario makes it necessary to stress on health as an integral part of development, supported by priority based investment. Further, the Declaration upholds the principle of social justice. With inequities widening in the present, the demand for social justice has only risen. Again, inequity has been recognized in government documents as an issue to be addressed.

The Alma Ata Declaration describes PHC as 'essential health care based on practical, scientifically sound and socially acceptable methods and technology made universally accessible to individuals and families in the community through their full participation and at a cost that the community and country can afford to maintain at every states of their development in the spirit of self-reliance and self-determination.'[11] This description is very critical especially in today's scenario. When we talk about practical and socially acceptable methods and technologies, we essentially thwart superimposed programmes and strategies. Thus, for instance, how practical is it to make population dependent or readymade sachets of oral rehydration solutions in the face of non-functioning health centres, missing health workers and poor connectivity? Or—as part of the malaria control strategy—providing 5" × 6" mosquito nets for houses that are not even 5" × 3" in dimension? Are there not many more cost-effective, efficient, and comprehensive strategies?

PHC as comprehensive health care providing for promotive, preventive, curative and rehabilitative services is a strategy often neglected in practice. It is of even more relevance today as a result of the changing epidemiological profile of India and the world, especially in the context of globalisation. Another critical aspect of PHC as envisaged in the Declaration is the need for other sectors. Such as agriculture and communications to work towards ensuring Health For All.

This is an indispensable aspect of any health strategy and its importance today stems again from the fact that most other sectors get priority over health. The Declaration also seeks to establish effective referral systems giving priority to those most in need, thus upholding the principle of social justice. Today, the better developed for the more capable states receive a better share of the Central Budget. This is the reality amongst us as citizens too. Consumerism and commercialization have commodified health; the more resources you have, the better your chances of receiving 'quality' medical attention. This, at the cost of the neglect of services, is used and needed by a majority of the population. Is the implementation of PHC failing in our country? Our health centres are understaffed (often the staff is non-existent!) and the quality and accessibility of health services is poor. Inequities exist amongst and within states. Even in the more developed states, ambiguities exist in the form of social maladies, like gender inequality manifested in female foeticide. India's situation thus becomes a very complex one, marked by serious aberrations even in the more developed states—a situation leading to a triple burden. The principles of equity and social justice require that the less developed regions be brought on par with the others, within the social realities of our country. This is necessary but becoming increasingly difficult.

Technology is necessary, yet expensive. We have not been able to find a way to handle technological advances within the issue of accessibility of health care for the masses. A doctor, who might have people at heart, is still a product of technological advances, which have strengthened the medical profession. Where technology is used for training them, doctors cannot be affordable for the people. Further, technology needs to be seen in view of drugs and diagnostics, both of which are going out of reach of people. The principle of social justice does not govern the actions of doctors. Technology has developed its own drive and dynamics. This is also an important issue behind the resource crunch.

The Declaration makes it necessary to make technology available for all 'at a cost that the community and country can afford to maintain'. It is a known fact that as a result of the low quality and poor availability of health care delivered by the government, the people have to utilise private profit making services—at a very high cost. Not only does this lead to indebtedness but also to irrational health care, possibly posing great risk, since the so-called 'practitioner' may not be qualified. Any document that lays down principles, which have standalone value as a result of their merit, can be most efficacious if used dynamically. The question here is this: are user charges against the principle of universal health care and social justice?

One has to argue with India's context where health is a state subject. It is important to know the process of decentralization, which was reinforced by the 73rd and 74th Amendments to the Constitution. Today, decentralization is viewed with a certain amount of disillusionment. It is believed that the states—while wanting less interference by the Centre—does not wish to devolve power to the panchayats either. Has the strategy of decentralization-aimed to ensure that the community's needs are expressed and managed by the community itself-failed?

In the post-independent period, several committees were formed to assess the health status and suggest health policy measures. India has two National Health Policies since 1947, one in 1983 and the other draft policy in 2001. Apart from these two policies various committees were formed. The first and foremost, before independence, was Bhore Committee. This is otherwise known as Health Survey and Development Committee. This was appointed by Government of India in October 1943 to survey the existing conditions with regard to health and to make recommendations for future developments. The committee submitted its report in 1946. The survey gave details about the then existing health conditions in India in volume one of the report. The committee recommended for the creation of a better standard of national health through the development of an organised health service on 'modern lines'. The committee, in those two volumes had dealt with India's health problems in order to present an adequate picture of the then existing state of affairs. Some of the important recommendations made by the committee in its report were the following:

"No individual should fail to secure adequate medical care because of inability to pay for it". "Health service should provide all consultant, laboratory and institutional facilities for proper diagnosis and treatment."[12] The committee emphasized on the preventive aspect of health care systems, the committee had recommended that, maximum of the medical relief and preventive health care should be provided to the rural population. The committee had recommended to bring the health services closest to the people. The committee for the first time had talked about the increasing awareness and local participation of people in health programmes and also to provide health education to masses.

Regarding the role of health care providers, the committee recommended that "doctor should be a 'social physician' who would protect the people from diseases and provide them happy life."[13] For the first time the report talks of 'social medicine', which widens the conception of disease from narrow view of tissue changes and microbial and other specific causes by the inclusion of social, economic and environmental factors which play an equally important part in causing of sickness. This also made a clear distinction between the curative and preventive aspect of health.

The committee had recognized the economic plight of the masses of India and the consequences of privatisation of health care, on the basis of that the existing condition of the medical services in the country should be free of cost for all section of the people in the society. On the other side, the contribution from those who can afford should be through the channel of general and local taxation. The committee left it for the Governments of the future to decide ultimately to all classes of people whether an insurance scheme would be more suitable. "For ensuring adequate health service for the vast rural population of the country and for overcoming the difficulty experienced in the past to attract medical practitioners to the countryside, so the committee recommended that the most satisfactory method of meeting the situation would be to provide a whole time salaried service, thus enabling governments to ensure that doctors are made available where their services are highly required."[14]

Bhore Committee had realised that, health problems cannot be dealt with fire-fighting approach and hence the committee had drawn up health plan in two parts, one a comprehensive programme for the somewhat distant future and other a short-term scheme covering two five years periods. In the long-term programme it was mentioned that, the treatment of disease would be approached not merely from the standpoint of providing the patient immediate relief, but also from that of attempting to remove the causes which are responsible for the condition. The hospital as an institution would play the dual role of providing medical relief and of taking an active part in the preventive campaign. "We consider that the health programme in India should be developed on a foundation of preventive health work and proceed in closest association with the administration of medical relief."[15]

The Bhore Committee was a landmark in the health policy of India. The committee reviewed health under public health, medical relief, professional education, medical research etc.

Despite all the above affirmative steps, it had many loopholes within it. The first and foremost thing is that it emphasized only on western system of medicine. In both its curative and preventive aspects of health, it talked only of Allopathic system of medicine. Nowhere in the report, they had mentioned about Indian systems of medicine such as Ayurvedic, Siddha, Unani etc. It overemphasized the 'modern' trends of health care delivery to Indian scenario without taking local conditions into consideration. There was confusion regarding, whether the service should be free or paid by the recipient. And the later, whether it should be a graded scale of payment so as to suit the level of patient's income, and whether such payment should be based on a full time salaried service of doctors or on private practitioners resident in each local area or settled there on a subsidy basis.

The report left it to the governments of future to decide ultimately whether medical service should remain free to all classes of the people or whether an insurance scheme would be more in accordance with the economic, social and political requirements of the country at that time.[16] The report says that 'the money for such special facilities, if they are to be developed, should be provided by the communities or groups which will be benefited by these services.'[17] Some other national health committees are discussed in the fourth chapter of this book.

Purpose of the Study

The purpose of the study is to explore the extent to which universal standards of right to health, health care or health protection are being shaped—and to some degree and level, recognized—under the rubric of a social or cultural entitlement within the law of human rights. It also examines the issues of indeterminacy, justifiability and progressive realization of present serious roadblocks to the goal of codifying and then implementing the right to health. While measured progress in meeting these first two challenges is occurring, the most contentious impediment remains: namely, determining the extent to which a sustained level of economic stability must be attained, in the first instance, before a state can seek to recognize, enforce and observe the standards of right to health at any minimal and maximal level.

In this context that the Universal Declaration of Human Rights, adopted by the United Nations, states that everyone has the 'right to adequate standard of living and well-being of his/her family including medical care' and also the World Health Assembly of WHO has resolved that 'the right to health is a fundamental right'. Fundamental rights are recognized in various constitutions of the world. It means to protect citizens against their violation by the executive actions of the state or by laws enacted by legislatures. It is common in the literature on law to refer to them as negative rights in the sense that what is guaranteed is freedom from the states interference, without due process, in the citizen's rights to such matter as life, personal liberty, equality of opportunity and so on. In contrast, the right to health care is primarily a claim to an entitlement, is a positive right, which can acquire an operational content only to the extent that the state is willing and able to ensure its realization. Not a protective fence as entitlements rights are contrasted with privileges, group ideals, societal obligations, or acts of charity, and once legislated they become claims justified by the laws of the state. (Chapman, 1993). The emphasis thus needs to shift from 'respect' and 'protect' to focus more on 'fulfil'. For the right to be effective optimal resources that are needed to fulfil the core obligations have to be made available and utilized effectively.

In the Indian Constitution, this obligation is placed in a number of Articles, which deal with 'Fundamental Rights' and 'Directive Principles of States Policy'. Article 13 says that laws inconsistent with or in derogation of the fundamental rights will cease to be law as the India, has the power to declare this *ultra vires*. Article 21 affirms protection of life and personal liberty. Here protection of life includes right to health which means medical aid in government hospital-failure on the part of the government hospital to provide timely medical treatment to the patient in need of such treatment, amounts to violation of the right to life. 'Directive Principles of State Policy', article 47 stipulates that 'the state shall regard the raising of the level of nutrition and the standard of living of its people and the improvement of public health as among its primary duties', article 39 calls on the state to protect the health and strength of workers, men, women, and to prevent the abuse of the 'tender age of children'. Articles 41 and 42 call upon the state to make effective provision for public assistance in case of old age, sickness, disability and for maternity relief. Is it to be realized at grass roots level? Is state withdrawing from public health sector? What then happens to article 47 of the Constitution of India read with article 21 and health provisions of UN Resolution 2200 (calls for member states to ensure among others 'the highest attainable standards of physical and mental health' under international covenant on economic, social and cultural rights approved by the UN General Assembly on 16th Dec., 1996).

Further, using human rights approach also implies that the entitlement is universal. This means there is no exclusion from the provisions made to assure health care on any grounds whether purchasing power, employment status, residence, religion, caste, gender, disability, or any other basis of discrimination. But this does not discount the special needs of disadvantaged and vulnerable groups who may need special entitlements through affirmative action to rectify historical or other inequities suffered by them.

Thus, establishing universal health care through the human rights route is the best way to fulfil the obligations mandated by international standards which influence the domestic constitutional provisions. International law, specifically ICESCR, the Alma Ata Declaration (details can find next part of the study), among others, provide the basis for the core content of right to health and health care. However, country situations are very different and hence there should be sensitivity to the specificity of each country. Country specific thresholds should be developed by indicators measuring nutrition, infant mortality, disease frequency, life expectancy, income, unemployment and underemployment, and by indicators relating to adequate food consumption. States should have an immediate obligation to ensure the fulfilment of this minimum threshold. However, in the long run we should realize the international standards set through several UN declarations and covenants and WHO indicators.

Approaches of the Study

The study adopts some of the relevant approaches to assess and evaluate the health and human rights approach which are outlined below:

A participatory analytic and reflective approach has been employed. This approach broadly includes the involvement of communities and stakeholders in decision-making, planning and implementation increases ownership and harness creative energies and resources – human, material and financial.

A public health and societal approach will be used to address determinants of ill health such as nutrition, water supply and sanitation, to reduce transmission of communicable diseases, and risk factors for diseases at population levels.

Public health aims to protect, promote, restore and improve the health of all people through collective action which is directly related to human rights.

The primary health care approach works together with public health and emphasizes principles of:

- inter-sectoral coordination at all levels, especially at the district, sub-division and village/municipal level.
- community participation and social control through Panchayati Raj Institutions, health committees and other institutionalized mechanisms for community feedback.
- equitable distribution of good quality health care, recognizing that health is a human right and there is need for social justice in health care.
- value of appropriate technology for health.
- adopting an inclusive approach with equal support to local health traditions, yoga, Indian systems of medicine, and homeopathy.
- referral systems and linkages between the primary, secondary and tertiary levels of health care.

Health financing, management and administration are critical support systems for the health sector. They will be developed through training, research and nurture. This approach also help to create people's awareness to realize the right to health at the grass roots level particularly but it also tries to make some change at all the levels in large scale.

The pro-poor approach: The co-relation between poverty and poor health is well known. It is not only the wage-loss during illness episodes or due to consequent disabilities that make the poor poorer, but also the sudden financial loss and debt-trap that make the situation worse for them. High out-of-pocket expenditure on treatment incurred by all sections of the community, as is evident from a variety of investigations in Orissa, leads to the conclusion that unless the State takes adequate care to protect the poor and the vulnerable from the adverse economic effects of diseases, any serious effort at sustainable socio-economic development will have no long-standing and favourable impact. At present, a very large portion of the public-provided services is consumed by the better-off than the worse-off for a variety of reasons. The policies and strategies therefore attempt to address this issue in every possible situation thereby indirectly helping in sustainable human development. Health improvement complements socio-economic development process by directly increasing human well-being and reducing economic risks and poverty. The policies and sector reform strategies contribute to health improvement by translating those strategies into actions that are cost-efficient in achieving health gains in the community, by reducing wasteful and inappropriate expenditure by the State as well as by the individual.

Statement of the Problem

Focusing on problems in health and human rights as the result of a situation of vulnerability, involves identifying its three components (accessibility, affordability, quality), and indicating its likely future performance in communities, households or individuals through empirical analysis. However, only accessibility can be described as population variables, whereas the remaining components require the study of diverse factors (social, economic, cultural, etc.), mostly contingent to the case in consideration.

Asking what secure access would mean points to the data needed. For example, does health centre provide secure access to health service? To find out, start by asking how many people are served by one health centre and from what distance. How capable are the medical staffs treating the illness they encounter? Track the stock levels of essential medicines, to see whether they can cater to the needs of the patients.

A dynamic process of changes and innovation is required to be brought about in the entire approach to health manpower development, ensuring the emergence of fully integrated bands of workers functioning within the "Health Team" approach.

Have we depended too much on the government as the 'saviour' and benefactor? Is it the states that constantly depend on central funds without contributing their share or is it the communities, who merely sits back and watch the government's effort—or lack of them—and use the first opportunity to criticize it for moving away from sacrosanct principles? At the same time, the government is also turning to the private sector (profit and non-profit) to help implement its programmes. Can we not use this to fight for space in decision making? Why do we continue to romanticise the role of the government?

Why did not the principles of the Alma Ata Declaration strike root? Was it too broad an agenda? Was it erroneous that its agenda was kept in the hands of medical professionals, not all of whom possess the sensitivity to understand complex social realities and needs? Social control for medical professionals is extremely important today. Historically, whenever doctors have been employed by the state, the medical profession has wielded significant power—one reason for their unresponsiveness. Thus, some social pressure must be exercised on the medical professionals.

The States would require careful review of the existing situation of health status, with special reference to the availability and dispersal of private practitioners and to take timely decisions in regard to health services at the grass roots level. Therefore, it needs right approach to address these important questions and queries. Here, field selection for study and its brief background to analyze the state of right to health and health standards is presented.

Selection of Field Site

Orissa has been taken as sample state for the study because this state is a backward state in every aspect. Hence, one has to give a brief background of the state to understand standard setting of human rights with special reference to right to health. Orissa formed on 1st April, 1936, lies on the East Coast of India, along the Bay of Bengal. It extends over an area of 1,55,707 square km. accounting about 4.87 per cent of the total area of India. According to the 2001 census, it has a total population of 36,804 million. Orissa is regarded as one of the poorest and least developed states in the country. The demographic composition reveals predominance of tribals, scheduled castes and small peasants. Administratively Orissa has three revenue divisions, 30 districts, 58 sub-divisions, 171 tahsils and 314 Community Development Blocks. On the basis of homogeneity, continuity and physiographical characteristics, Orissa has been divided into five major regions: the Orissa Coastal Plain in the east, the Middle Mountainous and Highlands Region, the Central plateaus, the western rolling upholds and the major flood plains. Agriculture provides employment to 77 per cent of the total employment of the state, paddy is the major crop in the state but most ironic aspect is that in the state of Orissa, the irrigation facility is less compared to other neighbour states. Orissa has an enormous mineral potential with its reserves of iron ore, manganese ore, limestone and graphite. However, the recurrent natural calamities like the cyclone, drought, flood coupled with the persistent resource constraint have been the major inhibiting factors for the growth and revival of the economy.

Orissa is presently implementing various National Health Programmes such as Tuberculosis, Malaria, Blindness, AIDS, Leprosy and RCH. In addition to this, the DFID has supported various initiatives such as Primary Health Care, Phase III (1997 to 2000); Rehabilitation and Reconstruction in cyclone affected areas (2000-2004) and strengthening of Sector Development of Health Care (2001 onwards) while the UNFPA is implementing the Integrated Population Development (IPD) project and the World Bank is supporting the Secondary and Primary Health Care Project (Health Systems Development Project) (1998-99 to 2004). In 2001, the Government of Orissa initiated a process to develop a medium term health sector strategy and a Health Vision 2010 document, which outlines strategies and points for action for development of the health sector in Orissa.

In spite of the efforts, Orissa has one of the lowest human development indicators and in health front, the IMR of Orissa stands at 65 against 58 for India. The per cent of underweight children is 44 per cent in Orissa against 46 per cent for the country as a whole. Even the percentage of institutional births is as low as 38.7 per cent for Orissa in comparison to 40.7 for the country as a whole (NHFS III).

Therefore, one has to know the demographics of the state at a glance and start analyzing the present situation of health in the state. The state has different people on the basis of caste and ethnicity. There are 62 scheduled tribes, and 93 scheduled castes in the state. More than 90 per cent of the people of the state who live in non-coastal districts are tribals. Whereas 37.08 per cent of people belong to socially, economically and politically deprived Scheduled Tribes and Scheduled Castes communities. The people living below the poverty line comprise 67.88 per cent of total population, 70.17 per cent of people live in rural, and 51.11 per cent in urban area. Of the total tribal and Scheduled Caste population, 95.38 per cent are distributed over 184 remote villages in the state. But the most unfortunate fact is that the primary health care facilities unavailable, inaccessible to desired extent in every remote village among the backward communities for whom health facilities have been envisaged.

Despite emphasis on strengthening local health care provision, concern remains regarding the rates of utilization of state-provided services within Orissa. The reported study examined patterns of service utilization across the rural population of Balasore district in Orissa, with special reference to perceptions of the availability and quality of state services at the primary care level. Apart from the state wide plan and programme, this study focuses on district level investment on health sector as to evaluate the health service delivery system in an effective way. Has the policy which is formulated by the government, reached to the grass roots level and to assess the district level strategy in the back of the profile of that particular district? Here Balasore district taken as a case study to know the state of right to health and accessibility to health care services.

The present study has been carried out in Balasore, one of the coastal districts, situated northern part of Orissa and south-eastern part of India. It lies on the northern most part of the state having 21°03′ to 21°59′ North Latitude and 86°20′ to

87°29′ East Longitude. Geographical area of the district is 36, 34 sqr. km. Midnapore district of West Bengal is in its North, the Bay of Bengal is on the east and Bhadrak district lies on the South whereas Mayurbhanj and Kendujhar districts are on its western side. As per the 2001 Census, the population is 20,23,000 comprising 10,38,000 males and 9,85,000 females.

Fertility Indicators

As per DRHS (RHS-RCH), 2002-2004, 24.5 per cent of the girls marry below the age of 18 years in Balasore district and 33.8 per cent of births are of order 3 and above. The district Crude Birth Rate (CBR) is 21 per 1000 population in 2005. The Couple Protection Rate (CPR) in Balasore is 34.62 per cent in (Source Year Book of H & FW, 2005) whereas the CPR for Orissa is 46.8 per cent and for India it is 48.2 per cent (As per NFHS-II). The Total fertility rate of Balasore district is 2.9 per cent (IIPS, 2001) which has come down substantially from 5.0 as per Census 1991. The percentage of 1 and 2 order births as per DLHS 2001 is 65.0 per cent.

Mortality Indicators

The Crude death rate of the district is 10 per 1000 population in 2005. The IMR for the District is 65 (Source – CDMO Office, Balasore) against the state as 77 (SRS-2004), this shows the district IMR is quite low in comparison to the state average. The MMR of the district is 315 per 1 lakh as per 2005 district data and the total number of maternal deaths is 121 as per the 2005-06 district data. For the year 2007-08 data is not available.

Morbidity Indicators: Communicable diseases like Malaria, Filariasis and Tuberculosis continues to be the major health problem in Balasore. Leprosy though prevalent has come down significantly. The HIV/AIDS situation has also become a matter of concern in the district. Filariasis is also seen in one of the blocks in Balasore.

Table 1.1 : Health Institutions in Balasore District

Name of the Health Institutions	*Number*	*Rented/Own*
No. of District Hospitals	1	Own
No. of Sub-Divisional Hospitals	1	Own
No. of Community Health Centres	6	Own
No. of Upgraded Primary Health Centres	1	Own
No. of Primary Health Centres (New) (Single Doctor PHC)	67	66 Own 1 adjusted in the Panchayat Building
No. of Primary Health Centres (Block PHC)	7	Own
No. of First Referral Units (F.R.U.)	5 (DHH, SDH, G.K. Bhattar Hospital, UGPHC Basta, Soro CHC-I)	Own
No. of Rural Family Welfare Centres	12	Own
No. of Urban Family Welfare Centres	1	Own
No. of Postmortem Centres	4	Own
No. of Sub-Centres (Including 12 main centres)	264	87
No. of A.N.M. Training Centre*	1	Running at DTU at present
No. of Ayurvedic Dispensaries	22 (Director of IM&H, Orissa)	
No. of Homoeopathic Dispensaries	30 (Director of IM&H, Orissa)	
No. of Municipality Dispensaries	3	

Source: CDMO Office, Balasore

* The ANM Training Centre of Balasore is running at Balasore District Training Unit. And at the present ANM Training Centre the CDMO office is functioning. ZSS-cum-CDMO office is under construction with support from EC SIP. As soon as the buliding is completed the CDMO office will be shifted to the new ZSS building and ANM Training Centre will shift from DTU and will run in the own ANMTC building of the district.

Administrative Structure

Administratively the District of Balasore has been divided into one Municipality, seven Tahsils, two Sub-Divisions, with three NAC, twelve Blocks, 289 GPs, twenty one Police Stations (2001 Census), 2952 villages, 2587 inhabited villages and 365 uninhabited villages. There are twenty five slums in Balasore Municipality with 29,713 populations, the slums people life is vulnerable in terms of personal hygiene and health conditions. Nobody bothers for them especially health worker and para-medical staff treat them as subhumans because they come from slum.

This district is backward compared to other coastal districts in the state in every aspects of the development. Therefore, from this district, two-sample hospitals with high concentration of Scheduled Caste, Scheduled Tribe and general caste population have been taken for the study; this includes one hospital located in the town and another situated in a remote village. One sample hospital is different from the other, on the basis of location, staff, beds, and hospital facility and also people's literacy rate, income level, employment opportunities and standard of living.

Objectives of the Study

- To focus on international and Indian legal instruments and standards relating to the right to health and their relevance to India.
- Examine the practices in the light of the standards and account for the gap between the promise and performance.

Methodology

The research tools adopted for the survey include structured schedules, interview guide, genealogies, observation guide and case studies. The structured schedules are included both open-ended and close-ended questions. Different sets of schedules were canvassed for collection of information on different units of observation. The schedules on village study cover the items like distances of villages from sub-health centre, PHCs and access to drinking water, approach roads, population size and composition, communication etc. Utmost importance was given to collection of information about health status and health care.

Genealogical charts, an anthropological method was prepared for each sample hospital for eliciting information on more reliable demographic socio-economic variable such as age, education, electricity, occupation, monthly income, family planning, socio-economic characteristics, infant and child mortality, etc.

A free associate type of group interviews and individual interviews were conducted. Case studies of ethnic social groups were gathered; individual doctors and village level health workers, and other health functionaries were contacted for information. The observation guides used for non-participant and participant observation at the hospital and village level.

Data Processing

The objectives formulated have been established or discarded on the basis of empirical data collected from the field study. The empirical evidence collected through the field study has been analyzed. The data from the secondary sources has been supplemented the results wherever necessary to analyze the data, as to establish the relationship among the variables. The simple statistical techniques such as scale, ratios and proportions have been used to substantiate the discussions on the basis of the findings of the study.

Scheme of the Book

The present book consists of seven chapters. The first chapter includes purpose of the study, ranging from statement of the problem, selection of field site, review of literature, review of health policies in post-independent India, rationale, objectives, methods of analysis, sources of the data, chapter schemes of the thesis, limitations of the study.

The second chapter starts with an introductory note on setting human rights standards: which includes the importance of the study. This introductory note introduces various facets of the study. It deals with an understanding health from human rights perspective, which covers the theoretical and philosophical foundations of the book. It broadly captures standard setting philosophy and its origin of the study, which gives the base on the present work.

The third chapter deals with the concepts, scope, definition and the sources of international human rights law, international treaties, customary international law, implementing the international right to health.

The fourth chapter covers the human rights standards in health: Indian scenario, delivery of health services in the public sector, organizational structure of the public health delivery system, goal-setting and strategic interventions, an overview of the evolution of the health system in India and peoples' perceptions and responses to right to health. It also covers health as human right in India: constitutional and legal dimensions, constitutional mandate to the state, health as right to life, states' obligation to preserve life, role of courts in realization of right to health and peoples' perceptions and their responses towards right to health.

The fifth chapter deals with the health care delivery in Orissa, genesis of health sector reforms in Orissa, Orissa health system development and public private partnership, process of decentralization, formation of district health committee and district overview. It also captures cases which stand as testimony to provide evidence that health as human rights.

The sixth chapter captures the basic information of the Balasore district in Orissa in the form of profile of the district. It includes statistical data and hospital administration, institutional arrangement, which is reference point to enter into rights discourse.

The last chapter attempts to provide summary. It covers reclaiming health an unfolding struggle for right to health. It also includes some suggestive measures for the better access to health for weaker sections of the society.

Limitations of the Study

This study is essentially focused on the standard setting exercise based on the secondary sources. It is an attempt to cover the whole debate to see the pattern and process of standard setting exercise. The empirical part of book is very limited.

The present survey includes both open-ended and close-ended questions, related to the topic. For the present study we adopt purposive sample design that has been chosen for convenience of the researcher. Even researcher faced difficulties while interviewing the respondents. The respondents in certain cases were reluctant in answering some of the questions related to government health policy and also human rights.

The nature of enquiry is limited, as it covers only ongoing patients, doctors and bureaucrats mainly of the two hospitals, for the reasons of constraints of time and resources. Therefore, the expectations that the debate raises could not be fully examined in the empirical part of the work. Study of Balasore, one district in Orissa—may not lend itself to valid generalizations for Orissa not to take of India as a whole. The study only provides some insight into the pattern but not yield a perspective.

END NOTES

1. Kumble, N.D. "Rural Health", Ashish Publication House, New Delhi, 1984.
2. Gillespie Stuart, "Struggle for Health", Concept Publishing House, New Delhi, 1993.
3. Balasubhramanyan, Vimal, "Women and the Burden of Child Health", *Economic and Political Weekly,* Issue 9, Vol. XXII, Bombay, 1987, p. 363.
4. Djukanovic and Mach, 1975: 15,18.
5. Cassen, R., "India: Population, Economy, Society", Macmillan Publication, London, 1978.
6. Ramalingaswami, P., "Dewesternising Medicine: the Indian Efforts", Health for All: An Alternative Strategy Report of the Indian Council of Social Science Research and Indian Council of Medical Research Joint Study 1980, Published by *Indian Journal of Community Medicine,* Vol. XIV, No. 4, New Delhi, 1989.
7. Roger Jeffery, "The Politics of Health in India", University of California Press, Berkeley, 1988, p. 116.
8. *Health Survey Development Report* (Bhore Committee), Government of India, New Delhi, 1946.

9. *Ibid,* II:17.
10. *Health for the Millions,* Vol. 30, Nos. 4 and 5, Oct.-Nov.-Dec., Governemt of India, New Delhi, 2003.
11. *Ibid.*
12. *Health Survey Development Report* (Bhore Committee), Government of India, New Delhi, 1946.
13. *Ibid.*
14. *Ibid*
15. *Ibid.*, Vol. IV, Summary.
16. *Ibid.*
17. *Ibid.* Vol. II, Chapter-II.

2

Right to Health
Understanding Health from Human Rights Concerns

Introduction

This chapter reflects the philosophical foundation of the setting human rights standards and right to health and it also traces the historical background of human rights and health issue. This study also focuses on the concept and history of standard setting exercise of human rights and right to health and gradual evolution of the concept in human civilization. This includes discussion on the law, ethics including bioethics which are essential for a deeper grasp of the essence of human rights standard setting and the process of enforcement.

In the past decade, the thinking has been that international action on human rights should move from setting legal standards to the implementation of existing standards. The usefulness of some new standards has been questioned, and there is evidence that disenchantment is gradually growing. At its simplest, the issue is that treaty making in the area of human rights has, in some ways, become complicated, and even in cases where a text is adopted, there is no guarantee that the treaty is effectively enforced. Recent negotiations on particular standards—for example, the Optional Protocols to the Convention on the Rights of the Health and the Convention against Torture and Other Cruel, Inhuman or Degrading Treatment or Punishment—show that some states are reluctant to support new and heightening standards.

This study examines and analyzes the effectiveness of the processes; the role of different factors within those processes, and also seeks to identify possible new avenues in standard setting. It is also an attempt to understand the processes involved in standard setting and draws lessons through the examination of different standards and their contexts. It also looks at fresh thinking of human rights experts who seek to initiate or advocate for new human rights standards and thinking or approach of officials engaged in inter-governmental and governmental organizations. The overall pursuit is to examine the process of relevance of standard setting in the heights discourse with specific focus on right to health.

Norm-Setting in International Law and Human Rights: Historical Antecedents

The normative regime of international human rights law to be specific originated in liberal theory and philosophy. The rise of the modern nation-state in Europe and its monopoly over violence and the instruments of coercion gave birth to a culture of individual rights to contain the abusive and invasive state. John Locke reduced this relationship between the state and the individual to a philosophy in his 'Two Treatises of Government.'[1] In liberal theory, individual rights act as a bar against the despotic proclivities of the state. It is on this theoretical foundation that international human rights law raises. Thus, the modern state is the primary guarantor of human rights, while it is at the same time the basic target for international human rights law.[2] For several centuries, however, these normative limitations remained the exclusive province of constitutional and other domestic legal regimes. The creation of a binding system of international human rights law did not happen until after World War II—following the abominations of the Third Reich. Human rights law is therefore at its core an internationalization of the obligations of the liberal state.

To be certain, the post-war international human rights regime did not spring into existence overnight. It has its historical antecedents in a number of mass struggles, international law doctrines, and institutions. These include anti-colonial struggles, state responsibility for injuries to aliens, struggles against (and from) religious persecution, the Mandates and Minorities Systems of the League of Nations, the protection of minorities, humanitarian intervention, international humanitarian law, the struggle for women's rights, anti-slavery campaigns, and anti-apartheid and other anti-racist struggles.

In its original formulation, international law was the exclusive preserve of the Society of Nations.[3] The responsibility for the initial construction of the basic principles of international law belonged to this small core of states. Standard setting and norm creation at the dawn of international law were therefore an exclusively European exercise. That is why the spirit of the discipline of international law, as well as its theoretical and philosophical predicates, is regarded as Eurocentric.[4]

International standard setting law, which was originally state-centred, exclusively governed relationships between nation-states. States alone made and applied international law. Thus, only a select few states were subjects of international law and therefore had any rights under this legal order. After World War I, however, several newly created international organizations were recognized as having some limited rights under international law. Generally, individual human beings did not have any international legal rights; as such, a state's treatment of its natural persons was not the business of any other state or of the international community.

With the passage of time, the individual started gaining currency in international law. The doctrine of humanitarian intervention, very early on in the development of international law, recognized "as lawful the use of force by one or more states to stop the maltreatment by a state of its own nationals when that conduct was as brutal and large-scale as to shock the conscience of the community of nations."[5] Later, the individual gained more protection from the nineteenth century treaties to ban the trans-Atlantic slave trade in Africans and the conclusion of treaties to protect Christians in the Turkish (Ottoman) Empire.

In the early twentieth century, the League of Nations provided that colonial powers observe the "principle that the well-being and development" of native [colonized] peoples "form a sacred trust of civilisation."[6] The League Covenant also called for "fair and humane conditions of labour for men, women, and children."[7] The International Labour Organization took up that challenge and produced a plethora of instruments on labour standards and worker's rights. The League also pushed for the development of an international system for the protection of minorities. International humanitarian law—the law of war—also provided for the care of the wounded or sick combatants and the protection of medical personnel and hospital facilities in wartime.[8]

While these international legal doctrines and institutions played a critical role in the early foundation of human rights norm-setting, popular mass struggles by marginalized groups and colonized peoples were no less important in giving content to the post-war human rights movement. Examples of these struggles are the anti-colonial and anti-racist movements by the peoples of different nation-states. These struggles for self-determination and independence have left an indelible mark on human civilization. The process of standard setting takes its own stance.

I. The Process of Standard Setting in Human Rights

The process of standard setting at the international level suggests complexity, negotiation, and consensus building. It also calls into play competing national interests, cultures, and ideologies. As if these aspects were not enough, more difficult matters of the asymmetry of power, the ability to participate effectively in the process, and the capacity to own both the process and the product come into play. Unpacking process, therefore, is a tricky and pivotal question. For it is quite often the case that control over the process makes the final outcome predictable and, sometimes, moot. Where complex and competing players exist, the process becomes as essential as the product itself. Thus, questions must be asked about fairness, transparency, ownership, democracy, and participation in any probing discussion of process.

There is, moreover, a tendency by those involved in the human rights discourse to use the terms "standard", "norm" and "right" interchangeably as though they were synonymous or have an identical meaning. Other terms with similar connotations, such as "entitlement" or "claim" are sometimes thrown in. All these terms conjure up the following images: ideal, threshold, floor, benchmark, aspiration and privilege. They suggest things that should be striven for and imply an expectation of the fulfilment of a promise or a duty. However, because the human rights corpus is a species of international Law—essentially a legal regime that binds states—it is imperative that analyses of the terms adopt a precise legal lens. The language of the law seeks precision about the legal meaning of words and determines their legal status and the nature of the obligations or privileges it envisages. In fact, it can be plausibly argued that the process of standard setting in human rights is a struggle over the meaning of language and its implications on the conduct of states. Perhaps the most elastic of these terms is the word "standard" itself, which has no particular legal meaning and does not necessarily imply a legal obligation of any kind. A standard is a vacuous, empty receptacle into which one can fit almost anything. It refers to a level of achievement or expectation that may carry with it moral, cultural, or other civilizational aspiration.

The UDHR, for example, which was initially only meant to carry moral authority referred to itself as a "common standard of achievement for all peoples and all nations."[9] It is almost certain that the UDHR would not have acquired its current authority had it been a legally binding instrument. It is in the flexibility of the term 'standard' that lies hidden therein its wide reach and scope. It can be argued that freeing the term from the narrow strictures of the law gives it more authority and propels it to the forefront as a universal civilizational value that knows no cultural or geographic boundary. In other words, a standard is a phenomenon that is above a mere legal rule; it is an inherent and self-revealing virtue, one that demands obedience without question. There are advantages, therefore, to employing the loose ended term particularly if one seeks a wider consensus without any obvious or immediate legal bond.

The term "norm" is more complicated than "standard" although it, too, has the advantage of transcending the narrow confines of the law. A "right" is the most crystallized of all these terms. It is the element that is laid bare once the other terms like standard and norm—are boiled down to their simplest forms. Arguably the single most important term in any legal regime, the word "right" is the foundation and basis of the human rights movement.

In human rights discourse, rights provide the avenues through which human dignity is secured and guaranteed. The term implies both a duty and the bearer of that duty. In human rights law, the state bears the primary duty of protecting rights, which are enjoyed by individuals and groups. A right is viewed as an entitlement.[10]

While the rule of law is the bar between tyranny and democracy, human rights are the most sacred of all legal entitlements. Once a claim achieves the status of a human right, it acquires the aura of irreversibility, irrevocability, timelessness, and universal validity. Human rights are regarded as the zenith of human civilization. A human right is a crystal clear phenomenon, an attribute that lacks the hazy outlines of a standard or a norm. It is in this respect that a right—in this case a human right—is a clear distillation and a more careful use of terminology than the more general "norm" or "standard." It is, therefore, important to note that the term standard encompasses both norms and rights. That is why the process and exercise of the creation of expectations and obligations in human rights can be referred to as standard setting, an expression that covers both binding and non-binding rules and codes of conduct.

On the other side of the argument is that while the modern Law of Human Rights may have a short formative period of no more than three centuries, both the principle and the history of the Dignity of Man—together with his common citizenship in society—can be seen for thousands of years. Indeed, almost from the very beginnings of recorded history of humanity, the quest for a validation of human rights has been found, not so much perhaps in reason, as with an instinctive feeling of what is both right and good.[11] Thus, it has been said, "Human rights have always existed with the human being", as with the concept of human dignity.[12]

Under one interpretation of human rights, they are seen as "non-positivistic, principled, legal limits to what states, state actors, and state agents can do to their citizens."[13] As such, they impose no obligations on states; rather, they impose limits to state action.[14] This view is drawn from the philosophy of the Bill of Rights and rooted in a neo-Lockean conception of the rule of law as a "commitment to a determinate set of legal rules."[15] In the international human rights community, however, a contrary view is taken—a view which holds to the notion that these rights either obligate state action under certain circumstances or, alternatively, obligate restraint by the state.[16]

Although a concrete notion of human rights appears absent from the Greek and Roman legal systems as well as the Chinese and other ancient civilizations[17], certain claims to parental authorship have—over time—been tied to Magna Carta 1215 and the Bill of Rights 1689, as well as the American Declaration of Independence, 1776, and the French Declaration of the Rights of Man and of The Citizen, 1789.[18] Yet, from the standpoint of historical accuracy, the French Declaration is seen correctly as the first document of its scope and nature which is reference to contemporary social, economic, and cultural rights styled originally as the rights to education, work, property ownership and social protection.[19]

Even though viewed as a type of generalized philosophical manifesto for the Western World, the French Declaration was not embraced by subsequent European constitutions.[20] Indeed, these new constitutions were seen as not only less pragmatic as the Declaration but they also were prone to de-emphasize "the philosophy of inalienable rights."[21] Rights were, thus, constitutional in origin. The European constitutions of the 19th century were the frameworks or mechanisms for declaring rights to be protected constitutionally within legal boundaries. Put simply, then, it was solely within the legislative power where fundamental rights were not only declared but limited.[22] Latin American constitutionalism de-emphasized the "inalienability of rights" and—instead—during the 19th and 20th centuries, chose to reference only those laws established by state authorities.[23]

In this study we focus more on the context of the Constitution of India, which is one of the most rights-based constitutions in the world. Drafted around the same time as the Universal Declaration of Human Rights (1948), the Indian Constitution captures the essence of human rights in its Preamble, and the sections on Fundamental Rights and the Directive Principles of State Policy.

The Constitution of India is based on the principles that guided India's struggle against a colonial regime that consistently violated the civil, political, social, economic and cultural rights of the people of India. The freedom struggle itself was informed by many movements for social reform, against oppressive social practices like *sati*, child marriage, untouchability etc. Thus by the mid-1920s, the Indian National Congress had already adopted most of the civil and political rights in its agenda. The movement led by Dr B.R. Ambedkar against discrimination of *Dalits* also had an impact on the Indian Constitution. In spite of the fact that most of the human rights found clear expression in the Constitution of India, the independent Indian State carried forward many colonial tendencies and power structures, including those embedded in the elite Indian Civil Service. Though the Indian State under Jawaharlal Nehru took many proactive steps and followed a welfare state model, the police and bureaucracy remained largely colonial in their approach and sought to exert control and power over citizens. The casteist, feudal and communal characteristics of the Indian polity, coupled with a colonial bureaucracy, weighed against and dampened the spirit of freedom, rights and affirmative action enshrined in the Constitution.

Over a period of 58 years, the articulation and assertion of human rights within civil society has grown into a much richer, more diverse and relatively more powerful discourse at multiple levels. A brief historical sketch of the different trajectories of human rights discourse will help us to locate human rights in the historical context.

There are four specific trajectories of human rights discourse in the Indian context:

- Civil and Political Rights,
- Rights of the Marginalized (such as Women, *Dalits* and *Adivasis*),
- Economic, Social and Cultural Rights, and
- The Right to Transparent and Accountable Governance.

Though each of these trajectories is interconnected, they were promoted by different sets of actors (often with varying ideological affiliations) at different points in time. There has always been tension and lack of mutual appreciation between those who promoted civil liberties and the left-oriented groups who worked towards the structural transformation of socio-economic conditions and consequently of the State.

As the concept of human rights was perceived as a western idea to gloss over inequalities and as a means of legitimizing the capitalist and imperialist projects of the west (particularly the US) the left-oriented groups were clearly skeptical about human rights, particularly as expressed by the civil liberties groups. Though in some quarters such skepticism still exists, there has been a greater recognition of the need to promote and protect human rights, in spite of the misuse of the human rights discourse by the new imperialist forces.

Rights need critical assessment to draw the clear-cut understanding of health rights. In attempting to distinguish human rights from fundamental constitutional rights, socialist jurisprudence sought to ignore any inherent or natural rights theories and treated them as philosophical rights—this, while recognizing the constitutionally created rights as political in origin. Even though constitutions drafted during the post-socialist period failed to follow the socialist concept of granted right, there remained a dilemma: how to develop a "middle-ground approach" which would validate the idea that "a consensus reached by the people at the constitution's adoption is the result of their recognition of some commonly accepted values."[24] It was all too apparent to those drafting new constitutions that securing fundamental recognition of a selection of core rights was not guaranteed by a designation that these rights were "natural."[25]

Indeed, throughout the subsequent history of human rights, "cultural relativism" has been a dominant force with which to reckon—for, the values of some people are not always capable of being judged by the norms shared by others.[26] Even with vagueness and imprecision as the all-too-often banner of contemporary human rights, a trend toward the "internationalization of human rights movements" is evidenced.[27] Yet, such a trend by no means can be seen as an integration of internationalization of human rights with special reference to international human rights movements. Rather, it must be accepted as "toleration for human rights which is monitoring by government and access to the most important human rights treaties."[28]

The crux of the argument is whether one can claim health as human right or it is merely a social service, if one claims health as human rights than what legal support does one require. The central thrust of the argument is that the enjoyment of the highest standard of human rights is one of the fundamental human rights of every human being, without distinction of race, religion, political belief or social condition. The Universal Declaration of Human Rights, Article 25 is concerned with the right to health. According to this Article, "everyone has the right to a standard of living, adequate for the health of himself, including food, clothing, housing, medical care and necessary services." The preamble of the World Health Organization states that the enjoyment of the highest standard of health is a fundamental right of every human being.[29]

Standard setting process entails sensitivity to ethics. Human rights constitute a set of norms governing the treatment by state and non-state actors or individuals and groups on the basis of ethical principles incorporated into national and international legal systems as the subject matter of norms in question relates to the treatment of human beings. Human rights overlap to a considerable degree with ethics (but should not be confused with ethics). Similarly, because human rights include the right to health and refer to essential social determinants of health and well-being of people, they overlap with many principles and norms of bioethics. However, human rights and bioethics differ in scope, sources, legal nature, and the mechanisms of monitoring and applying the norms.

The scope of bioethics is the ethical issues arising from health care and biomedical sciences, whereas that of human rights embraces the claims individuals and groups can legitimately make against state and non-state actors to respect their dignity, integrity, autonomy and freedom of action as defined in an officially endorsed set of standards or norms. Bioethics regulates clinical encounters with patients on the basis of principles such as beneficence, non-malfeasance, confidentiality, autonomy and informed consent; whereas human rights are the special rules agreed upon in a given society to achieve justice and well-being and overcome the pain and suffering that result from repression (somatic violence) and oppression (systemic violence).

The source of human rights is the norm-creating process of national and international legal systems, whereas that of bioethics is the deliberations and published opinions of leading thinkers, review boards and professional associations on the ethical issues they address. 'Source' is used here as the formal validation of normative positions rather than an abstract grounding of ethical reasoning in moral philosophy or a biological assessment of empathy or altruism. Bioethics and human rights share this deeper distal grounding but have recourse to different proximate sources. The proximate source of human rights is typically an international human rights treaty or declaration and of bioethics is a professional code or review board guidelines. Exceptionally, the proximate source is identical when an instrument of international law addresses directly an issue of bioethics and human rights, such as

UNESCO's Universal Declaration on the Human Genome and Human Rights or the Council of Europe's Convention for the Protection of Human Rights and Dignity of the Human Being with Regard to the Application of Biology and Medicine, both of 1997.

The legal nature of human rights norms ranges from merely aspirational claims to the justiciable and enforceable legally binding obligations. The former include non-binding norms through which advocates of various causes draw upon human rights discourse to seek social change. The latter refer to legally binding rules of domestic (normally constitutional) and international law requiring governments to respect, ensure, promote and fulfil certain norms, with opportunities for persons denied their rights, non-governmental organizations and various international agencies to obtain redress or change policy consistent with those norms. Insofar as those norms concern health and medicine, they contribute to the tasks of bioethics, although the legal nature of bioethical standards is less a matter of constitutional and international law than a field of inquiry, and reasoned philosophical discourse that may be used in law reform and litigation takes on a legal form through codes of conduct formally adopted by professional bodies with authority over the conduct of their members.

An important distinction may clarify further the difference between human rights and bioethics, namely that between 'rights' and 'human rights'. In ethics a right refers to any entitlement, the moral validity or legitimacy of which depends on the mode of moral reasoning the ethicist is using. In law, a right is any legally protected interest. In human rights discourse, a human right is a higher-order right authoritatively defined using the expression 'human rights' with the expectation that it carries a peremptory character similar to Rawls's idea of the "priority of liberty"[30] or Dworkin's "rights as trumps."[31] In other words, in case of conflict, human rights prevail over other (ordinary) rights. This distinction is relevant to both the natural law and positive law foundations of human rights.

As defined in natural law, a human right is usually considered inalienable, immutable and absolute, whereas in positive law it is dependent upon a political and legal process that results in a declaration, law, treaty or other normative instrument and may vary over time and be subject to derogations or limitations designed to optimize respect for human rights rather than impose an absolute standard. Although much confusion arises regarding moral and legal bases of human rights, the relationship between the two may be understood by considering that human rights emerge from claims of people suffering injustice, based on moral sentiment, but become part of the social order when they are proclaimed by an authoritative body, through a process that is law-based. During the process from moral sentiment to legal entrenchment, claims not yet formally recognized as human rights may nevertheless be legitimate and have consequences without being incorporated into binding law. However, the most solid basis for asserting that an act or omission is or is not in conformity with human rights standards is positive law. That is why the International Bill of Human Rights[32], along with the other human rights treaties of the UN and of regional organizations, constitutes the primary source and reference point for what properly belongs in the category of human rights.

The moral or natural law basis of human rights is essential to challenging abusive power and advancing human rights, but its universality may be questioned because it is culturally determined by contextualized moral and religious belief systems. The consensual or positive law basis of human rights reflects compromise and historical shifts but attains a higher degree of universality by virtue of the participation of representatives of virtually every nation in the norm-creating process.

The methods of monitoring compliance with human rights include moral judgments made with reference to recognized human rights, quasi-judicial procedures of investigation and fact-finding leading to official pronouncements of political bodies regarding compliance, and enforceable judicial decisions. Those of bioethics also include moral judgments made with reference to principles or codes of bioethics and official pronouncements of professional bodies that may result in altering research design or the behaviour or liability of health professionals in their relations with patients or in policies affecting the health of populations.

The overlap of human rights and bioethical discourse and differences between the two will become clearer as one clarifies the emergence of human rights in political and legal discourse, the content of the right to health as defined in human rights instruments, the other human rights as they relate to health and well-being, and the role and responsibility of health professionals, governments, international organizations and non-governmental organizations to respect, protect, promote and provide for these rights.

II. Emergence of Human Rights

The early formulation of norms we characterize today as human rights is inseparable from historical and philosophical manifestations of human striving for justice. The deepest origin of human rights no doubt derives from basic human instincts of survival of the species and manifestations of empathy and altruism that evolutionary biology is only beginning to explain.[33] Since human evolution is driven by reproductive selfishness, one could wonder why the human species would develop any ethical system, like that of human rights, according to which individuals manifest feeling for the suffering of others (empathy) and even more surprising act in self-sacrificing ways for the benefit of others without achieving any noticeable reproductive advantage. And yet, as Paul Ehrlich notes in "Human Natures", "empathy and altruism often exist where the chances for any return for the altruist are nil."[34] Natural selection does not provide the answer to moral behaviour as "there aren't enough genes to code the various required behaviours" but rather "cultural evolution is the source of ethics"[35] and therefore of human rights.

In legend, literature, religion and political thought, justice and eventually the concept of human rights became socially constructed over time into complex webs of social interaction striving toward a social order in which human beings are treated fairly as individuals and collectivities. The best-known histories of the human rights movement[36] tend to begin with the ancient religions and societies.

Religion and law have an ambiguous role in this historical process. The history of religions is replete with advances in the moral principles of behaviour 'many of which directly influenced the drafting of human rights texts' but also in crimes committed in the name of a Supreme Being. Similarly, the emergence of the rule of law has been critical to the advance of justice and human rights against the arbitrary usurpation of power in most societies but also in preserving the impunity of oppressors.

Scholars trace the current configuration of international human rights norms and procedures to the revolutions of freedom and equality that transformed governments across Europe and North America in the 18th century and liberated subjugated people from slavery and colonial domination in the 19th and 20th centuries. Enlightenment philosophers derived the centrality of the individual from their theories of the state of nature, social contractarians, especially Jean-Jacques Rousseau, predicated the authority of the state on its capacity to achieve the optimum enjoyment of natural rights, that is, of rights inherent in each individual irrespective of birth or status. He wrote in "Essay on the Origin of Inequality among Men" that "it is plainly contrary to the law of nature that the privileged few should gorge themselves with superfluities, while the starving multitude are in want of the bare necessities of life."[37] Equally important was the concept of the universalized individual ('the rights of Man'), reflected in the political thinking of Immanuel Kant, John Locke, Thomas Paine and the authors of the French and American Declarations. Much of this natural law tradition is secularized in contemporary human rights.

World War II was the defining event for the internationalization of human rights. In 1940, H.G. Wells wrote "The Rights of Man or What are We Fighting For?"; Roosevelt's four freedoms speech was given in 1941; the UN Charter established in 1945 an obligation of all members to respect and observe human rights and created a permanent commission to promote their realization; and the trial of Nazi doctors defined principles that were codified in the Nuremberg Code in 1946. In the war's immediate aftermath, foundations of human rights texts were adopted: the Genocide Convention and the Universal Declaration of Human Rights in 1948, the Geneva Conventions in 1949, followed in 1966 by the International Covenants on Human Rights. NGOs played a role in all of these developments and in subsequent drafting of treaties on the rights of the child, discrimination against women, and the International Criminal Court, as well as in the creation of investigative and accountability procedures at the intergovernmental level.

Drawing heavily on the debates in the Third Committee of the General Assembly in 1948, one finds that the philosophy of the Universal Declaration was linked to that of the French Declaration of 1789 but that 18th century deism had been replaced by 20th century secular humanism, as evidenced by the rejection of the explicit reference to "nature."[38] This is not only true for the legislative history of the Universal Declaration but is also an accurate characterization of the grounding of international human rights in the 21st century.

The valuation of every individual through natural rights was a break with the earlier determination of rights and duties on the basis of hierarchy and status. Commenting on the French Revolution's break with the past, Jürgen Habermas wrote that this "revolutionary consciousness gave birth to a new mentality, which was shaped by a new time consciousness, a new concept of political practice, and a new notion of legitimization."[39] Although it took more than a century for this new mentality to include women and slaves, the awareness that the "rights of man" should extend to all human beings was forcefully argued in the same period by Mary Wollstonecraft[40] and by the Society for the Abolition of the Slave Trade, founded in 1783. The movement to abolish slavery was the precursor of today's vast array of human rights non-governmental organizations (NGOs).

The secular tradition of human rights over the past three centuries has reflected a certain tension between political liberalism and democratic egalitarianism, between Locke and

Rousseau, between liberty and equality, between civil and political rights and economic, social and cultural rights. Marx and other socialist scholars questioned the "bourgeois" character of a limited interpretation of individual human rights. Community interest and egalitarian values are not the sole prerogative of Marxists and Socialists; they are reflected in the Universal Declaration's balancing of "bourgeois" liberal rights with duties to the community and social, economic and cultural rights as correctives to abuses of property rights. Significantly, the Declaration acknowledges that "Everyone has duties to the community in which alone the free and full development of his personality is possible."[41] While socialist thought and positions taken by Soviet bloc countries supported concepts of duties and economic, social and cultural rights, these are also deeply rooted in other cultural and political traditions, including European social democracy and Roosevelt's proposal for an economic bill of rights. The emphasis on community and duties is also found in conservative elements of some societies, like Islamic, Hindu and other Asian societies. The simultaneous affirmation of rights and duties, of protecting individual freedoms and meeting social and economic needs which refers to group rights and individual rights. It is also part and parcel of human rights, adding to it, complexity and depth to the norms, but also ambiguity and tension. Notwithstanding this balancing, the debate over the "universality" of human rights continues. The matter was not settled by the compromised language of the World Conference on Human Rights (Vienna, June 1993), according to which:

> "All human rights are universal, indivisible and interdependent and interrelated. The international community must treat human rights globally in a fair and equal manner, on the same footing, and with the same emphasis. While the significance of national and regional particularities and various historical, cultural and religious backgrounds must be borne in mind, it is the duty of States, regardless of their political, economic and cultural systems, to promote and protect all human rights and fundamental freedoms."[42]

This statement captures an important feature of human rights today, namely, the claim that they are universal and the reality of geo-cultural diversity. To understand it fully, the challenge this feature represents requires an understanding of the normative content of the current catalogue of human rights.

III. The Normative Content of Human Rights: The Right to Health

The current catalogue of human rights consists of some fifty normative propositions enumerated in the international bill of human rights, extended by a score of specialized UN treaties, a half-dozen regional human rights treaties, and hundreds of international norms elaborated in the fields of labour, refugees, armed conflict, and criminal law. This corpus of human rights law, enriched by declarations, programmes of action and other formulations of human rights in the process of becoming legally binding, is the source of the norms that properly fall with the category of international human rights.

The human rights framework takes on particular relevance for bioethics when the meaning, scope and practical significance of the right to health are considered. The right to health as understood in international human rights law is defined in Article 25 of the 1948 Universal Declaration of Human Rights (UDHR) ("Everyone has the right to a standard of living adequate for the health of himself and of his family, including food, clothing, housing, medical care and necessary social services"). Article 12 International Covenant on Economic, Social and Cultural Rights (ICESCR, 1966) which states "the right of everyone to the enjoyment of the highest attainable standard of physical and mental health."[43]

Variations on this definition are found in Article 5 (e) (iv) of the International Convention on the Elimination of All Forms of Racial Discrimination of 1965 ("The right to public health, medical care, social security and social services"), in Articles 11.1 (f) and 12 of the Convention on the Elimination of all forms of Discrimination Against Women of 1979 (CEDAW) ("the right to protection of health and to safety in working conditions, including the safeguarding of the function of reproduction"[and] to eliminate discrimination against women in the field of health care in order to ensure, on a basis of equality of men and women, access to health care services, including those related to family planning [and] ensure to women appropriate services in connection with pregnancy, confinement and the post-natal period, granting free services where necessary, as well as adequate nutrition during pregnancy and lactation) and in Article 24 of the Convention on the Rights of the Child of 1989 (CRC) ("the right of the child to the enjoyment of the highest attainable standard of health and to facilities for the treatment of illness and rehabilitation of health"). Regional human rights treaties also define the right, as in Article 11 of the European Social Charter of 1961 as revised in 1996 (states, obligation to take measures, to remove as far as possible the causes of ill health; to provide advisory and educational facilities for the promotion of health and the encouragement of individual responsibility in matters of health; to prevent as far as possible epidemic, endemic and other diseases, as well as accidents and the duty to ensure that any person who is without adequate resources and who is unable to secure such resources either by his own efforts or from other sources, in particular by benefits under a social security scheme, be granted adequate assistance, and, in case of sickness, the care necessitated by his condition); Article 16 of the African Charter on Human and Peoples' Rights of 1981 (the right to enjoy the best attainable state of physical and mental health [and the obligation of the state to] take the necessary measures to protect the health of their people and to ensure that they receive medical attention when they are sick); and Article 10 the Additional Protocol to the American Convention on Human Rights in the Area of Economic, Social and Cultural Rights of 1988 (enjoyment of the highest level of physical, mental and social well-being and measures to ensure "(a) Primary health care, that is, essential health care made available to all individuals and families in the community; (b) Extension of the benefits of health services to all individuals subject to the State's jurisdiction; (c) Universal immunization against the principal infectious diseases; (d) Prevention and treatment of endemic, occupational and other diseases; (e) Education of the population on the prevention and treatment of health problems; and (f) Satisfaction of the health needs of the highest risk groups and of those whose poverty makes them the most vulnerable").

In a General Comment on the Right to Health, the Committee on Economic, Social and Cultural Rights (CESCR) (created to monitor the ICESC) analyzed the normative content of the right in terms of accessibility, affordability, appropriateness and of quality of care, and specified the duties of the state to respect, protect and provide this right.[44] It also listed the following 14 human rights as integral components of the right to health: the rights to food, housing, work, education, human dignity, life, non-discrimination, equality, the prohibition against torture, privacy, access to information, and the freedoms of association, assembly and movement.[45] In other words, these related rights defined to a large extent the determinants of health.

The right to health does not mean the right to be healthy, since being healthy is determined in part by health care, but also by genetic predisposition and social factors. What is of greater significance for the realization of healthy lives is the extent to which respect for other human rights has a direct bearing on the right to health or on the social factors that contribute to healthy lives. The field of social epidemiology has excelled at establishing correlations between discrimination based on race, class or gender, denial of education and of decent working conditions, as well as other factors that contribute directly to increased rates of mortality and morbidity.[46] These social determinants may also be defined in human rights terms as deprivation of these health-related rights. The rapid survey which follows seeks to underscore the function of human rights as determinants of health by highlighting the normative content and their relation to health.

IV. Health-related Human Rights

Human rights have been categorized in various ways, such as economic, social and cultural or civil and political rights; as first, second, and third-generation or 'solidarity' rights are the most recently recognised category of human rights. Rights in this category include self-determination as well as a host of normative expressions whose status as human rights is controversial at present. These include the right to development, the right to peace, the right to a healthy environment, and the right to intergenerational equity.

The right to a healthy environment requires a healthy human habitat, including clean water, air, and soil that are free from toxins or hazards that threaten human health. The right to a healthy environment entails the obligation of governments to (i) refrain from interfering directly or indirectly with the enjoyment of the right to a healthy environment, (ii) prevent third parties such as corporations from interfering in any way with the enjoyment of the right to a healthy environment, and (iii) adopt the necessary measures to achieve the full realisation of the right to a healthy environment.

For the purposes of relating the core internationally recognized human rights to the realization of health and well-being, it is proposed here to group human rights into three categories, those that relate to the physical and mental existence of humans ("rights of existence"); those that relate to autonomy of thought and action of individuals ("rights of autonomous action"); and those that involve social interactions of individuals and groups from the family to the political, cultural and international communities ("rights of social interaction").

a. Rights of Existence

The right to death with dignity is sometimes claimed as the human rights grounding for domestic legislation on the subject. Although there is no explicit international human right to death, some scholars construe this right from various recognized rights, such as the rights to dignity and freedom from cruel, inhuman, or degrading treatment.

Another controversial aspect of the right to life is the tension between the claim that it includes the right to life of the foetus from the moment of conception and the claim that reproductive rights of the pregnant women include the right to voluntary termination of her pregnancy. The right to an abortion is recognized in various national legal systems but not explicitly in international human rights due to the large opposition by Catholic and Islamic countries.

The right to "a standard of living adequate for the health and well-being" of oneself and one's family was defined in the Universal Declaration of Human Rights as including "food, clothing, housing and medical care and necessary social services" as well as "the right to security in the event of unemployment, sickness, disability, widowhood, old age or other lack of livelihood in circumstances beyond [one's] control." Subsequently, the rights to health, work, safe and healthy working conditions (occupational health), adequate food and protection from malnutrition and famine, adequate housing, and social security (that is a regime covering long-term disability, old age, unemployment and other conditions) have been further elaborated. The rights to work and to decent conditions of work have been the responsibility of the International Labour Organisation since 1919, and specific rules have been developed through some 200 ILO conventions and recommendations, constituting a highly developed sub-field of human rights. The other rights relating to an adequate living standard have also been expanded upon by treaties, international conferences and summits, and the work of special rapporteurs and treaty bodies.

b. Rights of Autonomous Action

The great civil liberties, freedom of oral and written expression, freedom of conscience, opinion, religion or belief, as well as rights to a fair hearing and an effective remedy for violations of human rights, and protection of privacy in domicile and correspondence all support the autonomy of individuals to act without interference from the state or others. The implications for mental health of these freedoms are easy to identify. Similarly, freedom from arbitrary detention or arrest, from torture or other forms of cruel, inhuman or degrading punishment or treatment, and humane conditions of detention for those legally deprived of their liberty have obvious implications for physical and mental health. Human rights standards in UN and regional texts provide the definitions and means of redress for these rights. A separate but related human right is that of informed consent to medical experimentation, which was included in post-1945 enumerations of rights due to the abhorrent abuse of that right during World War II.

Freedom of movement means the right to reside where one pleases and to leave any country, including one's own, and to return to one's country. The right to seek and enjoy asylum from persecution is also a human right, which has been developed and expanded by international refugee law, the practice of the UN High Commissioner for Refugees and recent codes relating to internally displaced persons. This right, like many others, is not absolute; limitations may be imposed, for example, in time of epidemic, as long as certain safeguards, defined in human rights law, are observed.

c. Rights of Social Interaction

The third set of rights that are also determinants of health relate to the participation of individuals in their society. Social well-being 'an element of health' relates to group rights, education, family, culture, political and cultural participation, gender and reproductive rights, scientific activity, the environment and development, all of which are the subject of specific human rights.

The right to education includes compulsory primary education, availability and accessibility of secondary education and equal access to higher education, and the role of parents in choosing their child's educational institution. Several instruments relating to discrimination in education, technical aspects and content of education have been adopted by UNESCO. In addition to the right to education, rights of the child have been codified in several instruments, primarily the 1989 Convention on the Rights of the Child (CRC), which has been ratified by every county except the U.S. Defining a child as anyone under 18, the CRC makes 'the best interest of the child' the primary consideration and defines rights relating to the child's identity, health and access to health care, expression of opinion, conditions of adoption, and protection from abuse, torture, capital punishment, and traditional practices prejudicial to the child's health.

Health issues loom large in human rights standard-setting and policy determination regarding gender, sexual rights, and reproductive rights. The basic human rights texts have been supplemented by a specialized Convention on the Elimination of all forms of Discrimination Against Women (CEDAW) of 1979. Considerable advances in mainstreaming women's rights as human rights were made at the international conferences in Vienna (Human Rights, 1993), Cairo (Population, 1994), and Beijing (Women, 1995). Further developments have been made to deal with violence against women (through a 1993 Declaration and a Special Representative to study the problem) and traditional practices harmful to health, such as female genital cutting or mutilation, about which the World Health Organization, UN Children's Fund (UNICEF) and the UN Fund for Population Activities issued a statement in 1996.

Reproductive rights begin with "The right of men and women of marriageable age to marry and to found a family shall be recognised"[47] which is closely related to the right of men and women . . . to decide freely and responsibly on the number and spacing of their children. [CEDAW, Article 16 (1) (e)], and "to be informed and to have access to safe, effective, affordable and acceptable methods of family planning of their choice."[48] Various internationally approved programmes and plans of action have set out in considerable detail the specific ways in which this right can be realized.

Bioethical concerns overlap with human rights with respect to the right to enjoy the benefits of scientific progress and the right to scientific research.[49] The former refers to the positive and equitable use of scientific advances while the latter protects freedom to conduct research and disseminate results and the requirement of informed consent of human subjects.

In the same way that the distinction between civil and political and economic, social and cultural rights is losing its relevance in the post-Cold War, so too is the third category of solidarity or third generation rights less helpful than it was twenty years ago.[50] It referred to certain global values such as peace, a healthy environment, development, communication, humanitarian intervention or assistance and the like, which were raised to the level of human rights, notwithstanding the complex matter of defining the rights- and duty-holders and the precise obligations involved. While the literature continues to refer occasionally to all these values as constituting human rights, and some support exists in the literature and declarations of political bodies, two have become more systematically developed and enshrined in authoritative texts, namely the right to a healthy environment and the right to development.

The right to a healthy environment (or a related formulation such as "to live in an environment adequate for their health and well-being"[51]) has been recognized in some 90 national constitutions, including most national constitutions enacted since the 1992 Rio Conference on Environment and Development. South Africa's Constitution is exemplary in this regard: "Everyone has the right (a) to an environment that is not harmful to their health or well-being; and (b) to have the environment protected, for the benefit of present and future generations, through reasonable legislative and other measures that (i) prevent pollution and ecological degradation; (ii) promote conservation; and (iii) secure ecologically sustainable development and use of natural resources while promoting justifiable economic and social development."[52]

The right to development has been recognized in numerous UN resolutions and specifically in the 1986 Declaration on the Right to Development[53], as well as in the African Charter on Human and Peoples' Rights. The Declaration defines this right as "an inalienable human right by virtue of which every human person and all peoples are entitled to participate in, contribute to, and enjoy economic, social, cultural and political development, in which all human rights and fundamental freedoms can be fully realized."[54] The right implies that development policies of governments and partner agencies should "aim at the constant improvement of the well-being of the entire population and of all individuals, on the basis of their active, free and meaningful participation in development and in the fair distribution of the benefits resulting therefrom."[55] Now, the important issue has to be discussed in the light of health and human rights and modern concepts of health.

Health and Human Rights

Explanations for the dearth of communication between the fields of health and human rights include differing philosophical perspectives, vocabularies, professional recruitment and training, societal roles, and methods of work. In addition, modern concepts of both health and human rights are complex and steadily evolving. On a practical level, health workers may wonder about the applicability or utility ('added value'), let alone necessity of incorporating human rights perspectives into their work, and *vice versa*. In addition, despite pioneering work seeking to bridge this gap in bioethics, jurisprudence[56], and public health law[57], a history of conflictual relationships between medicine and law, or between public health officials and civil liberty advocates, may contribute to anxiety and doubt about the potential for mutually beneficial collaboration. Yet health and human rights are both powerful, modern approaches to defining and advancing human well-being. Attention to the intersection of health and human rights may provide practical benefits to those engaged in health or human rights work, may help reorient thinking about major global health challenges, and may contribute to broadening human rights thinking and practice. However, meaningful dialogue about interactions between health and human rights requires a common ground. To this end, following a brief overview of selected features of modern health and human rights, this chapter proposes a provisional, mutually accessible framework for structuring discussions about research, promoting cross-disciplinary education, and exploring the potential for health and human rights collaboration.

Modern Concepts of Health

Modern concepts of health derive from two related although quite different disciplines: medicine and public health. While medicine generally focuses on the health of an individual, public health emphasizes the health of populations. To oversimplify, individual health has been the concern of medical and other health care services, generally in the context of physical (and, to a lesser extent, mental) illness and disability. In contrast, public health has been defined as, "...(ensuring) the conditions in which people can be healthy."[58] Thus, public health has a distinct health-promoting goal and emphasizes prevention of disease, disability and premature death. Therefore, from a public health perspective, while the availability of medical and other health care constitutes one of the essential conditions for health, it is not synonymous with "health". Only a small fraction of the variance of health status among populations can reasonably be attributed to health care; health care is necessary but clearly not sufficient for health.[59]

The most widely used modern definition of health was developed by the World Health Organization (WHO): "Health is a state of complete physical, mental and social well-being and not merely the absence of disease or infirmity."[60] Through this definition, WHO has helped to move health thinking beyond a limited, biomedical and pathology-based perspective to the more positive domain of "well-being." Also, by explicitly including the mental and social dimensions of well-being, WHO radically expanded the scope of health, and by extension, the roles and responsibilities of health professionals and their relationship to the larger society.

The WHO definition also highlights the importance of health promotion, defined as "the process of enabling people to increase control over, and to improve, their health". To do so, "an individual or group must be able to identify and realize aspirations, to satisfy needs, and to change or cope with the environment."[61] The societal dimensions of this effort were emphasized in the Declaration of Alma Ata (1978), which described health as a "...social goal whose realization requires the action of many other social and economic sectors in addition to the health sector."[62]

Thus, the modern concept of health includes beyond health care to embrace the broader societal dimensions and context of individual and population well-being. Perhaps the most far-reaching statement about the expanded scope of health is contained in the preamble to the WHO Constitution, which declared that "the enjoyment of the highest attainable standard of health is one of the fundamental rights of every human being."[63]

A Provisional Framework: Linkages between Health and Human Rights

The goal of linking health and human rights is to contribute to advancing human well-being beyond what could be achieved through an isolated health- or human rights-based approach. This study proposes a three-part framework for considering linkages between health and human rights; all are interconnected, and each has substantial practical consequences. The first two are already well documented, although requiring further elaboration, while the third represents a central hypothesis calling for substantial additional analysis and exploration.

First, the impact (positive and negative) of health policies, programmes and practices on human rights will be considered. This linkage will be illustrated by focusing on the use of state power in the context of right to health.

The second relationship is based on the understanding that human rights violations have health impacts. It is proposed that all rights violations, particularly when severe, widespread and prolonged, engender important health effects, which must be recognized and assessed. This process engages health expertise and methodologies in helping to understand how well-being is affected by violations of human rights.

The third part of this framework is based on an overarching proposition: that promotion and protection of human rights and promotion and protection of health are fundamentally linked. Even more than the first two proposed relationships, this intrinsic linkage has strategic implications and potentially dramatic practical consequences for work in each domain.

The First Relationship : The Impact of Health Policies, Programmes and Practices on Human Rights

Around the world, health care is provided through many diverse public and private mechanisms. However, the responsibilities of public health are carried out in large measure through policies and programmes promulgated, implemented and enforced by, or with support from, the state. Therefore, this first linkage may be best explored by considering the impact of health policies, programmes and practices on human rights. The three central functions of health include: assessing health needs and problems; developing policies designed to address priority health issues; and assuring programmes to implement strategic health goals. Potential benefits to and burdens on human rights may occur in the pursuit of each of these major areas of health norms and standards.

For example, assessment involves collection of data on important health problems in a population. However, data are not collected on all possible health problems, nor does the selection of which issues to assess occur in a societal vacuum. Thus, a state's failure to recognize or acknowledge health problems that preferentially affect a marginalized or stigmatized group may violate the right to non-discrimination by leading to neglect of necessary services, and in so doing, may adversely affect the realization of other rights, including the right to "security in the event of...sickness (or) disability..." (UDHR, Article 25), or to the "special care and assistance" to which mothers and children are entitled (UDHR, Article 25).

Once decisions about which problem is to be assessed have been made, the methodology of data collection may create additional human rights burdens. Collecting information from individuals, such as whether they are infected with the Human Immunodeficiency Virus (HIV), have breast cancer, or are genetically predisposed to heart disease, can clearly burden rights to security of person (associated with the concept of informed consent) and of arbitrary interference with privacy. In addition, the right of non-discrimination may be threatened even by an apparently simple information-gathering exercise. For example, a health survey conducted via telephone, by excluding households without telephones (usually associated with lower socio-economic status), may result in a biased assessment, which may in turn lead to policies or programmes that fail to recognize or meet needs of the entire population. Also, personal health status or health behaviour information (such as sexual orientation or history of drug use) has the potential for misuse by the state, whether directly or if it is made available to others, resulting in grievous harm to individuals and violations of many rights. Thus, misuse of information about HIV infection status has led to: restrictions of the right to work and to education; violations of the right to marry and found a family; attacks upon honour and reputation; limitations of freedom of movement; arbitrary detention or exile; and even cruel, inhuman or degrading treatment.

The second major task of health is to develop policies to prevent and control priority health problems. Important burdens on human rights may arise in the policy-development process. For example, if a government refuses to disclose the scientific basis of health policy or permit debate on its merits, or in other ways refuses to inform and involve the public in policy development, the rights to "seek, receive and impart information and ideas...regardless of frontiers" (UDHR, Article 19) and "to take part in the government...directly or through freely chosen representatives" (UDHR, Article 21) may be violated. Then, prioritization of health issues may result in discrimination against individuals, as and when the major health problems of a population defined on the basis of sex, race, religion or language are systematically given lower priority.

The third core function of health, to assure services capable of realizing policy goals, is also closely linked with the right to non-discrimination. When health and social services do not take logistic, financial, and socio-cultural barriers to their access and enjoyment into account, intentional or unintentional discrimination may readily occur. For example, in clinics for maternal and child health, details such as hours of service, accessibility via public transportation and availability of daycare may strongly and adversely influence service utilization.[64]

It is essential to recognize that in seeking to fulfil each of its core functions and responsibilities, health may burden human rights. In the past, when restrictions on human rights were recognized, they were often simply justified as necessary to protect the health. Indeed, health has a long tradition, anchored in the history of infectious disease control, of limiting the "rights of the few" for the "good of the many". Thus, coercive measures such as mandatory testing and treatment, quarantine, and isolation are considered basic measures of traditional communicable disease control.[65]

The principle that certain rights must be restricted in order to protect the community is explicitly recognized in the International Bill of Human Rights: limitations are considered permissible to "(secure) due recognition and respect for the rights and freedoms of others and of meeting the just requirements of morality, public order and the general welfare in a democratic society" (UDHR, Article 29). However, the permissible restriction of rights is bound in several ways. First, certain rights (e.g., right to life, right to be free from torture) are considered inviolable under any circumstances. Restriction of other rights must be: in the interest of a legitimate objective; determined by law; imposed in the least intrusive means possible; not imposed arbitrarily; and strictly necessary in a "democratic society" to achieve its purposes.

Unfortunately, public health decisions to restrict human rights have frequently been made in an uncritical, unsystematic and unscientific manner. Therefore, the prevailing assumption that public health, as articulated through specific policies and programmes, is an unalloyed public good that does not require consideration of human rights norms must be challenged. For the present, it may be useful to adopt the maxim that health policies and programmes should be considered discriminatory and burdensome on human rights until proven otherwise.

This approach raises three related and vital questions. First, why should health officials be concerned about burdening human rights? Second, to what extent is respect for human rights and dignity compatible with, or complementary to health goals? Finally, how can an optimal balance between public health goals and human rights norms be negotiated?

Justifying health concern for human rights norms could be based on the primary value of promoting societal respect for human rights as well as on arguments of public health effectiveness. At least to the extent that health goals are not seriously compromised by respect for human rights norms, health, as a state function, is obligated to respect human rights and dignity.

However, it is also important to recognize that contemporary thinking about optimal strategies for disease control has evolved; efforts to confront the most serious global health threats, including cancer, cardiovascular disease and other chronic diseases, injuries, reproductive health, infectious diseases, and individual and collective violence, increasingly emphasize the role of personal behaviour within a broad social context. Thus, the traditional health paradigm and strategies developed for diseases such as smallpox, often involving coercive approaches and activities which may have burdened human rights, are now understood to be less relevant today. For example, WHO's strategy for preventing spread of the Human Immunodeficiency Virus (HIV) excludes classic practices such as isolation and quarantine (except under truly remarkable circumstances) and explicitly calls for supporting and preventing discrimination against HIV-infected people.

The idea that human rights and health must inevitably conflict is increasingly tempered with awareness of their complementarity. Health policy-makers' and practitioners' lack of familiarity with modern human rights concepts and core documents complicates efforts to negotiate, in specific situations and different cultural contexts, the optimal balance between health objectives and human rights norms. Recently, in the context of HIV/AIDS, new approaches have been developed, seeking to maximize realization of public health goals while simultaneously protecting and promoting human rights.[66] Yet HIV/AIDS is not unique; efforts to harmonize health and human rights goals are clearly possible in other areas.

The Second Relationship: Health Impacts Resulting from Violations of Human Rights

Health impacts are obvious and inherent in the popular understanding of certain severe human rights violations, such as torture, imprisonment under inhumane conditions, summary execution, and 'disappearances'. For this reason, health experts concerned about human rights have increasingly made their expertise available to help document such abuses.[67] Examples of this type of medical-human rights collaboration include: exhumation of mass graves to examine allegations of executions[68]; examination of torture victims[69]; and entry of health personnel into prisons to assess health status.

However, health impacts of rights violations go beyond these issues in at least two ways. First, the duration and extent of health impacts resulting from severe abuses of rights and dignity remain generally underappreciated. Torture, imprisonment under inhumane conditions, or trauma associated with witnessing summary executions, torture, rape or mistreatment of others have been shown to lead to severe, probably life-long effects on physical, mental and social well-being.[70] In addition, a more complete understanding of the negative health effects of torture must also include its broad influence on mental and social well-being; torture is often used as a political tool to discourage people from meaningful participation in or resistance to government.[71]

Second, and beyond these serious problems, it is increasingly evident that violations of many more, if not all, human rights have negative effects on health. For example, the right to information may be violated when cigarettes are marketed without governmental assurance that information regarding the harmful health effects of tobacco smoking will also be available. The health cost of this violation can be quantified through measures of tobacco-related preventable illness, disability and premature death, including excess cancers, cardiovascular and respiratory disease. Other violations of the right to information, with substantial health impacts, include governmental withholding of valid scientific health information about contraception or measures to prevent infection with a fatal virus (HIV).

As another example, the enormous worldwide problem of occupation-related disease, disability and death reflects violations of the right to work under "just and favourable conditions" (UDHR, Article 23). In this context, the World Bank's identification of increased educational attainment for women as a critical intervention for improving health status in developing countries powerfully expresses the pervasive impact of rights realization (in this case to education, and to non-discrimination on the basis of sex) on population health status.[72]

A related, even more complex problem involves the potential health impact associated with violating individual and collective dignity. The Universal Declaration of Human Rights considers dignity, along with rights, to be inherent, inalienable and universal. While important dignity-related health impacts may include such problems as the poor health status of many indigenous peoples, a coherent vocabulary and framework to characterize dignity and different forms of dignity violations are lacking. A taxonomy and an epidemiology of violations of dignity may uncover an enormous field of previously suspected, yet thus far unnamed and therefore undocumented damage to physical, mental and social well-being.

Assessment of rights violations' health impacts is in its infancy. Progress will require: a more sophisticated capacity to document and assess rights violations; the application of medical, social science and public health methodologies to identify and assess effects on physical, mental and social well-being; and research to establish valid associations between rights violations and health impacts.

Identification of health impacts associated with violations of rights and dignity will benefit both health and human rights fields. Using rights violations as an entry point for recognition of health problems may help uncover previously unrecognized burdens on physical, mental or social well-being. From a human rights perspective, documentation of health impacts of rights violations may contribute to increased societal awareness of the importance of human rights promotion and protection.

The Third Relationship: Health and Human Rights Exploring an Inextricable Linkage

The proposal that promoting and protecting human rights is inextricably linked to the challenge of promoting and protecting health derives in part from recognition that health and human rights are complementary approaches to the central problem of defining and advancing human well-being. This fundamental connection leads beyond the single, albeit broad mention of health in the UDHR (Article 25) and the specific health-related responsibilities of states listed in Article 12 of the ICESCR, including: reducing stillbirth and infant mortality and promoting healthy child development; improving environmental and industrial hygiene; preventing, treating and controlling epidemic, endemic, occupational and other diseases; and assurance of medical care.

Modern concepts of health recognize that underlying "conditions" establish the foundation for realizing physical, mental and social well-being. Given the importance of these conditions, it is remarkable how little priority has been given within health research for precise identification and understanding of modes of action, relative importance, and possible interactions.

The most widely accepted analysis focuses on socio-economic status; the positive relationship between higher socio-economic status and better health status is well documented. This analysis has at least three important limitations. First, it cannot adequately account for a growing number of discordant observations, such as: the increased longevity of married men and women compared with their single (widowed, divorced, never married) counterparts; health status differences between minority and majority populations which persist even when traditional measures of socio-economic status are considered; or reports of differential marital, economic and educational outcomes among obese, compared with non-obese women.

A second problem lies in the definition of poverty and its relationship to health status. Clearly, poverty may have different health meanings; for example, distinctions between the health-related meaning of absolute poverty and relative poverty have been proposed.[73]

A third, practical difficulty is that the socio-economic paradigm creates an overwhelming challenge for which health workers are neither trained nor equipped to deal. Therefore, the identification of socio-economic status as the "essential condition" for good health paradoxically may encourage complacency, apathy and even policy and programmatic paralysis.

However, alternative or supplementary approaches are emerging about the nature of the "essential conditions" for health. For example, the Ottawa Charter for Health Promotion (1986) went beyond poverty to propose that, "the fundamental conditions and resources for health are peace, shelter, education, food, income, a stable eco-system, sustainable resources, social justice and equity". Experience with the global epidemic of HIV/AIDS suggests a further analytic approach, using a rights analysis.[74]

More broadly, the evolving HIV/AIDS deadly disease has shown a consistent pattern through which discrimination, marginalization, stigmatization and, more generally, a lack of respect for the human rights and dignity of individuals and groups heightens their vulnerability to becoming exposed to HIV.[75] In this regard, HIV/AIDS may be illustrative of a more general phenomenon in which individual and population vulnerability to disease, disability and premature death is linked to the status of respect for human rights and dignity.

Further exploration of the conceptual and practical dimensions of this relationship is required. For example, epidemiologically-identified clusters of preventable disease, excess disability and premature death could be analyzed to discover the specific limitations or violations of human rights and dignity which are involved. Similarly, a broad analysis of the human rights dimensions of major health problems such as cancer, cardiovascular disease and injuries should be developed. The hypothesis that promotion and protection of rights and health are inextricably linked requires much creative exploration and rigorous evaluation.

The concept of an inextricable relationship between health and human rights also has enormous potential practical consequences. For example, health professionals could consider using the International Bill of Human Rights as a coherent guide for assessing health status of individuals or populations; the extent to which human rights are realized may represent a better and more comprehensive index of well-being than traditional health status indicators. Health professionals would also have to consider their responsibility not only to respect human rights in developing policies, programmes and practices, but to contribute actively from their position as health workers to improving societal realization of rights. Health workers have long acknowledged the societal roots of health status; the human rights linkage may help health professionals engage in specific and concrete ways with the full range of those working to promote and protect human rights and dignity in each society.

From the perspective of human rights, health experts and expertise may contribute usefully to societal recognition of the benefits and costs associated with realizing, or failing to respect human rights and dignity. This can be accomplished without seeking to justify human rights and dignity on health grounds (or for any pragmatic purposes). Rather, collaboration with health experts can help and voice to the pervasive and serious impact on health associated with lack of respect for rights and dignity. In addition, the right to health can only be developed and made meaningful through dialogue between health and human rights disciplines. Finally, the importance of health as a pre-condition for the capacity to realize and enjoy human rights and dignity must be appreciated. For example, poor nutritional status of children can contribute subtly yet importantly to limiting realization of the right to education; in general, people who are healthy may be best equipped to participate fully and benefit optimally from the protections and opportunities inherent in the International Bill of Human Rights.

Every country in the world has accepted that human rights are universal but all are challenged, in one way or another, to achieve progress with respect to those rights they neglect, however proud they may be of achievements with respect to other rights. The normative content of the corpus of human rights standards is probably the most complete catalogue of the determinants of physical, mental and social well-being. The methods of implementation or intervention to ensure compliance are not directly linked to medical and health practice as is the case with bioethics.

Another dimension is to analyse human rights and health which provides philosophical foundation to preserve human life. This preservation of life can be argued to be sacred, or important, whether it is viewed religiously, socially, economically and culturally. Religions universally value the preservation of life and the soul from the perspective of immortality. Socially, we need preservation of life so that we have like beings with which to interact. Economically, we need taxpayers and workers. Even the cultural places have an extremely high value on its personnel because of the costs of social norms and the necessary values and norms needed for interventions of certain activity. Thomas Hobbes[76] (1588–1679) felt that reason would allow man to figure out what must be done to preserve life. To this end, in his epic work, "Leviathan", he presents his rules, or Laws of Nature, and explains, "A law of nature (lex naturalis) is a precept or general rule, found out by reason, by which a man is forbidden to do that which is destructive of his life or taken away the means of preserving the same, and to omit that by which he thinks it may be best preserved.

Hobbes reasoned that every person has a "Right of Nature" in that, "every man has a right to everything, even to one another's body". In other words, anybody can do anything. However, as soon as we come to our senses we realize there is laws of nature that rein in this liberty. These laws that are put into place give us the concept of "obligation".

Hobbes presents three important laws of nature that cause us obligation in regard to our actions. Hobbes' laws involve (1) seeking peace, (2) laying down the right of nature and making covenants, and (3) performance of covenants. In following Hobbes' laws to the conclusion an argument can be made that a covenant exists between members of a society, though unwritten, to provide security or well-being for one another. Furthermore, since "we the people" are the government, such a covenant may actually exist between the members of a society and the government as to the provision of access to health care services.

Hobbes' first law is to seek peace, "that every man ought to endeavour peace, as far as he has hope of obtaining it; and when he cannot obtain it, that he may seek, and use, all helps, and the advantages of society. He follows this statement with the advisory that society should "seek peace, and follow it", and if a society cannot get peace, they must defend themselves.

In regard to health service, seeking peace and defending one's self can be manifested in the form of negotiations and the use of the electoral process to gain a favourable hearing on the argument that health service is a right to be shared by or available to all. However, this becomes difficult for the uninsured or the underinsured to pursue because they are without economic strength, many times they are racial minorities and can be marginalized by the political process.

Hobbes' second law, "lay down the right of nature", also applies and is extremely important. Here Hobbes indicates that we should lay down our right "to do anything" if others are willing to do the same. The rule "requires each of us to be satisfied with as much liberty toward other human beings as we are willing to allow them with respect to ourselves". When we give up liberty (or portions thereof) we can: "Renounce this right or transfer it to someone else. In engaging in either of these acts, we are removing an impediment to someone else's use of those same things or someone else's exercise of their right to them. In this way we are bestowing benefits on these other people. If we do not care who receives the benefit, we are said to renounce our right; if we wish the benefit to accrue to someone or more particular persons, we are to speak of transferring our right to them, which amounts to a gift. We may, then, either abandon our right or give it away to other people."[77]

This second law leads to the concept of contracts, or covenants. When people renounce or transfer the "right of nature" a contract, or covenant, is made. Covenants may "not be explicitly conveyed and acknowledged by words. The sign or indication of a contract may be by inference and be implicit or covert". Hobbes claims that, "generally a sign by inference of any contract is whatsoever sufficiently argues the will of the contractor". The "right" at stake here is the right of the medically needy to "transfer" their need (per Hobbes' theory) for health service to a society in which all of its members have pledged mutual cooperation by agreeing to Hobbes' second law. This acquiescence to Hobbes' second law has in fact occurred in our society although it seems not to have been acknowledged. Hobbes' third law regards the performance of covenants. When a covenant is made it is important that "men perform their covenants made: without which, covenants are in vain, and but empty words, and the right of all men to all things remaining, we are still in the condition of warren". If we have agreed to live in mutual security then we must make good on our promises, implied or otherwise.

The concept of "inference" or "implicitness", regarding Hobbes' second law, and the obligation of performance of covenants regarding the third law are very important. The citizens of the country have come to hope and expect availability of health care service access. The growing number of persons that are uninsured, or underinsured, have a limited access to prompt and adequate health care. The provision of health care is an implied covenant that the medically needy have hoped and expected society to embrace.

This constitutes a potentially rich framework for the improvement of health, which is the objective of the emerging sub-field of health and human rights.

Conclusion

The theory and philosophy helps in understanding the framework of standard setting exercise in the context of right to health. Standard setting exercise is not new in global as well as local level. The above arguments bring out the essence of standard setting and conceptualize the entire gamut of the debate ranging from global to local and theoretical to philosophical and also from policy formulation to implementation. It not only gives an outline of right to health and human right issues but it sparks the debate on standards, norms and values of the society. The argument also focuses on norm setting in international law and human rights, natural law, positive law and negative law. It captures the link between health and human rights in different ways and different context.

There is considerable interest in extending the concept of rights to social benefits, such as right health. There is little point in establishing such rights unless the loci of responsibility for delivering on them are clearly defined. It may be possible to establish international public health laws that set minimum standards for certain activities. This would define the responsibilities of the international community and national governments. The minimum standards could cover, public health programmes and services that address fundamental health right needs of the poor; essential regulation of the systems for training and supervision of health workers and distribution of drugs, provision of information on health problems, resource use and health sector performance. This may involve, for example, balancing measures to establish high standards for health insurance and provision of health care against the need to ensure that the poor have access to effective and affordable health services. International governance structures will be needed with the political legitimacy necessary to make and enforce to widen the scope of right to health. It would be difficult to reach international agreement on the kind of framework described above. However, an important first step is to move beyond idealised visions of a future international health system to a clear acknowledgement of reality and of the strategic options for change. This would provide a starting point for serious discussions.

In the next chapters, we begin with a brief review of how India's health care is delivered, focusing on the implications for its regulation. We then turn to see how the different approaches to overseeing the health sector are working in India, beginning with the formal administrative approaches. We then highlight consumer oriented approaches largely because this is a departure for the government into the area of health empowerment, and where there is now enough experience to see what effect it is having in health sector. We then turn to the other approaches that attempt to harness the standard setting for health care, notably contracting and professional self-regulation, before examining the prospects for new collaborative of health models of regulation involving institutionalized co-production.

We posit that in India, pursuing the traditional attempts to enforce the rules through administrative and bureaucratic controls are unlikely to add much value, largely because they fail to deal with the political economy and the social realities of health care. We look forward that Indian government should pay more attention to create norms that are currently working and are valued, and link them to open and negotiated standards that involve a wider range of actors in civil society. This would involve broader use of health and human rights oriented approaches, as well as institutionalized co-production. This approach would shift regulation from a state-led exercise to a more collaborative approach—a shift that is more in keeping with India's current and future health system. The law has to be enforced by the court. The main problem is not with the law as it exists on paper, but with the law as it is practiced. The limited ability to enforce civil and criminal laws in India is well known. Infractions that are considered criminal become difficult to prosecute, whereas the huge backlog of civil cases has overburdened the courts. In this environment, it is difficult to see how an emphasis on enforcement of legal instruments will have a major impact on health services in India in the near future.

Human rights of health need an international legal instrument to claim health as right but state has to recognize it. The law has to be enforced by the court and patient must get his/her rights which is recognized by Constitution of India. The above argument gives glimpse to understand the standard setting at different levels and different geographical boundaries. The slowness of standard-setting processes is a further deterrent. Even if there are exceptions to every rule, most recent negotiations have been cumbersome and long-winded, and their outcomes have been uncertain. Some texts have been watered down, others have been abandoned. The creation of standards is so time-consuming that many states have become reluctant to discuss and to take initiatives. Now we can discuss about the scope and methodology of study which plays pivotal role in the argument and also to claim health as human rights.

END NOTES

1. John Locke, "Two Treatises of Government", ed. by Peter Laslett, Cambridge University Press; 3rd edition, Cambridge, 1988.
2. Henry J. Steiner, "The Youth of Rights", 104 Harvard Law Review, Harvard, 917 (1991) [Reviewing Louis Henkin, 'The Age of Rights' (1990)].
3. James Crawford, "The Criteria for Statehood in International Law", 48 British Y.B. International Law, 93, 98 (1976-77).
4. See, e.g., John Norton Pomeroy, *Lectures on International Law in Time of Peace,* 4–5 (Theodore Salisbury Woolsey ed., 1886); Herbert Arthur Smith, *Great Britain and the Law of Nations,* 12 (1932–35); James Thuo Gathii, *International Law and Euro-centricity,* 9 Eur. J. Int'l L. 1, 184 (1998); Antony Anghie, *Finding the Peripheries: Sovereignty and Colonialism in Nineteenth-Century International Law,* 40 Harvard International Law Journal, 1, 40 (1999); Antony Anghie, *Francisco De Vitoria and the Colonial Origins of International Law,* 5 Social & Legal Study, 321 (1996).
5. Thomas Buergenthal, *et al., International Human Rights in a Nutshell* 3 (3rd ed., 2002).
6. League of Nations Covenant Article 22, available at http://www.yale.edu/lawweb/avalon/leagcov.htm.
7. *Ibid.,* Article, 23.

8. Geneva Convention for the Amelioration of the Condition of the Wounded in Armed Forces in the Field, 12 Aug. 1949, Articles, 1, 2, 6, 6 U.S.T 1864, 75 U.N.T.S. 31 (entered into force 21 Oct. 1950) (entered into force for U.S. 2 Feb. 1956).
9. UDHR, Supra Note 15, Preamble (Emphasis Added.)
10. Ronald Cohen, *Endless Teardrops: Prolegomena to the Study of Human Rights in Africa in Human Rights and Governance in Africa*, 3, 3–4, Ronald Cohen *et al.*, eds., 1993.
11. Fali Nariman, the Universality of Human Rights, 50 Revolution Instruments Community Jurist 9, 11 (1993).
12. Avery Dulles, *Human Rights: Papal Teaching and the United Nations,* America 14 Dec. 5, 1995.
13. Campbell, Tom, Jeffrey Goldsworthy, and Adrienne Stone (Edited) "Protecting Human Rights: Instruments and Institutions", Robin West, Article on "Human Rights, the Rule of Law and American Constitutionalism", Oxford University Press, Oxford, Chapter 4, 2003, pp. 93-96.
14. *Ibid.*, p. 93.
15. *Ibid.*, p. 95.
16. *Ibid.*, p. 93.
17. Michael D. Kirby, Paper, The Right to Health Fifty Years On—Still Skeptical?, Bagnoud Centre for Health and Human Rights, Harvard University School of Public Health, Cambridge, Massachusetts, Dec. 4, 1998, pp. 5, 6, Quoting Isaiah Berlin, 1 Berlin, "Two Concepts of Liberty in, Four Essays on Liberty", 118, 129, 1970.
18. Kirby, *ibid.* pp. 5, 6, Passim, R. H. Helmholz, Magna Carta and the Iuis commune, 66 U. CHI. Law Review 297 (1999); Akhil R. Amar, 'The Bill of Rights as a Constitution 100' Yale Law Journal, 1131, 1991.
19. *Ibid.* See P. G. Lauren, The Evolution of International Human Rights (1998); Stephen P. Marks, From the Single Confused Page to the Decalogue for Six Billion Persons: The Roots of the Universal Declaration of Human Rights in the French Revolution, 20 Human Rights Q. 459, 472 (1998). But see Hugo Adam Bedau, Anarchical Fallacies: Bentham's Attack on Human Rights, 22 Human Rights Q. 261 (2000).
20. Rett R. Ludwikowski, *Constitutionalization of Human Rights in Post-Soviet States and Latin America: A Comparative Analysis,* 33 GA. Journal of International Law & Company Law 1, 20 (2004).
21. *Ibid.*
22. Jeffrey Goldsworthy, *The Sovereignty of Parliament: History and Philosophy,* Oxford University Press, Oxford, 1999, pp. 9-21.
23. Ludwikowski, Supra Note 10, p. 21.
24. *Ibid.*, p. 22.

25. *Ibid.*, p. 22.
26. *Ibid.*, p. 23.
27. *Ibid.*, p. 40.
28. *Ibid.*, pp. 41-42.
29. The World Health Report 1998, Life in the 21st Century: A Vision for All, Report of the Director-General, World Health Organisation Geneva, Switzerland 1998.
30. John Rawls, *Justice as Fairness: A Restatement*, Harvard University Press, 2001, pp. 104-106.
31. Ronald Dworkin, *Taking Rights Seriously*, Harvard University Press, 1977, pp. 91-92 and 184-205; Ronald Dworkin, "Rights as Trumps", *Oxford Journal of Legal Studies*, Oxford, 1981, Vol. 1, pp. 177-212.
32. The International Bill of Human Rights Consists of the Universal Declaration of Human Rights of 1948, Office of the United Nations High Commissioners for Human Rights, Geneva, (UDHR) and the Two International Covenants of 1966—One on Civil and Political Rights, the other on Economic, Social and Cultural Rights.
33. Paul R. Ehrlich, *Human Natures: Genes, Cultures, and the Human Prospect*, Washington, D.C.: Island Press/Shearwater Books, 2000, pp. 305-331.
34. *Ibid.*, p. 312.
35. *Ibid.*, p. 317.
36. Paul Gordon Lauren, *The Evolution of International Human Rights: Visions Seen*, University of Pennsylvania Press, 1998, and Hersch Lauterpacht, International Law and Human Rights, Frederick A. Praeger, Inc., 1950, Reprinted by Garland Publishing, 1973.
37. Jean-Jacques Rousseau, *The Social Contact and Discourses (1762)*, tr. by G.D.H. Cole, rev. and augmented by J.H. Brumfitt and John C. Hall, updated by P.D. Jimack (1973), p. 117.
38. Johannes Morsink, "The Philosophy of the Universal Declaration", *Human Rights Quarterly*, The Johns Hopkins University Press, Vol. 6, 1984, p. 333.
39. Jürgen Habermas, *Between Facts and Norms: A Contribution to a Discourse Theory of Law and Democracy*, The MIT Press, Cambridge, MA, 1996, p. 467.
40. Wollstonecraft, Mary, *A Vindication of the Rights of Woman*, Ed. Miriam Brody Kramnick., Rev., ed. Harmondsworth: Penguin, 2004.
41. UDHR, Article 29.
42. World Conference on Human Rights, "The Vienna Declaration and Programme of Action", Office of the United Nations High Commissioner for Human Rights Geneva, Switzerland, June 1993, Para. 5.

43. International Covenant on Economic, Social and Cultural Rights, Adopted and Opened for Signature, Ratification and Accession by General Assembly Resolution 2200A (XXI) of 16 December 1966.
44. CESCR, General Comment 14: The Right to the Highest Attainable Standard of Health, UN Doc. E/C.12/2000/4, 4 July 2000, Para(s) 34-37.
45. *Ibid.*, Para. 3.
46. Lisa F. Berkman and Ichiro Kawachi (eds.), *Social Epidemiology,* Oxford University Press, London 2000.
47. International Covenant on Civil and Political Rights, Adopted and Opened for Signature, Ratification and Accession by General Assembly Resolution 2200A (XXI) of 16 December 1966, Article 23 (2).
48. Report of the International Conference on Population and Development, U.N. Doc A/CONF.171/13, Oct. 18, 1994.
49. ICESCR, Article 15.
50. Stephen Marks, "Emerging Human Rights: A New Generation for the 1980s?" *Rutgers Law Review,* vol. 33, no. 2, 1981, pp. 435-452; Philip Alston, *Peoples' Rights: Their Rise and Fall,* in Alston, *Peoples' Rights,* Oxford University Press, 2001, pp. 259-293.
51. UN General Assembly Resolution 45/94 of 14 Dec. 1990.
52. Constitution of the Republic of South Africa, as adopted on 8 May, 1996 and amended on 11th October, 1996 by the Constitutional Assembly, Article 12.
53. The Declaration on the Right to Development was Adopted by the General Assembly in its Resolution.
54. *Ibid.*, Article 1.
55. *Ibid.*, Article 3.
56. Ronald Dworkin, *Taking Rights Seriously,* Harvard University Press, Cambridge, 1978.
57. Scott Burris, "Rationality Review and the Politics of Public Health", *Villanova Law Review,* Published in United States, 34(1989):1933.
58. Institute of Medicine, *Future of Public Health,* (Washington DC: National Academy Press), 1988.
59. The International Bank for Reconstruction and Development, *World Development Report 1993: Investing in Health,* Oxford University Press, New York 1993.
60. World Health Organization, Constitution, in *Basic Documents,* 36th ed. (Geneva, 1986).
61. *Ottawa-Charter for Health Promotion,* presented at First International Conference on Health Promotion, Ottawa, November 21, 1986).
62. *Declaration of Alma Ata,* "Health for All" Series No. 1, World Health Organization, Geneva, September 12, 1978.
63. Supra Note 8.

64. Emily Friedman, "Money isn't Everything: Non-financial Barriers to Access", *Journal of the American Medical Association* 271, No. 19, May 18, 1994, pp. 1535-1538.
65. American Public Health Association, *Control of Communicable Disease in Man,* 15th ed., Washington, DC: APHA, 1990.
66. *AIDS, Health and Human Rights: An Explanatory Manual.* Geneva: International Federation of Red Cross and Red Crescent Societies and Francois-Xavier Bagnoud Centre for Health and Human Rights, Harvard School of Public Health, 1995, p. 162.
67. Geiger H.J., and Cook-Deegan R.M., "The Role of Physicians in Conflicts and Humanitarian Crises: Case Studies from the Field Missions of Physicians for Human Rights, 1988-1993," *JAMA* 270(1993), pp. 616-620.
68. Physicians for Human Rights, *Final Report of UN Commission of Expert,* UN Document S/1994/674 May 27, 1994.
69. Mollica RF and Caspi-Yavin Y. "Measuring Torture and Torture-Related Syndromes", *Psychological Assessment* 3, no. 4(1991): pp. 1-7.
70. Anne E. Goldfield, Richard F. Mollica, Barbara H. Pesavento, *et al.*, "The physical and psychological Sequelae of Torture; Symptomatology and diagnosis", *JAMA* 259, no. 18 May 13, 1988, pp. 2725-2730.
71. Metin Basoglu, "Prevention of Torture and Care of Survivors: An Integrated Approach", *JAMA* 270, No. 5, August 4, 1993, p. 607.
72. Supra Note 7.
73. Ichiro Kawachi *et al.*, "Income Inequality and Life Expectancy: Theory, Research and Policy", *Society and Health Working Paper Series May 1994,* No. 94-2, The Health Institute, New England Medical Centre and Harvard School of Public Health, Boston, 1994.
74. Global AIDS Policy Coalition, "Towards a New Health Strategy for AIDS: A Report of the Global AIDS Policy Coalition", MA: Global AIDS Policy Coalition, Cambridge, June 1993).
75. Jonathan M. Mann, Daniel J.M., Tarantola and Thomas W. Netter, *AIDS in the World,* Harvard University Press, Cambridge, 1992 and also Supra Note 30.
76. Hobbes T: Chapter XIV 'In Leviathan' Edited by: Tuck R., Cambridge University Press, Cambridge, 1996, pp. 91-100.
77. *Ibid.*

3

Right to Health

Sources of International Human Rights Law

This chapter searches the ways to assess health standard as set by the legal mandate, which requires societies through their governments assure adequate and affordable health care services. Thus, whether one recognizes right to health depends on one's political persuasion and moral values. International human rights law—which is now growing and enlarging—may provide a legal mandate for a right to health in India and other nations.

What is the "right to health?" This preliminary issue is the subject of much debate. It stresses the need for detailing meaningful definitions for health conditions. Most of the definitional issues raised by researcher with regards to "drowning" apply to the definition of 'Health'. Although concerns with health and disease have been a major pre-occupation of humans since antiquity, so, the use of the word 'health' to describe human 'well-being' is relatively recent. The word health was derived from the old English word 'hoelth', which meant a state of being sound, and was generally used to infer a soundness of the body.[1] Prior to enigmatic physician known as Hippocrates (c 460-377 BCE, or more appropriately, from around 5 BCE), health was perceived as a divine gift. Hippocrates was credited with the pioneering shift from divine notions of health, and using observation as a basis for acquiring health knowledge.

Scores of definitions of 'health' are available now in the literature. The most commonly quoted definition of health is that which is formalized by the World Health Organization (WHO) over half a century ago: "a complete state of physical, mental and social well-being, and not merely the absence of disease or infirmity."[2] Several other generally accepted definitions of the noun 'health' exist. Bircher defines health as "a dynamic state of well-being characterized by a physical and mental potential, which satisfies the demands of life commensurate with age, culture and personal responsibility"[3], while Saracchi defines health as "a condition of well-being, free of disease or infirmity and a basic and universal human right."[4]

Defining health as a human right, and determining what that means, presents some conceptual challenges. The public and scholarly discussion of health and human rights is relatively of recent origin. As late as 1994 it could still be said that, "Health and human rights have rarely been linked in an explicit manner. With a few exceptions, notably involving access to health care, discussions about health have not included human rights considerations."[5] Nonetheless, the idea that health is a fundamental human right was present at the birth of the human rights movement following the Second World War.

While the first intention of human rights as an international standard of law set forth in 1945 in the United Nations *Charter*, it was little more than an assertion of a commitment to promote and encourage "respect for human rights and for fundamental freedoms"[6], the meaning of the term human rights was quickly fleshed out. By 1946, the United Nations had shepherd into creation of the World Health Organization (WHO).

By 1948, the United Nations General Assembly adopted the *Universal Declaration of Human Rights*, an exposition on the nature and content of the term human rights that was subsequently developed into the *International Covenant on Civil and Political Rights* (ICCPR) and the *International Covenant on Economic, Social and Cultural Rights* (ICESCR).[7] After the formation of some of the international organizations the clear conceptual definition of health has come into existence. So, without the insights provided by the WHO definition of health, one might be misled to the conclusion that the human rights related to health, as articulated in the UDHR, as "right to life" (Art. 3) a "right not to be tortured" (with the health consequences associated with that [Art. 5]) and the right "to a standard of living adequate for the health…of himself [sic] and of his family, including food, clothing, housing and medical care" [Art. 25(1)].[8] However, in the light of WHO definition, the rights must be understood as health related human rights whenever they affect "physical, mental [or] social well-being." The definition therefore embraces the related rights though separate disciplines of medicine (focused on individual health) and public health.[9] Thus, the legal import of this broad definition is that the States not only have a duty to prevent or remove barriers to the realization and maintenance of physical, mental and social well-being, they also have an obligation to promote health, social, and related services, along with cultural reform to remedy potential social harms.[10]

Given this extremely expansive understanding of health, virtually every human right embodies an element of health. Thus, the WHO may reasonably assert that the human rights obligation of states to promote and protect health embodies a demand not simply to attend to the provision of "physical and mental health services, but to the justice of the foundations upon which societies function."[11] In assessing "health human rights" no limits apply. Not only do the instruments of the *International Bill of Rights* afford grounding, virtually every succeeding human rights instrument adds to the realm of health human rights. Whether it involves protection against genocide[12], war crimes[13], or racial discrimination, all have clearly recognizable effects on health and human well-being. Moreover, the United Nations and the international system were quickly supplemented by regional treaties and organizations in Europe, America and elsewhere, that echoed and sometimes advanced the ideas set forth in their international counterparts.

While the WHO definition of health justifies this broad understanding of health related human rights, many definitions become meaningless. If health is synonymous with human rights, health adds nothing to the conversation. Thus, it is useful to identify human rights to health as those rights whose derogation or promotion results in measurable effects in physical and/or mental health, either at the individual or social level. While making the concept of health related human rights more manageable, this limitation still allows for a very wide range of health rights. For example, the impairment of economic rights (such as unionization[14], rights to property[15], or a decent wage[16]) could clearly create a socio-economic status detrimental to a person's physical and mental health.[17] The health consequence of an impairment of these rights merely becomes one point of entry through which to consider the rights violation, or provides grounds for a legal or political compromise in the face of a conflict of rights.[18]

While health related human rights were clearly intended to be included within the catalogue of international human rights, the nature, extent and character of these health related human rights remains subject of debate. While those health rights arising under the ICCPR, the *Genocide* and other related conventions that protect the health of individuals from harmful state action (particularly actions that would directly threaten their right to life, or physical integrity or dignity)[19] are strongly protected, those health rights that may impose an affirmative duty upon the state to provide economic or social resources have traditionally been much more limited. For example, while the ICCPR mandates that member states have an affirmative, immediate obligation to protect all of the rights identified in the ICCPR (except for a limited number of political rights that may be derogated in times of public emergency), the ICESCR merely obligates State Parties to "undertake steps...to the maximum of its available resources...to achieve progressively the full realization of rights recognized in the [ICESCR]."[20] Thus, in evaluating any human health rights claim, it is important to determine the source and nature of the state obligation.

But for now, a right to health could be understood on a continuum. At a minimum, it could mean a right to conditions that protect health in the population. It might also include civil and political rights with respect to access to population-based and personal health care services. At most, it could also include provision of medical care for the diagnosis and treatment of disease and injury for those unable to pay.

Defining the content of a right to health is a formidable challenge. But the challenge should not impede the recognition and development of a human right to health in international human rights law. For such definitional problems attend many human rights and particularly those affirmative economic, social and cultural human rights that are now coming into their own in the post-Cold War World. Here, it is significant to note that the idea of an international human right to health which is gaining more attention these days.

Sources of International Human Rights Law

Notions of human rights are not new. The idea that individual human beings have human rights has its origins in the world's religions that recognize two basic precepts: (1) God, however revealed, values all human beings, and (2) human beings, in turn, are accountable to God for their actions toward other human beings whoever they may be.

We generally attribute the origins of modern notions of human rights to the Eighteenth Century Enlightenment and the English Revolution of the Seventeenth Century. The legacy of the Eighteenth Century Enlightenment and the English, American and French Revolutions was recognition of civil and political human rights for all people primarily in relation to their governments. The Eighteenth Century Enlightenment did recognize one economic right, the right to property, which served as the basis of the emerging economic system of capitalism in the Industrial Revolution.

Economic rights, in particular the human right to health, have different origins. They emerged primarily from the economic dislocations of the Industrial Revolution, which inspired many philosophers, including Karl Marx, to conclude that human beings also have rights to economic security. Notions of a positive right to health had its origins in the

Sanitary Revolution of the Nineteenth Century when public health reformers, also troubled by the economic dislocations of the Industrial Revolution and empowered with scientific advances, such as the germ theory of disease, pressed for state-sponsored public health reforms.

World War II and the establishment of the United Nations (UN) are the watershed events in the evolution of the modern corpus of international human rights law and the current international human rights system. The UN embraced the recognition and protection of human rights as a core strategy for world peace. Since the UN Universal Declaration of Human Rights in 1948[21], a substantial body of international law has developed recognizing basic human rights and their promotion and protection. In brief, there are two major sources of international human rights law that are relevant to the right to health: (1) international treaties of the UN and regional international organizations such as the Organization of American States, and (2) Customary International Law.

International Treaties

The 1948 UN Universal Declaration of Human Rights is not a treaty but a statement of policy and a call to action much like the Declaration of Independence. It affirmatively states a human right to health: "Everyone has the right to a standard of living adequate for the health and well-being of himself and of his family, including . . . medical care . . . and the right to security in the event of . . . sickness, disability . . . ."[22]

In the 1960s, the UN sponsored the development of two international covenants that articulate the human rights recognized in the UN Universal Declaration of Human Rights. These two covenants are the International Covenant on Civil and Political Rights (ICCPR)[23] and the International Covenant on Economic, Social and Cultural Rights (ICESCR).[24]

The International Covenant on Economic, Social and Cultural Rights (ICESCR)—the so-called Economic Covenant—is the most important in terms of the right to health. Article 12 of ICESCR states that the right to health includes "the enjoyment of the highest attainable standard of physical and mental health"[25], the relevant provisions of this covenant are presented in the Covenant on Economic, Social and Cultural Rights (ICESCR). The Article 12 talks that (1) "The State Parties to the present Covenant recognize the right of everyone to the enjoyment of the highest attainable standard of physical and mental health." (2) The steps to be taken by the States Parties to the present Covenant to achieve the full realization of this right shall include those necessary for: (a) The provision for the reduction of the stillbirth-rate and of infant mortality and for the healthy development of the child; (b) The improvement of all aspects of environmental and industrial hygiene; (c) The prevention, treatment and control of epidemic, endemic, occupational and other diseases; (d) The creation of conditions which would assure to all medical service and medical attention in the event of sickness.

The UN Committee on Economic, Social and Cultural Rights has responsibility for the promotion, implementation and enforcement of this covenant. A human right to health is also recognized in numerous other international human rights authorities that establish prohibitions against government conduct that is detrimental to health. Such treaties include the International Convention on the Elimination of All Forms of Racial Discrimination of 1965[26], the Convention on the Elimination of All Forms of Discrimination against Women of 1979[27], and the Convention on the Rights of the Child of 1989.[28]

The UN also has established several international agencies to promote economic and social development worldwide. The World Health Organization (WHO) has a legislative capacity to make international health regulations in addition to its health promotion functions.

In addition, regional international organizations have treaties and implementation bodies. The Inter-American system for the protection of human rights of the Organization of American States (OAS) is based on the OAS American Declaration of the Rights and Duties of Man[29] and the OAS American Convention on Human Rights[30], among other instruments. Specifically, Article 11 of the American Declaration of the Rights and Duties of Man states "[e]very person has the right to the preservation of his health through sanitary and social measures relating to food, clothing, housing and medical care, to the extent permitted by public and community resources."[31] The more recent Protocol of San Salvador specifies a human right to health in its interpretation of the OAS Convention on Human Rights.[32] Detailed provisions are presented in the Appendix of this thesis.

It is relevant to note that the 1993 Vienna Declaration and Programme of Action emphasize the fundamental interrelatedness of political and civil human rights and economic social and cultural human rights.[33] The Vienna Declaration specifically provides:

> "All human rights are universal, indivisible and interdependent and interrelated. The international community must treat human rights globally in a fair and equal manner, on the same footing, and with the same emphasis. While the significance of national and regional particularities and various historical, cultural and religious backgrounds must be borne in mind, it is the duty of States, regardless of their political, economic and cultural systems, to promote and protect all human rights and fundamental freedoms."[34]

The Vienna Declaration has become a crucial principle in international human rights law recognizing the irreducible truth that all human rights must be recognized if specific human rights are to have concrete meaning. A look to the body of international treaties that comprise the corpus of human rights law at first glance seems promising. However, these treaties bind only those nations that ratify them. The customary international law plays crucial role in health and human rights discourse. Therefore, it needs critical assessment to know how it is linked with health and human rights approach to establish the right to health.

Customary International Law

Customary International Law holds promise as an important source of international law with respect to human rights.

International Customary Law is interesting for it can legally bind nations regardless of treaty ratification. "Customary international law results from a general and consistent practice of states followed by them from a sense of legal obligation."[35] The two major elements of customary international law are state practice and *opinio juris*, a state's sense of legal obligation.

Customary international law also is promising when it comes to establishing a binding international human right to health in the nations of the world. Under the principles for the development of customary international law, widespread ratification of UN and regional treaties and other instruments recognizing international human rights can establish an international customary law of human rights. Specifically, treaties, declarations and other instruments become evidence of a general state practice in which states engage out of a sense of legal obligation. As evidence of general practice followed out of a sense of legal obligation, they establish the human rights obligations in the instruments as a customary international law. As international customary law, the obligations in the international human rights instruments then impose obligations on states. Thus, for example, the ICESCR is arguably customary international law due to its widespread acceptance internationally. As a consequence, it may be binding on all countries regardless of ratification.

Other law and practice in India and other nations provides evidence of custom regarding the international human right to health. Many nations, particularly Western democracies as well as many developing nations, establish an explicit right to health in their constitutions. The following pie chart presents the number of nations that have such provisions establishing a right to health in their constitutions. It also presents the number of nations that have signed UN or regional treaties and other instruments that recognize the human right to health.

As the health and morality of the people are essential to their well-being, and to the peace and permanence of the state, it shall be the duty of the legislature to protect and promote these vital interests. Here, different national constitutional provisions on health and human rights need to be explored, for example South Carolina's constitution designates health a

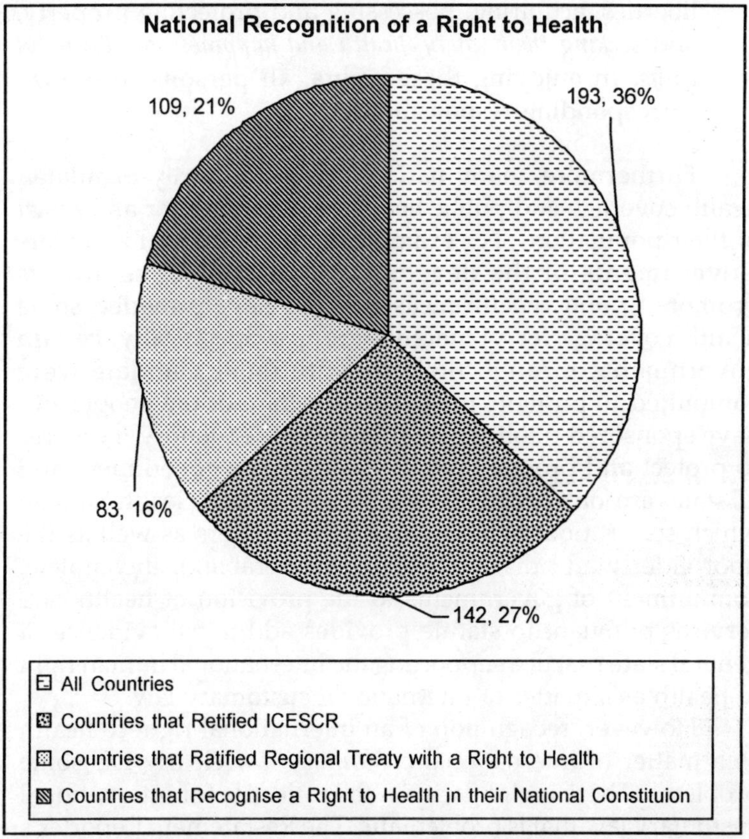

matter of public concern: "The health, welfare, and safety of the lives and property of the people of this State and the conservation of its natural resources are matters of public concern. The General Assembly shall provide appropriate agencies to function in these areas of public concern and determine the activities, powers, and duties of such agencies. [1970 (56) 2683; 1971 (57) 46]."[36] Montana's constitution is perhaps the most emphatic in providing a right to health as an affirmative matter in its section on inalienable rights:

> "All persons are born free and have certain inalienable rights. They include the right to a clean and healthy environment and the rights of pursuing life's with basic necessities, enjoying and defending their lives and

> liberties, acquiring, possessing and protecting property, and *seeking their safety, health and happiness in all lawful ways*. In enjoying these rights, all persons recognize corresponding responsibilities."[37]

Furthermore, many nations have statutorily-mandated health coverage and public health programmes for all or part of their populations. For example, both the Central and State Governments of the developing countries have always promoted public health measures and have provided some health coverage for vulnerable groups. Specifically, certain governments through their constitutional mandate were committed to promote the general welfare of the people and have sponsored public programmes and regulatory measures to protect and promote public health.[38] The government and all states are joint partners in the National Rural Health Mission which serves poor children and their mothers as well as the poor elderly and disabled. This considerable, if incomplete, commitment of governments to the provision of health care services pursuant to statute provides additional evidence of general state practice supporting the international human right to health as a matter of international customary law.

However, recognition of an international right to health as a matter of international customary law clearly has some problems. There is circularity in the rationale for international customary law that is problematic. The Restatement Reporter's comments layout some of the problems with customary international law as now defined:

> "Each element attempted definitions has raised difficulties. There have been philosophical debates about the very basis of the definition: how can practice build law? Most troublesome conceptually has been the circularity in the suggestion that law is built by practice based on a sense of legal obligation: how, it is asked, can there be a sense of legal obligation before the law from which the legal obligation derives has matured?"[39]

The reporter goes on to observe that "such conceptual difficulties, however, have not prevented acceptance of customary law essèntially as here defined" and opines that "perhaps the sense of legal obligation came originally from principles of natural law or common morality, often already reflected in principles of law common to national legal systems and practice built on that sense of obligation then matured into customary law."[40]

Customary international law—particularly as it pertains to economic rights such as the right to health—is also problematic from another perspective. What kinds of remedies attend the human right to health recognized under customary international law? Can an Indian citizen use in an international court to enforce this right? If so, can an international court rule that the Indian has some kind of obligation to provide the individual involved access to needed health care services? If not, what is the extent of the customary human right to health beyond a moral duty?

Implementing the International Right to Health

If there is a binding international human right to health, then how would it be defined and implemented? This is a challenge. In this effort, we should be imaginative. As researcher, we tend to think of administrative regulation and enforcement as well as judicial recourse as the primary mechanisms for assuring the implementation of rights. However, these models may not be particularly appropriate or effective when we are talking about what, at least in India and many other nations, is essentially a right to health under international customary law.

Such legalistic visions of the right to health may also not be appropriate or effective as there is still some uncertainty about the content of the international human right to health. Indeed, getting a handle on the content of the right to health is a necessary first step to effective implementation. But this is no easy task. To have meaning, the content of the right to health must be essentially the same for all nations and people. The implementation is dependent on the resources, as well as cultures of individual countries. How do we articulate the right to health in countries with vastly different economic resources and cultural traditions, multi-ethnic, multi-lingual and multi-religious country like India?

General Comment 14

The UN Committee on International Economic, Social and Cultural Rights—the treaty body responsible for implementing and monitoring ICESCR—has published a General Comment 14 to ICESCR that outlines the content to the international right to health.[41] This General Comment is extensive and quite specific and intended to apply to nations that have ratified the ICESCR. It addresses the content of the right to health and the implementation and enforcement of the right to health. It also provides remedies for individual parties who have been denied the human right to health.

General Comment 14 begins with some observations about the normative content of the right to health. Specifically, General Comment 14 states that "[t]he right to health is not to be understood as a right to be *healthy*" and that "[t]he right to health contains both freedoms and entitlements."[42] The General Comment 14 specifies the freedoms and entitlements as follows:

> "The freedoms include the right to control one's health and body, including sexual and reproductive freedom, and the right to be free from interference, such as the right to be free from torture, non-consensual medical treatment and experimentation. By contrast, the entitlements include the right to a system of health protection which provides equality of opportunity for people to enjoy the highest attainable level of health."[43]

General Comment 14 then observes that the right to health extends not only to timely and appropriate health care but also to the underlying determinants of health, such as access to safe and potable water and adequate sanitation, an adequate supply of safe food, nutrition and housing, healthy occupational and environmental conditions, and access to health related education and information, including on sexual and reproductive health.[44]

These provisions of General Comment 14 indeed prescribe a broad and inclusive conception of the content of the human right to health. General Comment 14 also provides that the health care system of a states party must have certain institutional characteristics to realize the right to health. These include the availability, accessibility, acceptability and quality of needed health care services and facilities. "Availability" means that the states party has sufficient facilities and services for the population given the country's state of development. Services include those that affect the underlying determinants of health, such as safe and potable drinking water. "Accessibility" to health care facilities and services include the four dimensions: non-discrimination, physical accessibility, economic accessibility (affordability), and information accessibility. "Acceptability" means that services and facilities must be respectful of medical ethics and culturally appropriate as well as being designed to respect confidentiality and improve the health status of those served. "Quality" means that services must also be scientifically and medically appropriate and of good quality.[45]

General Comment 14 imposes three types or levels of obligations: the obligations to *respect, protect* and *fulfil*. The obligation to *respect* requires states parties to refrain from interfering directly or indirectly with the enjoyment of the right to health. The obligation to *protect* requires states parties to take measures that prevent third parties from interfering with article 12 guarantees. The obligation to *fulfil* requires states parties to adopt appropriate legislative, administrative, budgetary, judicial, promotional and other measures towards the full realization of the right to health.[46] General Comment 14 also reaffirms that several "core" obligations have been established in prior international human rights instruments: These core obligations, as well as additional obligations, are as follows. General Comment 14, obligations regarding the human right to health, core obligations established in prior international human rights instruments:

- To ensure the right of access to health facilities, goods and services on a non-discriminatory basis, especially for vulnerable or marginalized groups;
- To ensure access to the minimum essential food which is nutritionally adequate and safe, to ensure freedom from hunger to everyone;

- To ensure access to basic shelter, housing and sanitation, and an adequate supply of safe and potable water;
- To providc essential drugs, as from time to time defined under the WHO Action Programme on Essential Drugs;
- To ensure equitable distribution of all health facilities, goods and services;
- To adopt and implement a national public health strategy and plan of action, on the basis of epidemiological evidence, addressing the health concerns of the whole population; the strategy and plan of action shall be devised, and periodically reviewed, on the basis of a participatory and transparent process; they shall include methods, such as right to health indicators and benchmarks, by which progress can be closely monitored; the process by which the strategy and plan of action are devised, as well as their content, shall give particular attention to all vulnerable or marginalized groups.

On the other dimension of obligations of comparable priority it reads in following manner:

- To ensure reproductive, maternal (pre-natal as well as post-natal) and child health care;
- To provide immunization against the major infectious diseases occurring in the community;
- To take measures to prevent, treat and control epidemic and endemic diseases;
- To provide education and access to information concerning the main health problems in the community, including methods of preventing and controlling them;
- To provide appropriate training for health personnel, including education on health and human rights.

General Comment 14 clearly addresses implementation. It imposes a duty on each states party "to take whatever steps are necessary to ensure that everyone has access to health facilities, goods and services so that they can enjoy, as soon as possible, the highest attainable standard of physical and mental health."[47] Implementation requires adoption of "a national strategy to ensure to all the enjoyment of the right to health based on human rights principles which defines the objectives of that strategy, and the formulation of policies and corresponding right to health indicators and benchmarks."[48] The national health strategy should also "identify the resources available to attain defined objectives, as well as the most cost-effective way of using those resources."[49] The national health strategy and plan of action should "be based on the principles of accountability, transparency and independence of the judiciary, since good governance is essential to the effective implementation of all human rights, including the realization of the right to health."[50]

General Comment 14 has extensive enforcement provisions and specifies violations of the right to health. The Comment explicitly provides that a states party which "is unwilling to use the maximum of its available resources for the realization of the right to health is in violation of its obligations under Article 12."[51] Further, if resource constraints make compliance impossible, the states party "has the burden of justifying that every effort has nevertheless been made to use all available resources at its disposal in order to satisfy, as a matter of priority, the obligations outlined above."[52]

General Comment 14 also specifies violations. For example, violations of the obligation to respect include "state actions, policies or laws that contravene the standards set out in Article 12 of the Covenant and are likely to result in bodily harm, unnecessary morbidity and preventable mortality."[53] Violations of the obligation to protect include "failure of a State to take all necessary measures to safeguard persons within their jurisdiction from infringements of the right to health by third parties."[54] Finally, violations of the obligation to fulfil include "failure of States parties to take all necessary steps to ensure the realization of the right to health."[55]

Finally, General Comment 14 accords remedies to individual parties. Specifically, any person or group victim of a violation of the right to health should have access to effective judicial or other appropriate remedies at both national and international levels. All victims of such violations should be entitled to adequate reparation, which may take the form of restitution, compensation, satisfaction or guarantees of non-repetition. National ombudsmen, human rights commissions, consumer forums, patients' rights associations or similar institutions should address violations of the right to health.[56]

General Comment 14 represents a significant step in delineating the international human right to state parties to the ICESCR. Despite General Comment's specificity, as well as flexibility, the issue of how General Comment 14 will be interpreted, implemented and enforced by states parties at different stages of economic development and with markedly different cultures and values will still be a challenge. In sum, the content of the international right to health remains a tough issue.

Realistic Implementation and Enforcement

When all is said and done, legal rights should be enforceable. Otherwise, we are back to where we began at the beginning of the first chapter of the thesis. The human right to health is just a moral right after all. Realistically, implementation and enforcement of the international right to health is difficult particularly if predicated on customary international law. Implementation requires affirmative action on the part of government, and implicates intervention in the internal domestic affairs of nations. India and other nations would probably not tolerate excessive interference in their domestic affairs that are specified in General Comment 14 if they have not ratified ICSECR. Further, given the diverse cultures and economic levels of the nations of the world, it is hard to envision a mandate that would implement the right to health that would be appropriate to all nations.

But if the international right to health is to mean anything at all, it does seem appropriate to impose some implementation obligations on states and also require some type of regulation to assure implementation and enforcement. We must allow states considerable latitude to define strategies for implementation within the national economic, social and cultural circumstances. Universal coverage through health insurance and health care plans may make sense for some states of India but is a ridiculous proposal for some other states. But if we allow such discretion, how do we not virtually vitiate the international right to health?

Proposed Approaches

Given economic, social and cultural differences among the nations of the world, we should take three major approaches: First, define universal outcome measures that measure compliance with the core state obligations of the human right to health; second, establish systematic reporting to responsible international bodies to monitor progress on implementation and compliance with international human rights obligations; third, highlight civil rights violations, such as discrimination against protected groups that inhibit access to health care services.

Use of Outcome Measures: The first approach outcome measures for measuring the implementation of the human right to health is essential. Outcome measures would also indicate where countries need to concentrate efforts to meet their obligations under the international human right to health. They also assist in establishing concrete goals for human rights implementation.

The UN and the WHO already appreciate the possibilities of reported data on outcome measures in monitoring compliance of states with international human rights obligations. In its *Human Development Report 2000*[57], the UN expressly recognizes a link between human rights and human development as well as the use of comparative data to measure compliance with international human rights obligations. Specifically, the UN acknowledges the potential use of such statistical indicators in human rights enforcement:

> "Statistical indicators are a powerful tool in the struggle for human rights. They make it possible for people and organizations—from grass roots activists and civil society to governments and the United Nations—to identify

important actors and hold them accountable for their actions. This is why developing and using indicators for human rights has become a cutting-edge area of advocacy."[58]

In this report, the United Nations has created four major indicators of economic development of use in measuring progress toward the achievement of economic human right. These are: (1) Human Development Index; (2) Gender Related Development Index; (3) Gender Empowerment Measure; and (4) Human Poverty Index. Further, in its *World Health Report 2000*, the WHO reports health system attainment and performance measures for member states. *World Health Report, 2000*, health system attainment and performance measures are:

- Health system attainment and performance in all Member States, ranked by eight measures.
- Basic indicators for all Member States Deaths by cause, sex and mortality stratum in WHO Regions.
- Burden of disease in disability-adjusted life years (DALYs) by cause, sex and mortality stratum in WHO Regions.
- Health attainment, level and distribution in all Member States Responsiveness of health systems, level and distribution in all Member States.
- Fairness of financial contribution to health systems in all Member States.

Establish a Comparative Reporting System: If a country meets these universal outcome measures specified in a systematic reporting system, responsible international bodies, as well as domestic constituencies, will assume that implementation and compliance have occurred. This approach mitigates the need for international bodies to delve deeply into the internal affairs of nations to assure implementation and compliance. The importance of comparative reporting and publication of comparative statistics can do much to advance the implementation of the human right to health, particularly with respect to state obligations to take affirmative measure to promote public health or expand health coverage.

The WHO has begun reporting country health statistics on a comparative basis. Specifically, in *World Health Report 2000*, WHO published its first comparative analysis of the world's health systems.

Highlight Civil Rights Violations: Highlighting civil rights violations, such as discrimination against protected groups with respect to health care services, can do much to promote the international human right to health generally. For example, elimination of discrimination against women, minorities and other disadvantaged groups in the provision of appropriate health care services can do much to promote the right to health generally. This approach reinforces the reproach of the 1993 Vienna Declaration quoted above that all human rights are highly interrelated.[59]

An example of the importance of recognizing the distinctions between the different types of rights that are subsumed in the larger right to health is the case of AIDS. According to women equal status in marriage and divorce and recognizing fully their civil and political rights does much to empower women in rejecting unwanted sexual relations with HIV-infected partners.[60] Clearly, recognition and enforcement of civil rights for women would do much to prevent HIV infection and associated AIDS.

Finally, what difference would it make to the nations of the world if there were a legal mandate for a human right to health? Such a legal mandate would play a tremendous role in making the promotion of public health and the expansion of health coverage a priority in all nations. Such recognition would encourage nations to promote health care programmes as a priority basis. Such promotion in recent years has been exceedingly difficult due to the supervision of the economies of debtor nations by the International Monetary Fund with its neo-conservative economic policies for debtor nations.[61]

Specifically, in the poor debtor nations of the world, recognition of a human right to health could shape lending policies of the International Monetary Fund and the World Bank in several ways. It could bolster efforts to protect infrastructure for the provision of health care services in a country by recognizing the importance of the right to health in the imposed economic development policies associated with international loans and economic assistance. Also, this right could end the disruptive practice of requiring user fees for the use of publicly funded clinics and other health care services—a widespread practice under neo-conservative policies of these lending bodies that has had a detrimental impact on health in poor debtor nations.

Conclusion

This chapter outlines the discourse about the international human right standards of health and what it could mean for our nation. We do think that the international human rights to health—as established under international customary law—arguably impose greater obligations on India with respect to health than we appreciate or recognize in our constitution. This chapter also throws light to broaden the scope of right to health with support of international legal instruments and national laws. The notion of enlarging health rights needs special attention to draw global legal norms which have been presented above. We are at a stage in history where political will to do something progressive is conspicuous by its absence. We may have constitutional commitments and backing of international law but without political will nothing will happen. To reach the goals of right to health, which are discussed above that the government agencies and the civil society or community based organizations, have to be involved in a very large extent and enlarge the scope of standard to realize right to health. The idea here is not to develop a plan of action but to indicate the various steps and involvements that be needed to build a consensus and struggle for right to health. It needs continuous negotiation and struggle to realize right to health. There is a huge gap between policy and its implication; policy does not have much problem in paper but problem lays when it turns into action or implementation. Therefore, country specific standard setting is value added one.

END NOTES

1. Dolfman, Michael L., "The Concept of Health: An Historic and Analytic Examination", *Journal of School Health,* Published by American School Health Association, Temple University, Philadelphia, Pennsylvania, 1973, Vol. 43, pp. 491-497.
2. WHO Preamble to the Constitution of the WHO as adopted by the *International Health Conference,* New York, 19-22 June 1946, and Entered into Force on 7th April, 1948.
3. Bircher J., "Towards a Dynamic Definition of Health and Disease", *Medical Health Care Philosophy,* Published by ResearchGATES, Scientific Society, 2005, 8(3) pp. 335-41.
4. Saracchi R., "The World Health Organisation needs to Reconsider its Definition of Health", *BMJ* 1997, 314:1409-10.
5. Jonathan M. Mann, Lawrence Gostin, Sofia Gruskin, Troyen Brennan, Zita Lazzarini, and Harvey Fineberg, "Health and Human Rights", 1994.
6. U.N. Charter Art. 1, Para 3.
7. G.A. Res. 2200 A (XXI), U.N. GAOR, 21st Session, Supp. No. 16, at 49, U.N. Doc. A/6316 (1966) (hereinafter ICESCR).
8. In terms of Health, the ICCPR and the ICESCR Essentially "Implemented" these Norms with Certain Elaborations, Such as the ICESCR'S Requirement that the States Parties "Recognized the Right of Everyone to the Enjoyment of the Highest Attainable Standard of Physical and Mental Health" and that the States Take Steps to Address Problems such as Infant Mortality, Environmental Pollution, Treatment of Epidemics and the Availability of Medical Care. *Ibid.* At Article 12
9. Mann *et al., supra* note 4, pp. 2-3.
10. Cook R.J. Chapter 1, "The Evolution of International Human Rights Relevant to Women's Health", in Women's Health and Human Rights: the Promotion and Protection of Women's Health through International Human Rights Law, Geneva, World Health Organization, 1994, pp. 1-4.
11. *Ibid.*
12. Convention on the Prevention and Punishment of the Crime of Genocide, approved for signature Dec. 9, 1948, 78 U.N.T.S. 277.
13. Geneva Convention, 75 U.N.T.S. 287 (August 12, 1949).
14. UDHR, Supra note 8, Article, 23, p. 4.
15. *Ibid.* at Article, 17, p. 1.
16. *Ibid.* at Article., 23, p. 3.
17. Nancy Adler *et al.,* "Socio-economic Status and Health: The Challenge of the Gradient", in *Health and Human Rights,* 181, Jonathan M. Mann *et al.*, eds., 1999.
18. See Infra Text at Notes 8-11.
19. ICCPR, Supra Note 9, Article 6; Convention on the Prevention and Punishment of the Crime of Genocide, Supra Note 15, Article II.

20. ICESCR, Supra Note 10, Article 2(1).
21. UN Universal Declaration of Human Rights, General Assembly Resolution, 217A (III), Article 13.1, U.N. GAOR, 3d Session, at 71, 74, U.N. Doc. A/810 (1948).
22. *Ibid.*
23. International Covenant on Civil and Political Rights, G.A. Res. 2200A (XXI), U.N. GAOR, 21st Session, Supp. No. 16, at 49, U.N. Doc. A/6316 (1966).
24. International Covenant on Economic, Social and Cultural Rights, General Assembly Resolution, 22001 (XXI), U.N. GAOR, 21st Session, Supp. No. 16, U.N. Doc. A/6316, 993 U.N.T.S. 3 (1966).
25. *Ibid.*
26. International Convention on the Elimination of All Forms of Racial Discrimination, Dec. 21, 1965, Article 5(d)(vii General Assembly Resolution, 2106 (XX), U.N. General Assembly Resolution, 20th Session, Supp. No. 14, at 47, U.N. Doc. A/6014 (1965), 660 U.N.T.S. 195, 222 (entered into force Jan. 4, 1969).
27. Convention on the Elimination of All Forms of Discrimination against Women, Dec. 18, 1979, Article 12, General Assembly Resolution, 34/180, U.N. GAOR, 34th Session, Supp. No. 46, U.N. Doc. A/34/36 (1980) (entered into force Sept. 3, 1981).
28. Convention on the Rights of the Child of 1989, Nov. 20, 1989, Article 24, General Assembly Resolution, 44/25, U.N. GAOR, 44th Session, Supp. No. 49, U.N. Doc A/44/49 (1989) (entered into force Jan. 4, 1969).
29. American Declaration of the Rights and Duties of Man, Mar. 30-May 2, 1948, O.A.S. Resolution XXX, Adopted by the Ninth International Conference of American States, Bogata Columbia, OEA/Ser. L/V/II, 23 doc., 21 rev. 6 (1948), Reprinted in Organization of American States, Basic Documents Pertaining To Human Rights in the Inter-American System, 1988, pp. 17-24.
30. American Convention on Human Rights, *Opened for Signatures,* Nov. 22, 1969, O.A.S. Official Records, OEA/Ser. K/XVI/II, doc. 65, rev. 1, corr. 2, 144 U.N.T.S. 123, 9 I.L.M. 673, 678 (1970), Reprinted in Organization of American States, Supra Note 13, pp. 25-54.
31. American Declaration of the Rights and Duties of Man, Supra Note 11, Article 11.
32. Additional Protocol to the American Convention on Human Rights in the Area of Economic, Social and Cultural Rights, Nov. 14, 1988, O.A.S. T.S. 69 at Article 10 (1988), Reprinted in The Inter-American System of Human Rights 500 (David J. Harris & Stephen Livingstone eds., 1998).
33. 1993 Vienna Declaration and Programme of Action, U.N. GAOR, World Conference on Human Rights, 78th Session, 22d Plenary Management, Part 1, Article 5, U.N, Doc. A/CONF 157/23 (1993).

34. *Ibid.*
35. *Ibid.*
36. South Carolina Constitution, Article XII, Section 1, Published by Legislative Printing, Information and Technology Systems, Columbia, 1895.
37. Montana's Constitution, Article II, Section 3, As Adopted by the Constitutional Convention March 22, 1972, and as Ratified by the People; June 6, 1972, Referendum No. 68, Published by Montana Legislative Services.
38. Lawrence O. Gostin, *Public Health Law: Power, Duty and Restraint,* Revised and Expanded Second Edition, The University of California Press, London, 2008, pp. 25-59.
39. Restatement, Third, Foreign Relations Law of the United States, 102, comment. 2, Published by Amer Law Institute, US, 1986.
40. *Ibid.*
41. United Nations, Committee on Economic, Social and Cultural Rights, U.N. ESCOR, 22d Session, *The Right to the Highest Attainable Standard of Health,* U.N. Doc. E/C, Dec. 4, 2000, ICESR General Comment 14 (2000).
42. *Ibid.* (emphasis in original)
43. *Ibid.*
44. *Ibid.*
45. *Ibid.*
46. *Ibid.*
47. *Ibid.*
48. *Ibid.*
49. *Ibid.*
50. *Ibid.*
51. *Ibid.*
52. *Ibid.*
53. *Ibid.*
54. *Ibid.*
55. *Ibid.*
56. *Ibid.*
57. Human Development Report 2000, Published for the United Nations Development Programme (UNDP), Oxford University Press, New York, 2000.
58. *Ibid.*, p. 89.
59. Supra Note 16 and Accompanying Text.
60. Gostin & Lazzarini, Supra Note 1, p. 46.
61. Walden Bello *et al.*, Dark Victory: the United States and Global Poverty (1999); Michael Chossudovsky, the Globalization of Poverty: Impacts of IMF and World Bank Reforms, Food Fast, NV, USA, 2000.

4

Human Rights Standards in Health

Indian Scenario

Human rights standards address the civil, political, economic, social and cultural sphere. Each human right, while formally belonging to one of those categories, in reality encompasses aspects of all of them. This is easily identifiable within the human right to health. Moreover, the right to health within the human rights framework is defined as the right to achieve the "highest attainable standard of health" not merely the absence of disease. Both of these aspects of human rights are consistent with a social determinant approach to health, as they take into account the wide array of factors that influence a person's overall health status. Finally, a human rights and health care delivery approach both have in common an assumption that the primary purpose of a health care system is preserving health, rather than addressing economic interests. This chapter broadly focuses on health delivery system in India and helps in examining them as against the global standards. The background of health policy since independence and evaluation of government reports, commission's recommendations and suggestions which we consider is of basic importance to know and explore the new dimensions of health rights. Second, it also presents the overview of health scenarios in India and standard setting norms in human rights and right to health which is a unit of analysis in this chapter. The argument flows from Alma Ata Declaration of 1978 and onwards.

The Alma Ata Declaration in 1978 gave an insight into the understanding of primary health care. It viewed health as an integral part of the socio-economic development of a country. It provided the most holistic understanding to health and the framework that States needed to pursue, to achieve the goals of development. The Declaration recommended that primary health care should include at least: education concerning prevailing health problems and methods of identifying, preventing and controlling them; promotion of food supply and proper nutrition, and adequate supply of safe water and basic sanitation; maternal and child health care, including family planning; immunization against major infectious diseases; prevention and control of locally endemic diseases; appropriate treatment of common diseases and injuries; promotion of mental health and provision of essential drugs. It emphasized the need for strong first-level care with strong secondary- and tertiary-level care linked to it. It called for an integration of preventive, promotive, curative and rehabilitative health services that had to be made accessible and available to the people, and this was to be guided by the principles of universality, comprehensiveness and equity. In one sense, primary health care reasserted the role and responsibilities of the State, and recognized that health is influenced by a multitude of factors and not just the health services. It also recognized the need for a multi-sectoral approach to health and clearly stated that primary health care had to be linked to other sectors. At the same time, the Declaration emphasized on complete and organized community participation, and ultimate self-reliance with individuals, families and communities assuming more responsibility for their own health, facilitated by support from groups such as the local government, agencies, local leaders, voluntary groups, youth and women's groups, consumer groups, other non-governmental organizations, etc. The Declaration affirmed the need for a balanced distribution of available resources (WHO: 1978).

Keeping this definition in mind, we now discuss whether this holistic concept has been utilized as a framework by policy-makers to develop various health policy documents, health committee reports and the five year plans since Independence so as to impact on the health system. After Independence, India adopted the welfare state approach, which was dominant worldwide at that time. As with most post-colonial nations, India too attempted to restructure its patterns of investment. During that time, India's leaders envisaged a national health system in which the State would play a leading role in determining priorities and financing, and provide services to the population. "If it was possible to evaluate the loss, which this country annually suffers through the avoidable waste of valuable human material and the lowering of human efficiency through malnutrition and preventable morbidity, we feel that the result would be so startling that the whole country would be aroused and would not rest until a radical change had been brought about" (Bhore Committee Report: 1946).

The emphasis of the first health report, i.e. the Health Planning and Development Committee's Report, 1946 (popularly known as the Committee Report) on the role of the State was explicit. It was a plan equivalent to Britain's National Health Service. Report was based on a countrywide survey in British India. It is the first organized set of health care data for India. The poor health status was attributed to the prevalence of insanitary conditions; malnutrition and undernutrition leading to high infant and maternal mortality rates; inadequacy of the existing medical and preventive health organizations; lack of general and health education; unemployment and poverty that produced adverse effects on health and resulted in inadequate nutrition; improper housing and lack of medical care. Intersectoral linkages were well discussed with nutrition, housing and employment as essential precursors for healthy living. It considered that the health programme in India should be developed on a foundation of preventive health work and proceeds in the closest association with the administration of medical relief. The Committee strongly recommended a health services system based on the needs of the people, the majority of whom were deprived and poor. It felt the need for developing a strong basic health services structure at the primary level with referral linkages. It also recommended the need to invest in the pharmaceutical sector to develop indigenous capabilities and reduce excessive reliance on multinational companies.

India was therefore one of the few developing countries which adopted a health policy that integrated the principles of universality and equity. Community participation and cooperative efforts to promote preventive and curative health work was important to achieve a vibrant health system. The Committee felt that large sections of the people were living below the normal subsistence level and they could not afford to pay for or contribute to the health services. It was decided that medical benefits would have to be supplied free to all at the point of delivery and those who could afford to pay should channel contributions through the mechanism of taxation. Though the report stated that "...it will be for the governments of the future to decide ultimately whether medical service should remain free to all classes of the people or whether an insurance scheme would be more in accordance with the economic, social and political requirements of the country at the time (Bhore Committee Report: 1946), one point was apparent—that no individual should fail to secure adequate medical care, curative and preventive because of the inability to pay for it. They recommended that State Governments should spend a minimum of 15 per cent of their revenues on health activities."

The National Planning Committee (NPC) set up by the Indian National Congress in 1938 under the chairmanship of Colonel S. Sokhey stated that the maintenance of the health of the people was the responsibility of the State, and the integration of preventive and curative functions in a single state agency was emphasized. The Sokhey Committee Report was not as detailed as the Bhore Committee Report but endorsed the recommendations of the Bhore Committee Report and commented that it was "of the utmost significance."[1]

The objectives of the First (1951-56) and Second Five Year (1956-61) Plans were to develop the basic infrastructure and manpower visualized by the Bhore Committee. Though health was seen as fundamental to national progress, less than 5 per cent of the total revenue was invested in health. The following priorities formed the basis of the First Five-Year Plan: provision of water supply and sanitation; control of malaria; preventive health care of the rural population through health units and mobile units; health services for mothers and children; education, training and health education; self-sufficiency in drugs and equipment; family planning and population control. Starting from the first plan, vertical programmes started, which became the centre of focus. The Malaria Control Programme, which was made one of the principal programmes, apart from other programmes for the control of TB, filariasis, leprosy and venereal diseases, was launched. Health personnel were to take part in vertical programmes. However, the first plan itself failed to create an integrated system by introducing verticality.

The concern of the Health Survey and Planning Committee (Mudaliar Committee: 1962) was limited to the development of the health services infrastructure and the health care at the primary level. It felt the growth of infrastructure needed radical transformation and further investment. Another major shift came in the Third Five Year Plan (1961-66) when family planning received priority for the first time. Increase in the population became a major worry and was seen as a hurdle to the development process. Although the broad objective was to bring about progressive improvement in the health of the people by ensuring a certain minimum level of physical well-being and to create conditions favourable for greater efficiency, there was a shift in focus from preventive health services to family planning. During the Fourth Plan (1969-74), efforts were made to provide an effective base for health services in rural areas by strengthening the PHCs. The vertical campaigns against communicable diseases were further intensified.

During the Fifth Plan (1974-79), policy-makers suddenly realized that health had to be addressed alongside other development programmes. The Minimum Needs Programme (MNP) promised to address all this but became an instrument through which only health infrastructure in the rural areas was to be expanded and further strengthened. It called for integration of peripheral staff of vertical programmes but the population control programme got further impetus during the Emergency (1975-77) and most of the basic health workers got sucked into the family planning programme. Meanwhile, the

Chaddha Committee Report (1963), the Kartar Singh Committee Report on Multipurpose Workers (1974) and the Srivastava Committee Report on Medical Education and Support Manpower (1975) remained focused on giving recommendations on how the health cadres at the primary level should be distributed. With the widespread disillusionment with vertical programmes worldwide and the need to provide universal health services came the Primary Health Care Declaration at Alma Ata in 1978, which India was a signatory to. The Sixth Plan (1980-84) was influenced by two policy documents: the Alma Ata Declaration and the ICMR/ICSSR report on 'Health for All by 2000'. The ICMR/ICSSR Report (1980) was in fact a move towards articulating a national health policy that was thought of as an important step to realize the Alma Ata Declaration. It was realized that one had to redefine and rearticulate and get back into track an integrated and comprehensive health system that policy-makers had wavered from. It reiterated the need to integrate the development of the health system with the overall plans of socio-economic and political change.

It recommended that the Government should formulate a comprehensive national health policy dealing with all dimensions e.g., environmental, nutritional, educational, socio-economic, preventive and curative. The National Health Policy (1983) attempted to incorporate all these. Provision of universal, comprehensive primary health services was its goal. A large number of private and voluntary organizations who were active across the country in the health field were to support the Government in its efforts to integrate health services. Evolving a decentralized system of health care and nationwide chain of epidemiological stations were some of the main recommendations.

Once again, a selective approach to health care became the focus when a strong lobby questioning the financial repercussions of the primary health care approach came up. Verticality was reintroduced as an 'interim' arrangement and interventions of immunization, oral rehydration, breastfeeding and anti-malarial drugs were suggested.[2] This was seen as a technical solution even before comprehensive primary health care could be realized. UNICEF too came out with its report on the state of the world's children health and suggested immunization as the spearhead in the selective GOBI-FF (Growth monitoring, Oral rehydration, Breastfeeding, Immunization, Food supplements for pregnant women and children, and Family planning) approach (Rifkin and Gill: 1986).

Programme-driven health policies were once again the central focus. Hence, the plan documents emphasized on restructuring and developing the health infrastructure, especially at the primary level. The Seventh Plan (1985-90) restated that the rural health programme and the three-tier health services system need to be strengthened and that the government had to make up for the deficiencies in personnel, equipment and facilities. The Eighth Plan (1992-97) distinctly encouraged private initiatives, private hospitals, clinics and suitable returns from tax incentives. With the beginning of structural adjustment programmes and cuts in social sectors, excessive importance was given for vertical programmes such as those for the control of AIDS, tuberculosis, polio and malaria funded by multilateral agencies attached with specific objectives and conditions. Both the Ninth (1997-2002) and the Tenth Five-Year Plans (2002-2007) start with a dismal picture of the health services infrastructure and go on to say that it is important to invest more on building good primary-level care and referral services. Both the plans highlight the importance of the role of decentralization but do not state how this will be achieved.

The National Health Policy (2002) includes all that is wanted from a progressive document and yet it glosses over the objective of NHP 1983 to protect and provide primary health care to all. The Policy document suggests that the integration of vertical programmes, strengthening infrastructure, providing universal health services, decentralization of the health care delivery system through Panchayati Raj Institutions (PRIs) and other autonomous institutions, and regulation of private health care but fails to indicate how it achieves the goals. It encourages the private sector in the first referral and tertiary health services. However, to understand the health right within the framework of standard setting one has to know the delivery of health services in the public sector.

Delivery of Health Services in the Public Sector

Health Systems an end in themselves or a means to achieving certain ends? Worldwide, there seems to be a consensus on measuring health systems in terms of improving the health status, enhancing patient satisfaction and providing financial risk protection. "In 2000, the World Health Organization (WHO) further expanded the definition of health. It includes a reduction in disparities for improving health status and sharing the financial burden in accordance with the ability to pay as being a fair form of health financing."[3] There is, however, notwithstanding the evolved standards, little consensus on what constitutes an ideal health system in universally acceptable terminology to enable better intercountry comparisons. This is because, unlike any other sector, health systems are highly contextualized and influenced by various exogenous factors such as societal values, epidemiology and disease burden, availability of financial resources, technical capacity, individual preferences and the nature of demand. Technological innovation in the health sector has improved the quality of life but has also increased costs. In countries that have no social insurance and where the role of the state is limited, people spend a substantial proportion of their incomes on seeking medical treatment, and in the process, get impoverished, thus widening disparities in the health status. To contain spiralling prices and distortions created by market failures such as moral hazard, asymmetry in information, induced demand etc., countries resort to multiple policy instruments. Health systems have five aspects or knobs that interact with each other and influence its basic nature and direction: (i) financial (tax, user fees, out-of-pocket expenditure, insurance), (ii) payment systems (how providers are paid: salary, per service rendered, capitation), (iii) organizational (manner in which the delivery systems are organized/structured), (iv) legal (regulatory frameworks), and (v) social (access to health information, advertising).[4] The effectiveness with which these instruments of state policy are designed and used determines the extent to which the health system is equitable, appropriate or fair. The health system in India consists of a public sector, a private sector and an informal network of providers of care operating within an unregulated environment, with no controls on what services can be provided by whom, in what manner, and at what cost, and no standardized protocols to help for measuring the quality of care. There are wide disparities in access, further worsened by the poor functioning of the public health system.

Evolution of the Health System in India: An Overview

The evolution of India's health system can be categorized into *three* distinct phases:

- Phase I (1947-83)—when the health policy was based on two principles: (i) that none should be denied care for want of ability to pay, and (ii) that it was the state's responsibility to provide health care to the people.
- Phase II (1983-2000)—when the first National Health Policy of 1983 articulated the need to encourage private initiative in health care service delivery, while at the same time expanding access to publicly funded comprehensive primary health care.
- Phase III (post-2000)—which is witnessing a further shift that has the potential to profoundly affect the health sector in three important ways: (i) the desire to utilize private sector resources for addressing public health goals; (ii) liberalization of the insurance sector to provide new avenues for health financing; and (iii) redefining the role of the state from being only a provider to a financier of health services as well.

Phase I (1947-83)

At the time of Independence, malaria affected almost a quarter of India's population; virulent diseases such as smallpox, plague and cholera were rampant, maternal mortality was over 2000 per 1,00,000 live-births and longevity of life was less than 32 years (Bhore Committee: 1946). While the public sector consisted of a few city hospitals, the private sector consisted largely of individual practitioners of Indian systems of medicine and licentiates practicing in villages, as family doctors. With meagre resources, this period saw the effective containment of malaria, bringing down the incidence from an estimated 750 lakh to less than 20 lakh, eradication of smallpox and plague, halving of the Maternal Mortality Rate (MMR), reduction of the Infant Mortality Rate (IMR) from 160 per 1000 live-births to about 105, containing cholera and increasing longevity of life to almost 54 years. Institutes of excellence such as the All India Institute of Medical Sciences (AIIMS) were set up for research and quality training, making India an exporter of highly trained medical doctors. These gains were in no small measure due to the strong foundation of public health on which the health system was grounded and the highly professionalized cadre of public health specialists who provided leadership from the front, camping in villages in hostile environmental conditions, whether to eradicate smallpox or supervise the malaria worker. However, under the overarching influence of modernization that characterized the post-colonial phase of global development, the urge to be on par with the western norms of modern medicine proved to be too strong to resist. India, unlike China, missed the opportunity to launch public health campaigns to promote, at the community and individual household levels, healthy lifestyles alongside expanding public investment to assure universal access to water, sanitation, nutrition and education. Instead, and more particularly during the 1960s and 1970s, public health campaigns were focused only on promotion of the small family norm and family planning. India also failed to utilize the strengths of the traditionally used and accepted modes of medical treatment and gave undue emphasis to allopathy, gradually laying the base for an expanded market for western style curative services, which are urban based as well as costly.

Phase II (1983-2000): The National Health Policy of 1983

Despite the remarkable achievements in disease control, the failure to control the population, the lack of access to basic health facilities in rural areas, and the international commitment to focus on providing comprehensive primary care as envisioned by the Alma Ata Declaration in 1978, led to the formulation of the National Health Policy of 1983. Limited resources to meet the growing demand for health services led to the articulation for private sector to shoulder some part of the burden. An estimated Rs. 6,500 crore worth of subsidy in terms of exemptions in customs duty for import of equipment, subsidized inputs such as land, etc. were extended to stimulate private investment in health. Alongside, the focus of state policy shifted to primary health care to reduce the iniquitous urban-rural divide and expand access to the rural populations, particularly the poor. Lack of resources resulted in segmenting health into independent silos of disease control programmes rather than visualizing health care as a continuum of service. Such segmentation led to simplistic formulations of the role of state being confined to primary health care and a selected list of diseases and health interventions, rather than being responsible for the well-being and health of the people. This phase witnessed an expansion of health facilities for providing primary health care in rural areas and the implementation of National Health Programmes (NHPs) for disease control under vertically designed and centrally monitored structures.

The adoption of this twin strategy had its advantages. With less than Rs. 200 per capita investment (2000), prioritization of interventions that benefit the poor and entail wide externalities, provided a moral and technical justification. Besides the establishment of health facilities in accordance with a population norm, guinea worm was eradicated and the disease load due to infectious diseases reduced and deaths averted. During the 1990s, with assistance from the World Bank, NHPs were upscaled with impressive outcomes: the cure rate of tuberculosis (TB) under the Directly Observed Treatment, the (DOTS) programme doubled and averted an estimated 50 lakh deaths, leprosy was eliminated except in 70 districts, the incidence of cataract as a cause of blindness reduced from 80 per cent to less than 50 per cent and the number of polio cases decreased drastically from 29,709 to about 100 (Table 4.1).

Table 4.1 : Evaluation of World Bank-funded Study in Four States under the State Health Systems

Programme	*Indicators*	*Current Status*
TB control (cure rate)	25 % (1997	86% (2003)
Control of cataract blindness/ number of surgeries	21 lakh (1995)	42 lakh (2003)
Control of Leprosy (prevalence per 10,000)	24 (1992)	2.44 (2003)
Control of HIV-per 1,000,000	3.5 (1998)	5.1 (2005)
Control of malaria in 8 project districts API 13.8 API	(1999) 9.5 API	(2002) In 32 out of 100 districts API fell below 2.
Reduction in polio cases	29,709	<100

Source : Ministry of Health and Family Welfare (MoFM), Government of Orissa.

Fiscal stress gave rise to innovation; various States attempted to improve the overall performance of public health facilities by a combination of policies—improved availability of inputs, greater flexibility in spending; defining responsibilities and rationalizing performance outputs; widening the scope for involvement of local bodies, Non-Governmental Organizations (NGOs), etc. Table 4.2 gives a broad idea of the policy areas, the direction and nature of such innovation and names of the pioneer states. The initiatives taken and the outcomes are impressive when analysed in reference to wide disparities in income and socio-cultural behaviour, a fast-changing economic scenario, comparatively unstable political environment in several States and a near stagnant average per capita investment in primary health care of Rs. 105. Despite the reduced health spending as a result of fiscal pressures that States faced during this period, most of them took advantage of available opportunities to achieve whatever they could, underscoring the fact that a limited level

Table 4.2 : Innovation in the Health Sector by States—1995-2000

Area of Innovation	*Broad Direction of the innovation and innovators*
Public-private partnerships	Handing over the management of public facilities to NGOs (Gujarat, Karnataka); Contracting private specialist services and outsourcing other services, such as diet, distribution of IEC materials, etc. (most States)
Decentralization	Transfer of budgets to and involvement of local bodies (Kerala, Karnataka, Himachal Pradesh, Orissa); Management Boards of Health Facilities (Rajasthan, Madhya Pradesh, Andhra Pradesh)
Human resources	Contracting professionals for service delivery-ANMs, doctors, surveillance, auditing, etc. (all States); Multiskilling, pre-internship training, Mandatory pre-post-graduate rural service (Orissa)
Financing	User fees and financial autonomy to hospitals (Madhya Pradesh, Rajasthan, Andhra Pradesh, Karnataka, Punjab, West Bengal, Maharashtra); Health insurance (Andhra Pradesh, Karnataka, West Bengal); Direct transfer of funds from GoI to districts under NHPs; Financial delegation of powers to PHCs, CHCs and district CMO (Tamil Nadu, Gujarat).
Accountability	Delegation of powers to district-level officials (Gujarat, Tamil Nadu, rationalizing responsibilities for better accountability, performance-based monitoring (Andhra Pradesh, Gujarat)
Community mobilization	Link couple schemes (Gujarat, Rajasthan); Village Planning and Community Health Worker (Madhya Pradesh, Uttar Pradesh)
Regulation/standard setting	Quality control circles (Gujarat); Blood transfusion standards (NACO); ISO certification (Karnataka, Himachal Pradesh) Ensuring the availability of essential drugs at health facilities under the Panch Byadhi Chikitsa Scheme (Orissa); Centralized drug procurement (Tamil Nadu, Orissa, Andhra Pradesh, Rajasthan)

Source: Initiatives from Nine States, MoHFW, GoI 2004.

IEC: Information, Education and Communication; GoI: Government of India; NHP: National Health Policy; PHC: Primary Health Centre; CHC: Community Health Centre; CMO: Chief Medical Officer; NACO: National AIDS Control Organization.

of investment can only give a commensurate level of outcome. Notwithstanding the above factors, five serious omissions occurred in the public health policy: (i) the private sector was encouraged without provisions for regulations, standards and accreditation processes; (ii) there was an absence of surveillance and epidemiological surveys to get a more accurate understanding of the changing profile of disease prevalence and incidence, which is necessary for measuring risk factors, designing interventions and launching information campaigns to reduce risky behaviour; (iii) advantage was not taken of the 73rd and 74th Constitutional Amendments for decentralizing programme implementation to the local bodies/community for increasing accountability in the system; (iv) neglect of research and development to promote technological innovation; and (v) inadequate investment in developing the critical mass of required skills and human resources. In other words, the governments ran public health programmes that would have been more cost-effective for the communities and local bodies and in the process neglected their more fundamental responsibility of governance—of laying down a framework, defining the rules of the game and monitoring systems to see that no player takes undue advantage in the health sector.

Phase III (post-2000) National Health Policy II, 2002

By 2000, India had not achieved 13 out of the 17 goals laid down in the first National Health Policy of 1983. Analysis of the 52nd Round National Sample Survey (NSS) on the utilization of health services showed that during 1986-96, there was a decrease in the utilization of public facilities for outpatient care from 26 per cent to 19 per cent; a decrease in access to free care from 19 per cent to 10 per cent and an increase in the number of persons not seeking care due to financial incapacity (Table 4.3).

State-wise comparisons show that the poorest in the poorer States of UP and Bihar had to pay substantial amounts for outpatient treatment and a low utilization of public

Table 4.3 : Utilization of Primary and Community Health Centres for Outpatient Care in Rural Areas

State	Utilization of PHC/ CHC for (Out of total OP) (%)	Utilization of PHC/ CHC for OP by the poorest 2 quintiles (Out of total PHC/CHC OP) (%)	Untreated ailments out of total number of ailments	Untreated ailments due to financial reasons (Out of total number of ailments) (%)	Average total household expenditure for treatment per ailment (OP) (in Rs.)
		Well performing States			
Kerala	5.4	49	11.7	1.5	119
Tamil Nadu	7.2	41.5	22.4	–	79
Andhra Pradesh	5.7	52.1	25.5	5.2	116
Maharashtra	6.5	47.7	11.4	2.9	144
Karnataka	11.0	55.1	22.3	2.6	91
		Moderate performing States			
Gujarat	9.9	29.3	8	–	144
West Bengal	4.3	49.1	19.9	4	105
Punjab	1.8	41.2	1	0.5	173
Haryana	5.1	23.5	3	–	183
		Poor performing States			
Rajasthan	10.2	44.1	10.2	6.2	172
Orissa	18.4	30.2	32.3	14.6	99
Madhya Pradesh	8.9	27.6	16.3	1.7	129
Uttar Pradesh	1.5	38.6	9.4	–	202
Assam and North-East	27.13	–	44	9.02	83
Bihar	2.0	19.6	21.9	5.5	220
All India	6.4	37.9	17.3	3.5	144

Source: Mahal A., Yazbeck A.S., Peters D.H., *et al.*, *The Poor and Health Service Use in India*. HNP Discussion Paper, Washington, DC, the World Bank, 2001.

PHC: Primary Health Centre; CHC: Community Health Centre; OP: Outpatient

Note: The total OP for a reference period of 15 days is 375.3 lakh. The total number of ailments (rural) is 408 lakh yearly. The average total expenditure for OP care is for the reference period of 15 days. Total expenditure includes medical expenditure and all expenses other than medical expense incurred by the household for availing the treatment.

facilities, which indicates a virtual breakdown of the public health system. On the other hand, in Assam and Orissa, a large proportion of persons did not avail of treatment at all. Read along with the number of untreated ailments due to financial reasons, the picture is dismal, as it further emphasizes the failure of the public health system in providing risk protection, since the average cost of outpatient treatment for every episode of illness is equivalent to three to five days' wage of one earning member of the family. To reduce the disease burden affecting the poor and alarmed by the falling levels in the utilization of public facilities, the government brought forth the National Population Policy (2000), the National Health Policy (2002), and the AYUSH Policy (2000), reiterating its resolve and commitment to achieve a set of goals by 2010. The goals envisaged are to increase public investment in health from the current level of 0.9 per cent to 2 per cent to 3 per cent; to increase the utilization of primary care facilities from less than 19 per cent to over 75 per cent; to reduce the MMR by three quarters from the current level of over 540 per 1000; to reduce the IMR from 62 per 1000 live-births to less than 30, eradicate polio, eliminate leprosy, reduce deaths on account of TB and malaria by over 50 per cent, etc. Many of these objectives are in consonance with the Millennium Development Goals (MDGs) for 2015. The following section highlights the systemic issues that may constrain from achieving these goals within the given time-frame unless addressed on priority. Some of the relevant data are presented below which has been already discussed above.

Organizational Structure of the Public Health Sector Delivery System

There has been a clear absence of any deliberate strategy to use the organizational tool for achieving public health goals, except family planning, until the Sixth Five Year Plan when, under the Minimum Needs Programme, concerted efforts were made to focus on expanding access to primary care in rural areas. Thus, built over the years, the public health delivery system consists of a large number of dispensaries, primary health care institutions, small hospitals providing some specialist services, large hospitals providing tertiary care, medical colleges, paramedical training institutions, laboratories, etc.

The failure to improve the health status, be accountable and responsive to people's needs or protect them from financial risk has brought into focus the functioning of the public health system, underscoring its failure in fulfilling such legitimate expectations. The focus of this section is to understand the causal factors that have led to such a failure. These causal factors can be divided into *three* broad groups:

1. Poor goal setting and lack of formulation of strategic interventions;
2. Management Failures;
3. Limited role of the State.

Goal-setting and Strategic Interventions

The public health system is inaccessible, disconnected to public health goals and inadequately equipped to address people's expectations. For the majority of citizens, the public health system is out of their reach due to distance, lack of money, lack of confidence in the system or the availability of a cheaper alternative. The organizational structure requires a villager to travel an average distance of 2.2 km to reach the first health post for getting a paracetamol; over 6 km for a blood test and nearly 20 km for hospital care. Given the poor road connectivity, the unreliability of finding the provider at the health centre, the indirect costs for transport and wages foregone, the marginal cost of availing a public service outweighs that of getting some treatment from the local quack. Further, even when accessed, there is no continuity of care guaranteed.[5] In other words, the segmentation of the health system into primary, secondary and tertiary, administered and monitored by different bodies, with none working in coordination, has resulted in the dilution of the concept of the integral nature of health where curative services are a continuum of the preventive and promotive health care.

Table 4.4 : Public health infrastructure in India, 1951-2001

Hospitals		*1951*	*1961*	*1971*	*1981*	*1991*	*1998*	*2000*
Hospital	Total	2694	3054	3862	6805	11174	NA	15888
	Rural	39	34	32	27			22
	Private				43	57		71.2
Hospital/ dispensary beds	Total	117000	229634	348655	504538	664135	NA	719861
	Rural	23	22	21	17			11.06
	Private				28	32		38.2
Dispensaries	Total	6600	9406	12180	16745	27431	NA	23.065
	Rural	79	80	78	69			53
	Private				13	60		57
PHCs		725	2695	5131	9115	18671	22149	22842
Sub-centres				27929	84736	130165	136258	137311
CHCs					761	1910	2633	3043

Source: Health Statistics/Information of India, CBHI, GoI, Various Years; *Rural Health Bulletin*, GoI 2002; National Health Policy, MoHFW, GoI, 2002.
PHC: Primary Health Centre; CHC: Community Health Centre.

In eight States, substantial investments were mobilized from the World Bank to upgrade, strengthen and establish hospitals at the district, sub-district and block levels. The comprehensive definition of the primary health infrastructure (Health for All Report of 1980) got a further distortion with the Community Health Centres (CHCs) rechristened as First Referral Centres (FRUs), divorcing them from their contextual framework. In Andhra Pradesh, Karnataka, Punjab, etc. the World Bank-funded CHCs were brought under the administrative control of autonomous Directorates dealing with secondary level hospitals while those CHCs not covered under the project are continued to be administered by the Director of Health Services. An evaluation report of West Bengal, AP, Karnataka and Punjab showed that while these states were successful in improving the quality of care in urban and semi-urban areas (Table 4.5), an expected outcome, such as, for example, an increase in institutional deliveries was not realized. Had the focus been on establishing the referral system and linkages with the other World Bank-assisted disease control and Reproductive and Child Health (RCH), investments made for strengthening the health systems would have had a considerable impact on reducing maternal, neonatal and infant deaths, or deaths due to malaria, TB which require hospitalization? This experience clearly demonstrates that mere increase in investments in infrastructure does not automatically translate into better health outcomes.

It also underscores the urgent need for conceptual clarity on the expectations of the organizational structures that have been established and the urgent need for standardization of facilities across the country. Shortage of funds has been primarily responsible for the non-availability of facilities in accordance with the norms set by the government; and inadequate provisioning of critical inputs such as drugs, equipment, facilities such as operation theatre, etc. Due to lack of budgets and the pressure to achieve targets, several States upgraded the two-roomed subcentres to PHCs with no place for laboratory, examination, pharmacy, etc. Most of them are non-functional. There are PHCs with over 33 subcentres and there are subcentres which cover over 200 habitations. It is estimated that 25% of people in Madhya Pradesh and Orissa, and 11% in Uttar Pradesh could not access medical care due to hospital location reasons (NSS-India Health Report: 2003). The question that then arises is to what extent is infrastructure an important determinant in health outcomes? Is there any association? Box 1 reveals the mockery we have made of the health care service delivery system by having subcentres function in non-standardized places denying dignity and privacy to women who visit the ANM for treatment and care. Some of the evidence gives the levels of utilization of the PHC facilities. It links outcomes with the infrastructure to examine if there is any such association. What emerges from the data is that while in the poorer performing States, the ratio of facilities to 100,000 population are on par with the rest of the States, and even better than that in Andhra Pradesh and West Bengal, the health outcomes are poor. This shows that it is not mere establishment of a physical facility but a combination of factors such as distance, availability and quality of skills, adequacy of infrastructure and access to alternative sources of care that seem to influence health-seeking behaviour and determine outcomes which have been captured by a set of indicators such as complete immunization, percentage of those severely malnourished, full antenatal coverage, safe and institutional deliveries and finally, the IMR and the under five mortality rate (U5MR). While it is clear that infrastructure development had little linkage to goal setting, it is also seen that policy interventions *per se* often lacked focus, were not based on hard evidence, and had weak institutional capacity to translate policy into action.

Table 4.5 : Evaluation of World Bank-Assisted for State Health Systems

State/year of project	*Increase in the utilization of out-patient care(%)*	*Increase in the utilization of in-patient care (%)*	*Increase in laboratory tests (%)*	*Additional beds (% increase)*	*Increase in bed occupancy (%)*	*Reduction in institutional deliveries 1999-2003*
Karnataka (1996-2001)	72.2	83.3	29.0	29.3	10.8	From 55% to 33%
West Bengal (1996-2004)	44.6	29.3	54.4	12.9	71.6	From 77% to 74%
Punjab (1996-2003)	115.9	65	456.6	45.6	14.4	From 97% to 26%
Andhra Pradesh (1995-2002)	102.2	100	Not available	67.3	Not available	From 35% to 33%

Source : *Implementation Completion Report*, World Bank, Washington, DC, 2004.

Lack of Focus, Evidence and Capacity

Lack of Focus: Vertical Versus Horizontal Programmes

Box 1 : The State of India's Health Delivery System

In one district, where the NCMH took up a facility survey, officials stated that 90% of the 369 ANMs did not reside in the area of their jurisdiction—a situation referred to in Rajasthan and Gujarat as 'up-down'—and that with just Rs. 75 per month as rental most subcentres were functioning in verandahs. Now the rent has increased to Rs. 250 but the 'verandahs cannot be left as dues have to be paid'! Due to lack of any facility and privacy, the ANM does not provide any maternal services.

The NHP 1983 made a strong policy commitment to establish a comprehensive primary health care, based on the active involvement of the community and intersectorally linked to non-health determinants such as water, sanitation, etc. Such an approach if implemented would have helped avert an additional 15 lakh infant and 8,00,000 maternal deaths. Gains could have been impressive. However, the NHP was hardly implemented. Instead, largely due to resource constraints, strategies contrary to what was stated in the policy, were adopted (such as the selective primary health care approach). The adoption of the strategy of selective primary health care, running counter to the vision of a comprehensive primary health care laid down in the NHP of 1983 was on account of resource constraints. Compulsions to prioritize resulted in selecting interventions based on the criteria of the extent to which the disease/condition affected the poor disproportionately more, was technically feasible to implement and could be made available at comparatively low cost, and to be implemented vertically from the centre. Evidence from community-based experiments and surveys however tell another story. They conclusively show that people have other health needs and expectations from their health system which make integrated approaches more effective, efficient and, in the long run, more sustainable. The experiments also show that vertical programmes fail to integrate with the provisioning of general health services, weaken the health system as a whole and, over a period of time, get disconnected from local health problems, priorities and the community itself. These observations find resonance in the experience gained so far. A range of health needs such as treatment for debilitating fever that incur wage losses for the labourer, treatment for epilepsy, uterine prolepses, infertility or menstrual problems affecting women's ability to work are concerns that are ignored as public health systems narrowly focus on achieving programme targets: sterilization, immunization, collection of blood smears in case of fever, providing drugs to sputum positive persons etc. In fact, even under a programme such as the RCH, which is expected to be gender-sensitive, due to its vertical, target-oriented nature, the number of women receiving postmortem care was very low (NFHS-II). Given the large number of domiciliary deliveries, the health workers visited an average of 5.1 per cent mothers within one week of delivery and 16.5 per cent mothers within 2 months of delivery. In Madhya Pradesh, these figures were 1.8 per cent and 10 per cent and in Uttar Pradesh 2 per cent and 7.2 per cent, respectively. This not only explains the reason for such high neonatal mortality but also the unattended morbidity which in these two States was reported to have affected nearly 17 per cent women, while 10 per cent to 13 per cent suffered heavy women health problem (NFHS-II, 1998-99). Such postmortem morbidities go unmonitored, as they are not a part of the programme targets to be achieved. Apart from such distortions, vertical programming with line item-wise budgeting provides little flexibility for front-line workers responsible for delivering care, making integration difficult as seen in the case of HIV with Family Welfare or providing treatment for malaria or TB to pregnant women.

Another example of a narrow, programmatic approach is TB. While there is no doubt about the technical efficacy of Directly Observed Treatment (DOTS) for curing TB, there is some concern about the techno-managerial approach to a disease that is embedded in the biosocial determinants of poverty, poor housing, illiteracy, financial problems, migration, and low resilience to the initial side-effects of the drugs affecting the ability to work. The DOTS programme is a highly sophisticated one and very well designed, ensuring the availability of microscopes, trained manpower and drugs etc. but has little effort or budgetary resources for tackling the root cause of the disease, for spreading awareness about the programme, for social mobilization to see that people in need get the treatment. In an attention to the social causes or community involvement can result in dropouts or the very poor not being able to access or continue with the treatment, for example migratory labour. Besides, a legitimate concern expressed widely is the potential for increase in primary Multi-Drug Resistant (MDR) TB, which is currently estimated to be

2.8 per cent in North Arcot near Chennai. This is largely on account of the existence of multidrug regimens being administered by doctors in the private sector and the tendency of shopping that patients resort to, on an average about six to nine providers, before finally reaching the DOTS centre. Such frequent switching of doctors by the patients is not only draining their financial base but also, with the irrational prescriptions given, could well be contributing to drug resistance. MDR TB is not only far more expensive to treat but may also not be treatable. Yet, India barely has a surveillance network to closely monitor this aspect. The story of TB reiterates the need for social/community control on the process and the need for adopting a public health approach to the disease.[6]

Weak Evidence Base for Interventions

Neither the Ministry at the Centre nor at the State level has adequate in-house capability to design research studies, collect data and analyze research findings of the various health interventions to enable evidence-based policy-making. Substantial resources are being spent on programmes and interventions that have a poor evidence base. For example, there is no evidence to indicate the current burden of malaria, or maternal mortality. Similarly, hardly any studies are available to assess the efficacy of the use of a drug or of a treatment protocol in different settings and conditions for formulating differential strategies to suit the diverse conditions prevailing in India.

Such non-availability of good quality research for evidence based policy formulation is one instance of the health delivery system missing the woods for the trees. For example, the principal goal of the National Reproductive Health Programme is to reduce maternal mortality. Over 1,00,000 women die every year due to pregnancy-related reasons that necessitate skilled attendance and some surgical interventions. The international definitions of skilled attendants disqualify either the Traditional Birth Attendants (TBAs) or the 18 months' trained ANMs. Surgical interventions on the other hand require a minimum infrastructure such as access to blood, an operation theatre, access to personnel skilled in surgery and administration of anesthesia, etc. Public policy should in all these years have to focus on making investments on development of infrastructure and building-up a professional and skilled cadre of attendants for facilitating safe and institutional deliveries. The failure to link intervention with evidence has resulted in poor outcomes.

The organizational strategy consisted of three concepts: (i) Village-level clinics conducted by a professional health team consisting of a medical doctor, a trained nurse, laboratory assistant, etc. to provide Antenatal Care (ANC) and examine other ailments, with the auxiliary nurse attending to mandatory registration of all pregnant women, other public health duties and promoting institutional deliveries, etc; (ii) Investment in establishing well-equipped Maternal and Child Health (MCH) clinics/hospitals for delivery; and (iii) a strong Health Management Information System (HMIS) and monitoring system including a regular medical audit of every maternal death for taking corrective action. Compared to the above factors, India for several years promoted training of village-based TBAs, consistently lowered the quality of training and competencies of the ANMs and neglected supervision and monitoring. Resorting to such low-cost solutions helped avoid committing resources required for the establishment of the requisite infrastructure and human resource development. The example of MMR is useful as it is a good proxy for demonstrating the effectiveness of the health system. A similar mismatch between goal and strategic intervention is evident in the case of reducing the IMR. While 40 per cent of deaths take place within one week of birth, and nearly 23 per cent on account of upper respiratory tract injections and diarrhoeal diseases, strategies required to address these causal factors have been overshadowed by the immunization programmes, particularly the one for polio. The single-point pursuit of polio eradication has resulted in adversely affecting the routine immunization programme, which was initiated in 1986 as a Technology Mission for achieving full protection against all vaccine-preventable diseases by 2000. As per a household survey conducted in 1998 and again in 2003 (Indian Institute of Population Sciences: 2004), the data for 220 districts showed that in the majority of the districts, there was either a declining performance or no improvement at all under the Universal Immunization Programme (UIP). Second, the high percentages of drop-outs for Oral Poliomyelitis Virus (OPV3) indicated the wrong perception among mothers of the need to adhering to the immunization protocol (Table 4.6). Discussions with field staff seemed to suggest that this decline was largely on account of the emphasis given to polio, which not only commanded better resources and visibility in the media but also consumed nearly one-third of the time, 30 times the cost and exhausted the staff in 2003, the Government of India (GoI) had to dispatch half the departmental officers to oversee the Pulse Polio Initiative (PPI) Round due to resistance from the local staff which had got tired of participating in one campaign after another—4 rounds of PPI with each round requiring one whole month of preparation, two family health awareness programmes camps of the National AIDS Control Organisation (NACO), health *melas* of the GoI, leprosy household rounds for identification of left-out cases, registration of patients with guinea worm infection, RCH camps, family planning targets, and so on. Such isolated programmatic approaches have made it impossible to allow the health system to develop. Therefore, even as we get set to achieving zero polio prevalence in India, the question remains as to whether vertically driven strategies

Table 4.6 : Universal Immunization Programme

Vaccine	*Positive decline*	*Stagnant*	*Improved*
BCG	13.2	72.3	14.5
DTP	40.4	53.8	5.8
OPV3	54.1	43.6	2.3
Measles	30.0	57.7	12.3
Full immunization	48.2	43.2	8.6

Source : *IIPS*, GoI.

BCG: Bacille Calmette-Guérin; DTP: Diphtheria, Tetanus, Pertussis; OPV: Oral Poliomyelitis Vaccine.

implemented in a campaign mode, which are also resource intensive and neglect equally important public health functions, are worthwhile.

Inadequate Capacity to Plan and Implement at the Centre, State and District Levels

Failure to develop a public health cadre and widening the eligibility criteria to include clinicians, without making public health training a mandatory requirement for working in posts that need public health skills, have adversely affected the implementation of public health programmes. Non-reservation of posts or the absence of a dedicated public health cadre have also reduced the employability of persons trained in public health resulting in an accumulated shortage of the critical mass of epidemiologists, biostatisticians and other personnel. With radiographers, orthopaedicians, surgeons working as an Additional Chief Medical Officers (ADMO) in charge of the RCH programme or programmes for malaria or TB, or IAS officers as project officers of HIV/AIDS, etc., the lack of technical capacity in providing the required level and quality of leadership at the State/district-level has been a serious handicap. Mavlankar (Mavlankar: 1999), persuasively argues that one reason for the successful implementation of the maternal health strategies is that the availability of technical capacity to design and monitor at all levels, from the village to the Central Government. In India with a billion populations has one Director—level officer for MH in the Ministry of Health at the Centre. Besides the gross inadequacy of the number, technical posts in the Central Government are manned by personnel drawn from the Central Health Service with no fixed tenure or any pre-qualifications. For example, a Director of MH should have knowledge of public health, obstetrics and midwifery and related fields. While so the personnel of the Central Health Service have a distinct handicap of not only not having these technical qualifications but also no experience of working in a PHC or a CHC, made worse with no field training upon recruitment as is the case with Indian Administrative Service (IAS) officers.

Lack of technical expertise and non-availability of the critical mass or a minimal number at the Central and State levels are reasons for public health programmes lacking in focused designing, development of national treatment protocols and standards, the non-integration with other related sectors/ programme such as TB with HIV, HIV with MH, MH with malaria, health with nutrition or water, etc.; or absence of technical leadership in States and districts on the operationalization of interventions based on technical norms; or assessing and building up of technical skills and human resources required by the programme. Most importantly, this absence of adequate technical skills have also been responsible for the near absence of operational research for obtaining the evidence base for designing better targeted programmes in keeping with the wide social and geographical disparities that characterize India. Instead, at the Central and State levels, almost 40 per cent of the time of these ill-equipped officers in charge of complex programmes is spent in attending to administrative duties.

The situation in the States is no better. A survey conducted in six States to assess the technical capacity of these States for Maternal Health (MH) programmes, (or for that matter malaria) showed that except one Deputy Director-level officer in Kerala, in none of the other five States of Tamil Nadu, Maharashtra, Rajasthan, Gujarat and Chhattisgarh was there even one officer exclusively earmarked for monitoring the maternal health programme (Mavlankar: 1999). The situation in the districts is worse. The void in the unavailability of such capacity for surveillance and monitoring at district levels has temporarily been addressed under the TB control and Polio Pulse programmes by taking persons on a contract basis—many from the government itself, thus further weakening the already fragile technical capacity required for implementing the large number of government programmes. In addition, there is also the question of the State Governments' ability to sustain these programme-based consultants after withdrawal of external support.

The collection and review of data is hardly given any importance, leave alone analyzing it for future planning.

Monitoring is essentially confined to the bare minimum of NHP targets and now, polio pulse immunization targets. In the absence of any system of surveillance or epidemiological data gathering, planning interventions lack an evidence base and also make it impossible for the system to be responsive to felt needs. A study conducted in Zenana Hospital in Udaipur, Rajasthan found that during 1983-93 nothing had changed despite the improved road network and awareness levels.[7]

The researcher further observes that the failure of the system to provide ambulance services, which resulted in incurring expenditures on transport ranging between Rs.150 and Rs. 300, borrowed from moneylenders 'leaving the people poorer both materially and emotionally when despite their desperate efforts the woman's life could not be saved'. The study also showed that during this period while there was a drop in eclampsia, there was a six-fold increase of deaths on account of malaria induced anaemia and abortions induced by unqualified practitioners. Abortion and emergency obstetric services remain almost unavailable to the vast majority of the rural women.

Inconsistent Procedures

Rules and procedures do not synchronize with objectives of a programme or foster any accountability among the functionaries. For example, unsafe abortion is said to cause at least 8 per cent of all maternal deaths. Yet field surveys showed that untrained and unqualified providers in the informal sector routinely conduct illegal abortions. This flourishing clandestine business is because of government procedures that take over 15 months for getting a centre certified the conflicting provisions such as the requirements for a person trained in medical termination of pregnancy to be working at the centre, but then having no facilities to train such private providers, etc. It is for such reasons that a large State like Rajasthan has only 338 certified private facilities with 78 per cent of them in nine districts, five districts having no private facility and 6 having one.[8] With no effective intervention to ensure government facilities having all the required skills, equipment and drugs, the number of deaths due to unsafe abortions remains high.

Management Failures

Management failure due to a combination of reasons such as low budgets, untimely and irregular supplies, corrupt practices and poor governance has adversely affected the functioning of the health system. The dispersed and disaggregated nature of responsibilities and conflicting job profiles make accountability a difficult proposition. While the Secretary of the Department of Health has no control on when and how much money will be made available to implement programmes, the Medical Officer (MO) in the peripheral centre has no administrative powers over the front-line workers and other functionaries working under him. With most supplies such as vaccines and drugs being provided by the Centre for the NHPs, the States have little control to ensure outcomes, as in several instances procurement delays by the Centre can take as long as over one financial year, affecting the credibility of the system. All these factors have serious implications for the quality of management and efficiency.[9] We now discuss the most frequently cited and widely accepted reasons for management failure.

Performance-Based Monitoring

There is absence of accountability in the system. To this end, Andhra Pradesh introduced performance-based monitoring in 1998-99. Primary health facilities, where the maximum absenteeism among doctors and health workers was observed and were graded into four categories based on programme targets/achievement indicators, scores/grades were given. This was then the basis for review at the highest level. It enabled identification of the problems and corrective action to be taken. Under various programmes and in some States, such performance-based monitoring is done but is neither timely nor systematic, except under the donor-funded programmes of blindness, TB Control Programmes and the Pulse Polio Initiative. It is however pertinent to note that an estimated 1500 consultants were appointed by WHO at the field level to monitor the TB and polio control programmes. In addition, common to these three programmes is the extensive computerization of monitoring and review systems that provided access to information at the district level. Such systems need to be adopted by other programmes and also for other aspects of implementation.

Absenteeism from Place of Work

A majority of doctors opt for specialization and/or urban practice. The reluctance to serve in rural areas has become a major impediment in the government's ability to provide health services to the rural population. Not surprisingly, absenteeism among doctors and front-line workers from their place of work is high. A study conducted by the World Bank (2004) and other studies (Mohan *et al.*: 2003; Rao: 2003) show absenteeism ranging from 40 per cent to 45 per cent among doctors working in primary health centres. The World Bank Study based on a simple regression analysis showed the relationship between income and absenteeism, which suggested that higher income States have lower rate of absenteeism with point value at 0.001, meaning that every increase of Rs. 1,000 State per capita income is associated with a reduction in absence of 1 per cent point, with p values on the co-efficient on income at 0.13. However, this is a crude analysis as, at another level, absenteeism is high in these rich States where doctors are also engaged in private practice. Punjab has the lowest utilization of public facilities only because of large-scale absenteeism of doctors.[10]

Quality of Service Delivery—An Imbalanced Mix of Inputs

Vehicles without POL budgets, beds without washing allowances, X-ray machines lying idle for the want of consumables or maintenance budgets, empty shelves in pharmacy counters, etc. also contribute to management failure.

In addition, quality is also perceived to be low due to the often unfriendly, rude, corrupt behaviour of the personnel working in these facilities, distance, inconvenient timings and lack of reliability in the availability or the skill of the provider, etc. reflecting management failure. The subcentres are never open as the single ANM is required to undertake village visits, attend to fixed day immunization schedules, domiciliary deliveries, disseminate health information, oversee the work of the TBA, coordinate with the anganwadi worker (AWW), conduct household survey, attend review meetings in PHCs and maintain records, etc. With better rearrangement of these factors utilisation can be drastically improved.

Box 3 : Management Issues in the Rural Health Care

Doctors do not stay at PHCs and absenteeism among PHC staff is high.
Training during MBBS is not geared to impart skills for providing service in rural areas.
Doctors need to be provided financial and non-financial incentives for staying in rural areas.
There is a need for increasing para-medicalization of primary health care services.

Lack of Policies for Human Resource Development

The recruitment policy is a contributory factor for the lack of motivation among doctors to provide services in rural areas. Quite often, post-graduate students are recruited by the governments and placed at PHCs where the skills acquired by them during post-graduation are of little relevance. This is made worse by the lack of equipment, drugs and adequate caseload. Similarly, there is almost always a mismatch of skills gynecologist is posted at a CHC where there is no anesthetist resulting in the underutilization of skills. Likewise, transfers are often arbitrary and without adherence to any norms, resulting in the low morale of doctors. Even the States that do have a transfer policy rarely adhere to it. Recently, there was an instance in a State where at a CHC all the seven doctors were transferred out in one go, leaving behind a hapless lot of patients. Often, the skills needed or acquired in a training programme are not taken into consideration. Therefore, under the NHP, money may be spent in training a doctor in anesthesia, Intra Ocular Lens (IOL) implantation surgery, or a Manual Vacuum Aspiration (MVA), but fail to impact on the programme as, more often than not, on return from training, he or she is posted to a place where the acquired skills are not required or the required equipment is not available. The absence of transparent transfer policies, norms for deployment of personnel, and reward for merit, are some of the factors contributing to the deviant behaviour among providers. Therefore, the professional commitment is getting diluted in health sector.

Limited Promotional Avenues

In many States (such as Orissa, Bihar, Uttar Pradesh, Rajasthan) an MO often gets the first promotion after 15-20 years of service. There are many doctors who continue to remain MOs without promotion while their counterparts in civil services might have been promoted from the post of an SDM to Special Secretary or even Secretary and from Accounts Officer to Financial Advisor. Career stagnation affects the morale. In Madhya Pradesh, the Departmental Promotion Committee (DPC) meeting has not been conducted in the past 20 years. In Chhattisgarh, all chief medical officers have been posted on an *ad hoc* basis.

Poor Payment Systems and Dual Practice

To compensate for the relatively low salaries, doctors are permitted private practice after office hours or are given a non-practising allowance, often 25 per cent of the basic pay. Lack of monitoring and effective supervision at times, collusive relationships which are causes for the abuse of this facility affecting patient care in public facilities. Due to financial constraints, most States have now stopped recruiting MOs in the regular pay scales and instead are now offering contractual services for as small a remuneration as Rs. 8,000 per month, a strategy which has a high turnover with doctors joining services only for getting rural service experience for admission to Post-graduate Entrance Examination, or as a makeshift service for preparing for the PG entrance exams, or joining service and just lingering on to it in the hope that some day their services might get regularized. Time has come to review such arrangements keeping a long-term perspective in view. Doctors, particularly, specialists need to be paid better and there is a need to sanction posts of specialists and public health managers in hospitals at district and State levels. Low cost solutions or decisions based on present day contingencies cannot sustain the system which will develop fissures, and cost more to repair.[11]

Poor Facilities at Work

The most demotivating factor is the lack of appropriate facilities and required inputs to enable a qualified doctor to do his best for his patient and derive job satisfaction. In addition, lack of decent housing facilities and educational facilities for their children are further contributory factors to the reluctance to work in rural and underserved areas. The working conditions of nurses/midwives are worse, ranging from the lack of basic amenities such as toilets to physical safety. Inadequate and unreliable supply of inputs, absence of supervision and technical guidance, limited opportunities for career advancement, absence of accommodation with over 60 per cent of the subcentres functioning in rented places hired for about Rs. 100-300 per month, and often doubling up as a part of her residential accommodation are other factors that contribute to sub-optimal outcomes. Initially, subcentres were envisaged to consist of a multipurpose worker (male) (MPW-M) and one multipurpose worker (female) (MPW-F). However, 60 per cent of the posts of MPW-M are lying vacant, thereby increasing the workload of the ANM and affecting the ANM's quality of services. In the community setting, female health functionaries face many problems with regard to transportation, accommodation, gender-based harassment and lack of security, in addition to lack of incentives, stagnation of career due to inadequate development opportunities and inadequate provision for living with the family and education of their children.[12]

Corruption

This then brings us to the key issue of corruption. As per Transparency in India, health has the maximum public interaction and is the second most corrupt sector. The Karnataka Lok Ayukta has estimated that at least 25 per cent of the budget is siphoned off through corruption practices. An analysis of the Lok Ayukta shows that all categories of government health functionaries—*ayahs* and ward boys to nurse, doctors and specialists—are involved. Corrupt is in many areas ranging from indulging in unauthorized private practice to issuing medical certificates, transfers, postings, recruitment, in 'tolerating' absenteeism, etc. The most sensitive areas are in the procurement of drugs and licensing of blood banks, where unlicensed manufacturers have been recipients of orders and action on spurious drug suppliers tardy.

BOX 4 : The ANM—First Interface with the Community

The ANM still continues to be the only worker for delivery of primary health care in rural areas in the public sector. She is presently working in isolation without a team and with no support or supervision from either the Lady Health Visitor (LHV) or the Medical Officer. She is overloaded with too many functions and activities to be delivered at too many places to too many groups of clienteles. She is required to deliver health services, travel, educate communities, counsel clients and mobilize communities. She has to fill in several registers and submit several reports. The mean number of years of gap between her obtaining qualification and joining service is 4.2 years. Few subcentres operate from government-owned buildings which are poorly maintained and many are in rented buildings. The subcentre is a small area and cannot accommodate an examination or labour table, and the supplies are inadequate, irregular and erratic. About 40 per cent to 62 per cent ANMs do not live at headquarters, the most common reason for their non-availability being security concerns. In about half the cases, the subcentre, are located far from the village.

Source: Ranga Rao, 2003, Mohan *et al.*, 2003.

The pervasive spread of corruption is not limited to the public sector. The private sector is also working under low thresholds of integrity. Patients are exploited by being made to undergo unnecessary tests only for making money. Providers in private practice are seen to own pharmacies and diagnostic centres. They get 'cuts' and commissions for referrals and such fee splitting is the mainstay of many doctors' monthly earnings. There are adequate studies that have shown the disproportionately large number of caesarean sections 66 per cent of all deliveries in private hospitals in Kerala.[13] The rate of hysterectomies being performed among young women is one example of the absence of ethical standards that need to be effectively countered by fostering transparency, widening participation, strictly enforcing inspections and, above all providing leadership, in technical, administrative and political organizations in reiterating and reasserting value systems.

Enforcing good management and governance is then absolutely essential since the implication of bad practices in the health sector hurts persons who are poor and suffer the double tragedy of being sick. No market can function or sustain itself unless there is a minimal level of integrity, fair play and rule of law. Therefore, if insurance and contracting the private sector are to be the new ways of expanding access and financing health, then it is essential that values of probity, nurturing of informed consumers and wider participation through good governance be ensured. Consumer forums, patient management committees, village health committees, patients/ citizens' charter, Transparency Act, right to information, imparting of value systems and training in management practices, e-governance, redressal systems, etc. are some of the instruments that need to be employed by the government for counter-checking malpractice and to realize the patients' rights at the grass roots levels.

Lack of Discipline and Work Ethic

In India, government employees often explain the omissions or commissions on 'lack of political will'. It is however, a fact that more often than not, there is large-scale abdication of responsibility at the field levels, say for example when a head of the department or a CMO does not undertake field visits, conduct review meetings, monitor the implementation of various activities, attend office on time and check attendance registers, listen to grievances, fill vacancies, promote people, punish the wrong, reward the good, then there is abdication of duty. When the CMO 'allows' doctors and other functionaries to absent themselves from duty, then it is collusion. No amount of funding or administrative reforms can help till there is an overall institutional discipline enforced at all levels and pride for good work instilled. Creating such an environment again carries the implication of having systems and tools that facilitate its emergence. Therefore, it needs effective institutional arrangement not only to supervise the overall administrative service of the top but also to carry out the detail functionaries of the organization as well as grass roots problems. The critical factor may be personal commitment of head of the department which is required at all levels to maintain harmony among the staff and health problems of the society.[14]

Use of IT for Better Decision-Making

Effective leadership rests on access to organized information which is increasingly becoming possible due to e-governance. Information about health inputs and outcomes, achievement of targets and goals are necessary for formulating policies and monitoring activities, they are related to technology, human resources or infrastructure. Since quality monitoring based on performance indicators on a concurrent basis is fundamental to curbing errant behaviour, the need for the use of IT cannot be overstated. IT should be used for record maintenance, monitoring supply and inventory control, tracking events and disseminating information to consumers. This would place a great amount of power in the hands of the government to guide, monitor and correct. Such data analysis also reduces subjectivism in transfer policies and personnel development, and ensures transparency in all transactions, the only check to abuse of discretionary power. Besides, even for patient care through the use of telemedicine, or establishing call centres for giving instant advice on coping with a small emergency or advising which hospital to check into etc. technology has the solution. Such a system development will become even more important with the government shifting its role as a financier of services rather than a provider; as a regulator of providers; and as the final protector of patient and consumer rights to medical practices that are safe and appropriate.

Urgent Need for Infusion of New Skills

What emerges from the recounting of the several areas of management failure particularly at the point of service is the need to institute a class I All India cadre of Public Health Managers—directly recruited and trained in public health and posted at district levels, like the IAS officers. Over a period of time these young recruits will become the backbone for providing leadership in the public health area. Such persons need not necessarily be doctors—they could be from a wide variety of related disciplines such as a PG in microbiology etc. but possess a Masters in Public Health. In such a system, those keen to specialize can gradually be veered to work in the hospitals and be provided career opportunities to work in teaching hospitals and super specialize etc. Such options for human resource management will be critical for steering the country from out of the veritable mess we are in presently.[15]

Dysfunctional Structure—the Role of the State

Though health is a State subject, the Central Government has certain powers and responsibilities related to the control of infectious diseases, family planning, education, drugs and research. Therefore, the departments dealing with health and family welfare, at the Central and State levels are large in terms of the human resources employed and the wide span of work covered. At both levels, there are several directorates headed by doctors and technical units dealing with the myriad issues in the health sector. For discharging their multiple functions of provider, regulator, facilitator, educator and promoter, the departments employ a large number of technical people—doctors, nurses, paramedical staff, etc. for running hospitals, dispensaries, health centres, medical colleges, nursing schools, and public health laboratories, for inspecting the quality of food and pharmaceutical products, for providing information on public health issues, production of vaccines, etc.

Structurally, the administrative units do not take into their purview the functioning of the private sector, which is seen as an independent, autonomous entity. This disassociation is in part due to the fact that various Ministries administer matters that directly effect health outcomes and have no mechanism to ensure coordination among them. For example, in the Central Government, the pharmaceutical industry is under the Ministry of Chemicals, policies related to import or export of drugs and technology are the responsibility of the Ministry of Commerce, drug regulation is under the Ministry of Health, programmes related to nutrition are part of the Department of Women and Child Welfare, while water and sanitation is looked after by the Ministry of Rural Development, research in medical diagnostics or vaccines by the Department of Biotechnology, health insurance by the Ministry of Finance, etc. Such intense fragmentation across departments and States is the single most important factor that confines the Ministry of Health to narrowly focus on the implementation of budgeted programmes and activities. The second structural mismatch is the fragmentation of the Ministry itself: into the Departments of Health, Family Welfare and AYUSH. Such fragmentation that took place in the 1990s had negative downstream effects down to the implementation level, making inter-programme integration problematic, diluting the technical capacity to think holistically and duplicating resource use. For example, the Reproductive and Child Health (RCH) programme rarely addresses HIV/AIDS, malaria or tuberculosis (TB). Likewise, the programme for malaria control has no indicator focusing on pregnant women; or nutritional deficiencies in the child health programmes.

In addition to the inadequate technical oversight, the departments also function more like 'casualty wards' where managing themselves rather than the system has taken centre stage.[16] The Department of Health, for example, spends over three-quarters of the time addressing VIP claims under the Central Government Health Scheme (CGHS); sanctioning medical colleges; procuring medical drugs and supplies, and transferring doctors and court cases. Lastly, the problem of governance, whether at the Centre or States, has also been compounded with the frequent shifting and transfers of Ministers and officers. During 1998-2003, there were five Ministers in the Central Government and as many Secretaries.

Restructuring of the Administrative Departments

The issues raised above have been felt for a long time. The Ministry of Health itself commissioned studies to restructure its organization to face the emerging challenges. The three reports: Administrative Staff College of India (1986); the Bajaj Committee (1996) and the Centre for Policy Research (2000) made some important recommendations which are waiting to be implemented:

- Constitute Hospital Committees and delegate administration to them;
- Outsource and decentralize promotional and publicity functions;
- Convert the CGHS to an autonomous board;
- Constitute an Advisory Body to advise the Ministry on policy issues;
- Decentralize planning and programme formulation to States, confining the Centre to monitoring adherence to national policy goals and providing technical support;
- Outsource procurement to an independent body;
- Establish a Federal Drug Authority and a Commission for medical education;

- Transfer all Delhi-based hospitals to the Delhi Government and make the Central hospitals autonomous;
- Merge all the three departments;
- Create an Indian Medical Service such as the Indian Administrative Service (IAS);
- Establish an institutional mechanism for interdepartmental coordination;
- Establish a manpower-planning cell in the Ministry.

Implementation of the above recommendations would 'free' the Ministry of Health at the Central and State levels to address more important issues of governing the health system as a whole. In other words, the Ministry of Health is not only expected to be concerned with the implementation of its programmes but the functioning of the health system comprising both the public and private sector, by diligent oversight safeguarding the interests of the public in general and patients in particular. Such a change in understanding of the functional responsibilities would not only require space in terms of time but also capabilities and skills to address such a role. Organizational structures reflect the objectives and aims of a policy. For example, since RCH objectives emerged as a consequence of the failure of a family planning strategy, it was added on to the Family Planning Programme and renamed as Family Welfare (FW), explaining the anomalous position of the DGHS who does not have any role in the technical aspects of the RCH programme. In the districts, such disassociation of FW from the technical head, namely the Director of Health Services, has had a negative impact on the technical quality of the programme. In States where the Health Department is divided into Health and FW, implementation of the FW programmes has been problematic due to non-alignment between authority and responsibility. Due to these factors, recently, the two departments have been merged at the Centre. While this is a positive step, there is still need to restructure the set-up on a functional basis all through the chain.

Case for Systemic Reforms: Restructuring Institutional Frameworks

The process for systemic reform will need to start from the Central Ministry of Health, looking at the big picture which has been setting standards and laying down rules and regulations to be followed by all stakeholders; mobilizing resources; providing leadership based on its knowledge and technical superiority; facilitating and steering the health system to ensure that the goals of equity, efficiency and quality are met. Such a role would require the Central Ministry to restructure its work allocation based on functional homogeneity.

The Ministry should also shift from micromanagement by divesting and delegating powers and authority to functional units. There is also an urgent need to establish new institutions, such as an autonomous institute for health information and disease surveillance, a food and drugs authority; a social health insurance corporation to take care of government employees and the labour in the organized sector by merging the CGHS and the Employees State Insurance Scheme (ESIS); enable the Indian Council of Medical Research (ICMR) to have more autonomy (such as the National Institutes of Health, USA) by generating its own resources; and outsourcing all procurement work to professional bodies. The manpower and time that would be available with the removal of this historical burden of functions would enable the Ministry to discharge its stewardship functions which require laying down standards on health infrastructure and quality, classification of diseases, costs and norms for monitoring utilization levels, carrying out research to evaluate the cost-effectiveness of the various interventions being implemented, training, etc.

The functions listed under the stewardship role are not simple, and entail mobilizing multidisciplinary groups and collecting and collating evidence for revising existing policy or formulating a new one. Standard setting is a tedious process and has cost implications. For example, setting a standard to include five ultrasound tests for an antenatal protocol would have substantial financial implications, besides driving investment to expand availability of this technology, though there is no evidence to establish its efficacy in assuring better outcomes of pregnancy. Likewise, it is through research that long-term consequences of policies need to be studied before taking decisions. For example, India's hasty decision to relax vigil in the 1970s and disbanding the malaria programme resulted in its resurgence in a form more serious and also more expensive.

Such decisions therefore need inputs from public health specialists as well as economists to state which interventions work and which do not, and what policies should be adopted and why. If public policies fall short it is because such expertise is sadly lacking and in short supply in the country. Thus, good governance is not only dependent on political commitment but also having the appropriate tools, instruments and information. Bad poiicies need not only be the result of careless oversight or narrow sectional interests, but also due to lack of evidence and information. In addition to the above, the administrative departments of health, including those at State levels, need to achieve greater efficiency in reference to some aspects described below.

Regulation in the Health Sector: Accreditation of Facilities

The role of the government in the health sector is to look after patients' welfare. Drawing up legislation in a sector like health is complex and requires an understanding of the incentives or disincentives such legislation may have on human behaviour and a balanced approach. For example, if the legislation is too inflexible and specific, putting all risks on the provider, then it may result in mindless litigation, increasing defensive medicine and higher costs for the patient, endanger the patient-doctor relationship which should be based on trust and entail harassment and outright corruption at the hands of the bureaucracy. If, on the other hand, it is too considerate to provider concerns, the patient may end up getting shortchanged. Besides, it is the enforcement of the laws that is more important. In other countries, inspectors and assessors sent to evaluate provider facilities for accreditation or licensing are trained, so that at all times the focus is on achieving the objective of increasing awareness and creating a sense of accountability among providers regarding the quality of patient care, and not the blind and mindless application of a standard or a rule. Thus, supervision requires being supportive, not prescriptive or fault-finding, as the objective is not to drive away the providers but to persuade and convince them of the need to adhere to quality and patient safety. This calls for a different mindset to be cultivated through intensive training programmes and performance monitoring systems. Supportive supervision is a new skill that needs to be nurtured in the government sector.

The key challenge to governance is the enforcement of regulations related to the 'quack' or the unqualified practitioner in the villages. In a setting where the public health system does not function and the private sector is too expensive, it is the quack who meets the social need. Rational arguments of quality or harmful practices, lack of qualification, etc. do not matter as, for the people; the quack is able to provide instant relief to a need at affordable cost. How then does the Government achieve its norms for quality and standards of patient care while allowing this clearly illegal and perhaps harmful practice to continue? Good governance would require a political will to resolutely enforce discipline and make the public health system work, besides educating the people on the rational use of medical practices or drug use.

Devolution of Authority—The District Societies: A Mechanism for Better Utilization of Funds

A major problem being faced by the Department of Health was untimely the release of funds. Routinely, Central assistance meant for specific programmes would be diverted by the State finance departments for tiding over their ways and means position, resulting in delayed release of funds, stalling the implementation of health programme activities. Therefore, under the National Programme for the Control of Blindness, district societies for blindness control programmes were first constituted during the early 1990s. Under this arrangement funds were directly released to the district societies.

This mechanism was subsequently used by all programmes resulting in the constitution of over four to five societies, one each for TB, Blindness, Malaria, RCH, and Leprosy. The experience has been a positive one as it has enabled better absorption of funds and quicker implementation. The experience of district societies is now being used to integrate them into District Health Societies so as to facilitate district-level health planning and monitoring activities to achieve health goals.

A pilot study conducted on the functioning of these different societies in the district of Orissa brought forth some interesting suggestions in following points:[17]

- Develop capacity for better management through training;
- Establish more rigorous monitoring and programme review systems to improve outcomes and ensure cost-effective utilization of funds;
- Standardize reporting and auditing formats; and
- Sensitize officers on programme goals and objectives, and increase the involvement of civil society to reduce the temptation to misuse or misallocate funds.

Based on the above, training in data analysis and planning processes, developing indicators for performance review and monitoring for corrective action will need to be accorded priority focus. The societies also need better expertise, persons trained in health economics, financial planning, statistics and data analysis, epidemiology etc. In the absence of such expertise and evidence-based planning, the tendency is to merely repeat what was being done earlier, nullifying the benefits of a bottom-up planning concept. Resources are not only financial. It is the government's responsibility to monitor the availability of human resources as well. What skills are needed, what are being produced, where and by whom are they being utilized, where are they concentrated, etc. are the sort of issues that should attract priority attention, as 5-8 years are needed before the required human resources are available? Past neglect of human resources is the cause for today's imbalance in skills mix, acute shortage of trained nurses. This function will gain even greater importance in future years as with the General Agreement on Trade in Services (GATS), more professionals from India will be able to find employment abroad. The government needs to establish mechanisms to know the migration flows of skill and identify areas of shortage so that corrective action can be taken in advance.

Local Bodies

In the health sector in India, decentralization has to be viewed, not only in the context of devolving authority and power to States by the Centre, to districts and States but to the multilayered local bodies as well. Such devolution of authority has taken place only in Kerala. Kerala has invested both time and resources in systematically focusing on building capacity for governance among elected leaders. Leadership and governance means having the ability to plan, budget, implement, manage, monitor, review and accept responsibility for the decisions taken. The strategy of the 'big bang' approach adopted in Kerala where, in one sweep, functions, powers and responsibilities were transferred rather than the usual cautious approach, of training and building capacity before delegating responsibility, has proved to be successful compared to the experience of other States where devolution has been incremental, halting and sporadic.

Devolution of powers has, however, not been easy. The Kerala experience shows that despite the transfer of some proportion of the budgets and bringing all-district level institutions under the control of the local bodies, the benefits in terms of health indicators have not really been visible.[18] This is largely because of the lack of technical guidance at the Panchayat level, lack of standardization of facilities laying down clearly the functions, duties, responsibilities and outcomes of health personnel working in facilities located at different levels, lack of clarity and clear delineation of what services ought to be available where, making it difficult for the local bodies to understand what exactly should be their priorities and areas of focus. Lack of integration between different systems of medicine, ego problems between the highly educated doctor, senior in rank, to functionaries of the local government, dual control, multiplicity of bodies handling health budgets such as the Chief Medical Officer (CMO), hospital superintendent, zilla parishad, district societies for each national programme, hospital development committees, etc. are other reasons that were found to have complicated matters. Kerala is therefore now working towards evolving minimum standards of care and conduct, a citizen's charter and community-based monitoring of health programmes. Decentralization to local bodies has been under consideration for several years but was never implemented in true spirit due to various reasons. The attitude towards the involvement of local bodies has nearly always been to sensitize the representatives and use them in an advisory capacity or for execution of government works under the Rural Development Programme. In the health sector, utilization of the local bodies as agents of change or in social mobilization has been minimal and perfunctory. Experience shows that unless the local bodies are provided funds, specific responsibilities and powers, the benefits of decentralized systems cannot be fully realized.

In this context, it would be useful to keep in mind the international experience in fiscal decentralization as they provide a few lessons to be learnt based on certain principles.[19] For fiscal decentralization, all aspects and components need to be addressed such as:

- Assignment of expenditure responsibility to local governments to be followed by revenue responsibilities;
- Availability of a strong state ability to monitor and evaluate the intergovernmental fiscal system;

- Devolution of powers and responsibilities in keeping with capabilities;
- Linking of revenue-raising and expenditure decisions;
- The intergovernmental system should be designed to match a set of clearly specified objectives, kept simple and flexible, while at the same time be subject to the discipline of budget constraints.

Applying these principles will mean having a clear-cut delineation of duties and functions to be carried out by the local bodies at different levels *vis-à-vis* the government departmental hierarchies; the financial implications of those functions and systems for utilization and reporting; and finally the kind of authority, powers, or control they have on the functionaries responsible for discharging those duties.

Such delineation needs to be based on clear government orders or legislation as the case may be and backed by intensive training and guidelines provided in simple, easy-to-understand formats. Without such a systems approach merely 'orienting' locally elected representatives to be 'involved' in health activities is as valuable as the paper on which it is written. Given the vastness and diversity, India will find it difficult to reverse the trend on communicable diseases such as malaria and TB unless the local bodies and the wider community are also fully involved. However, such involvement needs to be formalized. For example, the local bodies should be made responsible and accountable for certain health actions, registering births and deaths, carrying out all anti-malarial activities such as plugging the breeding grounds of mosquitoes, etc. In fact, later when social health insurance picks up, it will be necessary to have such a capability available at the local level for making the health insurance scheme function at minimal cost. Wider participation of the communities through village health committees working in coordination with management committees at higher-level facilities is the only way the health system can be made more accountable to the people they are meant to serve. More inclusive approaches and greater democratization is essential if health gains are to be achieved.

The initiatives would remain platitudes unless there is close monitoring by the State and provisioning of technical advice. This would require having a team at Primary Health Centres (PHCs) and Community Health Centres (CHCs) to work exclusively on the development of the community-based strategies—the village health workers, village health teams, local bodies, etc. In the absence of such administrative restructuring to guide, facilitate and supervise the development of the demand side of the health system, decentralization may not really go beyond tokenism.

One has to analyse the fact that without support of legal instruments or documents, it would not be possible to claim health as a human right. Both international legal instruments and national laws are important in examining the rights standards and how it is realised at the ground level. This is done with support of cases. It brings a couple of Orissa health cases, which are relevant to the present study. Hence, a series of argument gathered to prove health as human right. Both favourable and unfavourable cases are presented here to substantiate the above argument and to see that how the standards are set through the constitutional and judicial process in India. This helps in understanding how the scope of the standards got enlarged.

Constitutional Mandate to the State

The obligation of the State to ensure the creation and the sustaining of conditions congenial to good health is cast by the Constitutional directives contained in Articles 39(e) (f), 42 and 47 in part IV of the Constitution of India.[20] State has to direct its policy towards securing that health and strength of workers, men and women, and the children are not put to health hazards and that citizens are not forced by economic necessity to enter avocations unsuited to their age or strength [Article 39(e)] and that children are given opportunities and facilities to develop in a healthy manner and in conditions of freedom and dignity and that childhood and youth are protected against exploitation and moral and material abandonment [Article 39(f)]. The State is required to make provision for just and humane conditions of work and for maternity benefit (Article 42). It is the primary duty of the State to endeavour for raising of the level of nutrition and standard of living of its people and improvement of public health and to bring about prohibition of the consumption, except for medicinal purposes of intoxicating drinks and of drugs which are injurious to health (Article 47). Protection and improvement of environment is also made one of the cardinal duties of the State (Article 48 A). The State Legislature is (under entry 6 of the State List) contained in the Seventh Schedule to the Constitution, empowered to make laws with respect to public health and sanitation, hospitals and dispensaries. Both the Centre and the States have power to legislate in the matters of social security and social insurance, medical professions, and, prevention of the extension from one State to another of infections or contagious diseases or pests affecting man, animals or plants, by entries 23, 26 and 29 respectively contained in the concurrent list of the Seventh Schedule.

Health as Right to Life

Article 21 of the Constitution guarantees protection of life and personal liberty by providing that no person shall be deprived of his life or personal liberty except according to the procedure established by law. As a result of liberal interpretation of the words 'life' and 'liberty', Article 21 has now come to be invoked almost as a residuary right. Public interest petitions have been founded on this provision for providing special treatment to children in jail; against health hazards due to pollution; from harmful drugs; for redress against failure to provide immediate medical aid to injured persons; against starvation deaths; inhuman conditions in after-care home and on scores of other aspects which make life meaningful and not a mere vegetative existence. A positive thrust is given to the nature and content of this right by the Apex Court imposing a positive obligation upon the State to take effective steps for ensuring to the individual a better enjoyment of his life. The Supreme Court has held that the right to live with human dignity enshrined in Article 21 derives its life and breath from the directive principles of State policy particularly Articles 39(e) and (f), 41 and 42 and would therefore include protection of health as envisaged in the directives.

The expanded meaning of right to life is wholly justified, for, without health of a person being protected and his well-being being looked after, it would be impossible for him to enjoy other fundamental rights such as rights to freedom of speech and expression, to move freely throughout the territory of India, to practice any profession or carrying on any trade, occupation or business, to form associations guaranteed by Article 19 in a positive manner. Without a guarantee of health and well-being most of these freedoms cannot be exercised fully. To make other rights meaningful and effective right to a healthy life is the basis underlying the constitutional guarantees. All that the courts have done is to provide redressal by a meaningful and just interpretation to the right to life and commanding enforcement of the duties of a welfare State. The Court itself being an authority and therefore 'State' within the meaning of Article 12 which definition is made applicable by Article 36 to part IV containing the Directive Principles of State Policy, has to bear in mind these directives in its decision making process.

State's Obligation to Preserve Life

Article 21 casts an obligation on the State to safeguard the right to life of every person, preservation of human life being of paramount importance. The Apex Court has held that whether the patient be innocent person or be a criminal liable to punishment under the law, it is the obligation of those who are in charge of the health of the community to preserve life so that innocent may be protected and the guilty be punished. A doctor at the government hospital positioned to meet this State obligation is, therefore, duty bound to extend medical assistance for preserving life. Every doctor, whether at Government Hospital or otherwise, has a professional obligation to extend his services with due expertise and care for protecting life. It has been held that this obligation is total, absolute and paramount, and laws of procedure, whether in Statutes or otherwise, which would interfere with the discharge of this obligation cannot be sustained and must therefore give way to higher standards. A doctor does not contravene the law of the land by proceeding to treat the injured victim on his appearance before him either by himself or being carried by others.

In a welfare State the primary duty of the government is to secure the welfare of the people. Providing adequate medical facilities for the people is an essential part of the obligations undertaken by the government in a welfare state. The government discharges this obligation by running hospitals and health centres which provide medical care to the person seeking to avail of those facilities. The government hospitals run by the State and Medical Officers engaged therein are duty bound to extend medical assistance for preserving human life. Failure on the part of a government hospital to provide timely medical treatment to a person in need of such treatment results in violation of the injured victim's right to life guaranteed by Article 21.

Responsibilities of Municipalities and Panchayats

Article 242 of the Constitution provides that the Legislature of a State may by law, endow the municipalities with such powers and authority as may be necessary to enable them to function as institutions of self-government and provide with respect to the performance of functions and implementation of schemes as may be entrusted to them including those in relation to the matters listed in the Twelfth Schedule to the Constitution which include at item 6, 'Public health, sanitation conservancy and solid waste management'. Similar provision is made for the panchayats under Article 243-G read with the Eleventh Schedule (item 23), of the Constitution. Various municipal laws prescribe duties of such local authorities in the sphere of public health and sanitation which include establishment and maintenance of dispensaries, expansion of health services, regulating or abating harmful or dangerous trades or practices, providing a supply of water proper and sufficient for preventing danger to the health of the inhabitants from the insufficiency or unwholesomeness of the existing supply, public vaccination, cleansing public places and removing noxious substances, disposal of night soil and rubbish, providing special medical aid and accommodation for the sick in the time of dangerous diseases, taking measures to prevent the outbreak of diseases etc. Therefore, whenever there is failure of these statutory obligations of the local authorities, the citizens can approach the High Court under Article 226 of the Constitution for seeking a mandamus to get the duties enforced.

There is, however, a significant difference between local government authorities and the State health authorities, the latter having enormous powers to make available financial resources and make key appointments. Healthy alliances between the two types of authorities are crucial, if health is to be effectively promoted. This continues to be one of the areas of tension between these two levels of the authority.

Right to Health: Judicial Activism

Health as stated earlier is a state of complete physical, mental and social well-being. The term 'health' implies more than mere absence of sickness as held by the Supreme Court. The Apex Court in India has played a significant role in realization of the right to health by recognising the right as a part of the fundamental right to life and issuing suitable directions to the State authorities for the discharge of their duties. The Court has recognised that maintenance of health is a most imperative constitutional goal whose realisation requires interaction of many social and economic factors.[21]

In this context the theory of the inter-relatedness between rights was famously articulated in the *Maneka Gandhi*[22] decision. This became the basis for the subsequent expansion of the understanding of the 'protection of life and liberty' under

Article 21 of the Constitution of India. The Supreme Court of India further went on to adopt an approach of harmonization between fundamental rights and directive principles in several cases. With regard to health, a prominent decision was delivered in *Parmanand Katara* v. *Union of India.*[23] In that case, the court was confronted with a situation where hospitals were refusing to admit accident victims and were directing them to specific hospitals designated to admit 'medico-legal cases'. The court ruled that while the medical authorities were free to draw up administrative rules to tackle cases based on practical considerations, no medical authority could refuse immediate medical attention to a patient in need. The court relied on various medical sources to conclude that such a refusal amounted to a violation of universally accepted notions of medical ethics. It observed that such measures violated the 'protection of life and liberty' guaranteed under Article 21 and hence created a right to emergency medical treatment.[24]

Another significant decision, which strengthened the recognition of the 'right to health', was that in *Indian Medical Association* v. *V.P. Shantha.*[25] In that case, it was ruled that the provision of a medical service (whether diagnosis or treatment) in return for monetary consideration amounted to a 'service' for the purpose of the Consumer Protection Act, 1986. The consequence of the same was that medical practitioners could be held liable under the act for deficiency in service in addition to negligence. This ruling has gone a long way towards protecting the interests of patients. However, medical services offered free of cost were considered to be beyond the purview of the said Act.

With regard to the access and availability of medical facilities, the leading decision of the Supreme Court was given in *Paschim Banga Khet Mazdoor Samiti* v. *State of West Bengal.*[26] The facts that led to the case were that a train accident victim was turned away from a number of government-run hospitals in Calcutta, on the ground that they did not have adequate facilities to treat him. The said accident victim was ultimately treated in a private hospital but the delay in treatment had aggravated his injuries. The Court realized that such situations routinely occurred all-over the country on account of inadequate primary health facilities. The Court issued notices to all State Governments and directed them to undertake measures to ensure the provision of minimal primary health facilities. When confronted with the argument that the same was not possible on account of financial constraints and limited personnel, the Court declared that lack of resources could not be cited as an excuse for non-performance of a constitutionally mandated obligation. The Court set up an expert committee to investigate the matter and endorsed the final report of the said committee. This report contained a seven-point agenda addressing several issues such as the upgrading of facilities all-over the country and the establishment of a centralized communications system amongst hospitals to ensure the adequacy and prompt availability of ambulance equipment and personnel. Some commentators have argued that by recognizing a governmental obligation to provide medical facilities, the Court has created a justiciable 'right to health'.

The judgment of the Supreme Court in *Nilbati Behra* v. *State of Orissa*[27] case holds that in view of the fundamental right to life (Article 21 of the Constitution)[28] the Government cannot claim 'sovereign immunity' for liability for the negligence of its employees.

The right to health and health care is protected under Article 21 of the Constitution of India, as a right to life and reach of which can move the Supreme Court on High Court through writ petition. Practice of medicine is capable of rendering great service to the society provided due care, sincerity, efficiency and skill are observed by doctors. When doctors performed their duties towards the patient negligently in a Government hospital, the servants of the state violated the fundamental right of the patient, guaranteed under Article 21 of the Constitution.

Medical profession has its own ethical parameters and code of conduct. 'Services' of medical establishments are more of purchasable commodities and the 'business' attitude has given an impetus to more and more malpractices and instances of neglect. But the question is, whether, on the whole, branding the entire medical community as a delinquent community would serve any purpose or will it cause damage to the patients. The answer is, no doubt, the later. It is not that measures to check such dereliction are absent. Victims of medical negligence, considering action against an erring doctor, have *three* options:

a. Compensatory mode—Seek financial compensation before the Consumer Disputes Redressal Forum or before Civil Courts,
b. Punitive/Deterrent mode—Lodge a criminal complaint against the doctor,
c. Corrective/Deterrent mode—Complaint to the State Medical Council demanding that the doctor's license be revoked.

Jurisdiction of Civil Court was never disputed but its scope was limited for damages only. In the recent times, professions are developing a tenancy to forget that the self-regulation which is at the heart of their profession is a privilege and not a right and a profession obtains this privilege in return for an implicit contract with society to provide good competent and accountable service to the public. The self-regulator standards in the profession have shown a decline and this can be attributed to the overwhelming impact of commercialization of the sector. There are reports against doctors of exploitative medical practices, misuse of diagnostic procedures, brokering deals for sale of human organs, etc. It cannot be denied that black sheep have entered the profession and that the profession has been unable to isolate them effectively. Two basic propositions laid down in law regarding liability for negligence are: firstly, 'Breach of Duty' to care and secondly, standard of care, i.e. the practitioner must bring to his task a reasonable degree of skill, knowledge and exercise a reasonable degree of care with caution. Supreme Court has made necessary guidelines for protection in order to secure life and health of individuals which are elaborated in the case presented in this study.

Health Right of Workmen

The importance of health promotion at the workplace is increasingly recognized particularly in larger organisations. Health promotion at workplace reduces absenteeism and can lead to gain in productivity. The Supreme Court surveyed in CESC case various functions of the State to protect safety and health of the workmen and emphasized the need to provide medical care to the workmen to prevent disease and to improve general standards of health consistent with human dignity and right to personality. It was held that medical care and health facilities not only protect against sickness but also ensure stable manpower for economic development. Facilities of health and medical care generate devotion and dedication among the workers to give their best physically as well as mentally, to productivity. It was held that the medical facilities are, therefore, part of social security and like gilt-edged security; it would yield immediate returns to the employer in the form of increased production and would reduce absenteeism. Just and favourable conditions of work imply ensuring safe and healthy working conditions to the workmen. The periodic medical treatment invigorates the health of workmen and harnesses their energy resources. Prevention of occupational disabilities enthuses them to render efficient service which is a valuable asset for greater productivity to the employer and national production to the State. Medical facilities, therefore, is a fundamental human right to protect his health. It was held that health insurance, while in service or after retirement was a fundamental right and even private industries are enjoined to provide health insurance to workmen.

The expression 'life' as held by the Supreme Court does not connote mere animal existence or continued drudgery through life but has a much wider meaning which includes right to livelihood, better standard of life, hygienic conditions in workplace and leisure. Continued treatment, while in service or after retirement is considered to be a moral, legal and constitutional concomitant duty of the employer and the State. Right to health and medical care is a fundamental right under

Article 21 read with Articles 39 (c), 41 and 43 of the Constitution to make the life of workman meaningful, held the Supreme Court in *C E & R C* v. *Union of India*.[29] The Court directed that the workers who suffered from asbestosis—an occupational health hazard, should be paid compensation by the concerned establishments. All the asbestos industries were directed to maintain and keep maintaining healthy record of every worker up to a minimum period of 40 years from the beginning of the employment or 15 years after retirement or cessation of employment whichever is later, to adopt the Membrane Filter test to detect asbestos fibre, and to compulsorily insure health coverage to every worker. The Union and the State Governments were directed to review the standards of permissible exposure limit value of fibre/cc in tune with the international standards reducing the permissible content.[30]

Health Right of Mentally Ill

Ranchi Mansik Arogyashala, a mental hospital located at Kanke near Ranchi once upon a time enjoyed international reputation and patients from outside India used to come for treatment there. But the complaints that the Supreme Court received about the institution were of a serious nature. During the pendency of the matter, the Supreme Court therefore gave interim directions for:

1. increased daily allocation for diet to patients,
2. supply of pure drinking water to the hospital,
3. restoration of proper sanitary conditions in the bathrooms and toilets of the hospital,
4. supply of mattresses and blankets to the patients,
5. immediate removal of ceiling limit which was in vogue in respect of costs of medicines allowable for each patient and for providing them medicines as prescribed by the doctors irrespective of the costs, and
6. appointing a qualified psychiatrist and a medical superintendent for the hospital.

The Supreme Court held that running of the mental hospital was in the discharge of the State's obligation to the citizens and the fact that a huge amount was required to be spent by the public exchequer was not of any consequence. The State has to realise its obligation and the government of the day has got to perform its duties by running the hospital in a perfect standard and serving the patients in an appropriate way. When the directions given by the Court not complied in an effective way by the governmental authorities, the Supreme Court found that the institution cannot be run as a mental hospital of that magnitude unless there was a change in the administrative set up and a new service to patient oriented thrust was to be given to the institution. A Committee was therefore constituted for the management of the mental hospital and directions were given to the State of Bihar to provide for a basic fund of Rs. 50 lakhs to be spent for the improvement of the hospital in a manner approved by the Committee. It was directed that the quality of the hospital should improve and the patients should have the benefit of modern scientific treatment having regard to the fact that the method of care and attention for the mentally ill had undergone a sea change.

Noticing that even patients who had cured were kept as inmates for prolonged periods it was held that hospital is not a place where cured people should be allowed to stay. It was found necessary that there should be a rehabilitation centre for those who after getting cured are not in a position to return to their families or on their own seek useful employment. Thus, a rehabilitation programme was also treated as a part of health care. Sometimes, patients also take advantages to use hospital for long time after they get proper treatment from the hospital. The following points would provide a base for clear understanding of the court direction and medico-legal cases.

Court Directives in Medico-Legal Cases Requiring Emergent Treatment

There was reluctance on the part of the doctors to treat medico-legal cases until clearance was given by the police authorities.

There was also an instinct to avoid attending legal proceedings due to the inconvenience involved. The following case explains the points.

A scooterist was knocked down by a speeding car. Seeing that the profusely bleeding scooterist a person who was on the road picked him up and took him to the nearest hospital. The doctors refused to attend on the injured and asked the man to take the patient to different hospital located 20 kms away, which was authorized to handle medico-legal cases. The Samaritan, without losing time, carried the victim to the other hospital, but before he could reach there, the victim succumbed to his injuries. The Court held that every doctor has a professional obligation to treat the injured victim and extend his services with due expertise for protecting life and the doctor does not contravene the law by proceeding to treat the injured victim. The court directed wide publicity to its decision to ensure that every doctor wherever he would be in the territory of India should forthwith be aware of this position.[31]

Rights of Patients Undergoing Ophthalmic Treatment at Eye Camps

The problems of the ophthalmic health status of the Indian citizen are of a complex dimension causing an understandable concern. The very large number of cases of impairment of visual perception in the country needs the purposeful involvement of voluntary social organisations so as to provide an augmented, broad-based, participatory medicare for the general improvement of the tone of ophthalmic health in the country. The Government of India has evolved a comprehensive policy and programme for control of blindness which amongst other things, envisaged a programme for the promotion of eye care through 'eye camps' organised by social and voluntary organisations and to provide financial assistance.

In *A.S. Mittal* v. *State of UP*, the Supreme Court was confronted with a case where the eyes of 84 out of 108 patients who were operated (88 for cataract), in an 'eye camp' were irreversibly damaged owing to a post-operative E-coli infection of the intra-occular cavities of the operated eyes, which mishap was undisputedly due to a common contaminating source being the 'normal saline' used in the eyes at the time of surgery. The Court examined whether the existing guidelines prescribing norms and conditions for conducting 'eye camps' laid down by the government were sufficiently comprehensive to ensure the protection of patients, who were generally drawn in such eye camps from the poorer and the less effluent section of the society and issued directions to the government to incorporate the following suggestions made by a sub-committee of the Indian Medical Council in the revised guidelines:

1. The operations should only be performed by qualified experienced ophthalmic surgeons and an 'eye camp' should not be used as a training ground for post-graduate medical students.
2. There should be a pathologist available to examine urine, blood etc.
3. Preferably, a dentist should also be present to check teeth for sepsis.
4. A physician for general medical check-up of the patients should also be there.
5. All medicines to be used must be of standard quality duly verified by the doctor in charge of the camp.

On Medical Negligence

The patient has a right to be treated with a reasonable degree of care, skill and knowledge. A mistake by a medical practitioner which no reasonably competent and careful practitioner would have committed is nothing short of negligence. But the law recognizes the dangers which are inherent in surgical operations, where the operations is a race against time, the court makes greater allowance taking into account the 'risk-benefit' test.

In Dr. *L.B.Joshi* v. *Dr. T.B. Godbole,* the Supreme Court held that a person who holds himself out ready to give medical advice and treatment impliedly undertakes that he possesses skill and knowledge for the purpose. He owes a duty of care to the patient in deciding whether to undertake the case and what treatment to be given. A breach of such duty gives a right of action to the patient for negligence of the doctor.

Medical practitioners do not enjoy any immunity from an action in tort, and they can be used on the ground that they have failed to exercise reasonable skill and care. The Supreme Court has held that the fact that they are governed by the Indian Medical Council Act and are subject to the disciplinary control of the Medical Councils is no solace to a person who has suffered due to their negligence and the right of such person to seek redress is not affected. Service rendered to a patient by a medical practitioner (except where the doctor renders service free of charge to every patient or under a contract of personal service), by way of consultation, diagnosis and treatment, both medical and surgical, was held to fall within the ambit of 'service' as defined in section 2(1)(O) of the Consumer Protection Act, 1986.

On Quality of Blood for Transfusion

While transfusion of blood can save life of a needy patient, it can take away life if contaminated. In part XII-B of the Drugs and Cosmetics Rules, 1945 provisions are made to regulate blood collection and storage by prescribing the equipment and supplies required for a blood bank.

In a Public Interest Litigation serious deficiencies and shortcomings in the matter of collection, storage and supply of blood through various blood centres were highlighted before the Supreme Court and directions were sought to the Union of India and States to take steps for obviating the malpractices, malfunctioning and inadequacies of the blood banks. The Supreme Court constituted a Committee to examine the draft schemes suggested by the Petitioner and the Union of India. The Committee made a report proposing an action plan. Keeping in view the report of the Court Committee, the report of the Experts Committee set up by the Indian Red Cross

Society and the programme that was being implemented by the National Aids Control Organisation, the Court held that the Government should take suitable action as per the immediate implementation and long-term implementation plans suggested by the Court Committee and gave the following directions:

1. The Union of India should take steps to establish a representative body to be known as National Council of Blood Transfusion as a registered society to be funded by the Government of India with empowerment to raise its own funds from trade, industry and individuals.
2. The State Governments should establish State Councils in consultation with the National Council and they should be funded by the Government of India and the State Governments, with empowerment to raise its own funds.
3. The programmes and activities of the National and State Councils shall cover the entire range of services related to the operation and requirements of blood banks including:
   (a) launching of effective motivating campaigns for stimulating voluntary blood donations.
   (b) launching programmes of blood donations in educational institutions, among the labour, industry and trade establishment and organisations of various services including civic bodies.
   (c) training of personnel in relation to all operations of blood collection—storage and utilization, separation of blood groups, proper labelling, proper transport, quality control and cross-matching of blood, separation and storage of blood components and all the basic essentials of the operations of blood banking.
4. The National Council should undertake training programmes, establish institution for research in collection, processing, storage, distribution and transfusion of human blood and its components.

5. The National Council should take steps for starting Special Post-graduate courses in medical colleges in blood collection, storage, transfusion etc.
6. Donations to the National and State Councils may be made tax-free by the Government of India.
7. The government should ensure that the blood banks operating in the country are duly licenced in a year.
8. Professional donor system should be eliminated in two years by the governments.

Protection Against Injurious Drugs

With the onward march of science and complexities of living processes, hitherto unknown diseases are notified. New and emerging diseases, combined with the rapid spread of pathogens resistant to antibiotics and of disease carrying insects resistant to insecticides, are daunting challenges to human health. The gap between the ability of microbes to mutate into drug-resistant strains and man's ability to counter them is widening fast. To meet the new challenges new drugs have to be found. The Central Government is by section 26A of the Drugs and Cosmetics Act, 1940 empowered to prohibit in public interest, manufacture, sale or distribution of any drug which is likely to involve any risk to human beings or animals or if does not have the therapeutic value claimed.

In *Vincent Panikurlangara* v. *Union of India*, directions were sought from the Supreme Court for banning import, manufacture, sale and distribution of the drugs which were recommended for banning by the Drugs Consultative Committee and for cancellation of all the licences authorising such drugs. Taking note of the fact that the WHO on the basis of expert advice, was of the view that human ailments can be treated effectively with 285 basic drugs, the Supreme Court observed that the Central Government on the basis of expert advice can indeed adopt an approved national policy and prescribe an adequate number of formulations which would on the whole meet the requirement of the people at large. While laying down guidelines, injurious drugs must be totally eliminated from the market, and great care in this regard has to be taken. Drugs as are found necessary should be manufactured in abundance and their availability to satisfy every demand should be ensured. The State's obligations to enforce production of qualitative drugs and elimination of injurious ones from the market must take within its sweep an obligation to make useful drugs available at a reasonable price so as to be within the reach of a common man, which would involve regulating the price. It may be that on account of the cost of a particular medicine of improved quality it will have to sell at a higher price, but, for every illness which can be cured by treatment, the patient must be in a position to get its medicine. It was held that this is an obligation on the State in view of the fundamental directives of State policy enshrined in Part IV of the Constitution. The Supreme Court gave a direction to the Central Government to examine the objections raised in the petition against the drugs or refer them to the consultative Committee for examination and take a decision within six months.

One disturbing trend noticed by the Court was that there was no adequate response from the bodies like Medical Council of India, the Indian Medical Association and the Drugs Medical Council of India despite notices by the Court.

It was held that these bodies are not litigants and do not have a choice of keeping away from the Court like private parties in ordinary litigations opting to go *ex parte.* It was observed that, when the Court invited them to come forward and place their views on the relevant aspects, an attitude of callous indifference could not be appreciated.

Welfare of Children

In *Sheela Barse (II)* v. *Union of India,* the Supreme Court held that the nation's children are a supremely important asset. Their nurture and solicitude are our responsibility. Children's programmes should find a prominent part in our national plans for the development of human resources, so that our children grow up to become robust citizens, physically fit, mentally alert and morally healthy, endowed with skill and motivations needed by the society. By definition health encompasses with physical, mental and social well-being, therefore, this section is coming under the health and human rights purview. The state has to provide basic nutrition and health facilities to all its citizens including children.

Conclusion

Human rights standards address the civil, political, economic, social and cultural sphere. Each human right, while formally belonging to one of those categories, in reality encompasses aspects of all of them. This is easily identifiable within the human right to health. Moreover, the right to health within the human rights framework is defined as the right to achieve the "highest attainable standard of health" not merely the absence of disease. Both of these aspects of human rights are consistent with a social determinant approach to health, as they take into account the wide array of factors that influence a person's overall health status. Finally, a human rights and public health approach both have in common an assumption that the primary purpose of a health care system is preserving health, rather than addressing economic interests.

But a human rights approach is not merely consistent with a social determinant/public health model. It can also be employed as a tool to strengthen and promote, through policy and education, such a model. In the context of reproductive health, it brings greater definition and clarity to the parameters of what should be considered reproductive health concerns, and what are acceptable policy measures to influence or coerce reproductive health outcomes. This study addressed how that tool can be employed and the components and principles within the human rights framework of particular relevance to right to health matters.

The overview of the plans and policy reports not only throws light on the gap between the rhetoric and reality but also the framework within which the policies have been formulated. There has been an excessive preoccupation with single purpose driven programmes. Above all, the spirit of primary health care has been reduced to just primary level care. The health reports and plans mostly concentrated on building the health services infrastructure and even this lacked a sense of integration. Most of the policy reports miss out on the importance of a strong referral system. Instead, there has been more emphasis on building the primary level care and even that has lacked proper implementation. The Bhore Committee report and later, the Primary Health Care Declaration discussed the operational aspects of integrating the other sectors of development related to health. The multi-sectoral approach that is much needed and the intersectoral linkages that are essential for a vibrant health system have not been well thought out, and there has been no plan drawn out for it later. The outline of plan documents and their implementation have been incremental rather than being holistic. It is important to question whether it is only the low investment in health that is the main reason for the present status of the health system or is it also to do with the framework, design and approach within which the policies have been planned.

Technological advances, investment and good policies can be turned to naught in the presence of a system lacking in leadership, direction and a core sense of integrity pervading all levels of health care. Unless all stakeholders are motivated by a set of values—of compassion and human concern for the sick and ill, of not accepting a system which allows people to be denied care only because of circumstances beyond their control, of a minimal sense of equality and dignity among all the health system will continue to reflect the cement and mortar issues of the expanding medical and drug industry, which can, in the absence of the guiding hand of the state, degrade human suffering into an opportunity for making profits. It then becomes critical to define the role of the State as the current utilitarian liberal approach of the health sector offers no acceptable solution. The issue is broader and needs to be examined within the context of the principles that underlie the concept of social contract of Rousseau or sense of justice of

Rawls. If these principles enshrined in our Constitution are adhered to, then the State will need to intervene both intelligently and firmly.

END NOTES

1. "Health and Family Planning Services in India: An Epidemiological, Socio-cultural and Political Analysis and a Perspective", *Lok Paksh,* New Delhi, 1985.
2. Warren, K.S., "The Evolution of Selective Primary Health Care", *Social Science and Medicine,* Centre for Communication Programmes, Johns Hopkins Bloomberg School of Public Health, 1988, No. 26 (9), pp. 891-898.
3. *The World Health Report 2000, Health Systems: Improving Performance,* World Health Organisation, Geneva, 2000.
4. Hsiao, William C., *Unmet Health Needs of Two Billion: Is Community Financing a Solution?,* Discussion Paper on Health, Nutrition, and Population Family (HNP) of the World Bank's Human Development Network, The International Bank for Reconstruction and Development/The World Bank 1818 H Street, Washington DC, 2001.
5. Sen, P.D., *Community Control of Health Financing in India: A Review of Local Experiences,* Bethesda, Maryland, Abt Associates, Partnerships for Health Reform, xvii, Technical Report No. 8 USAID Contract No. HRN-5974-C-00-5024-00) October 1997, p. 83.
6. Atre, S.R., Mistry, N.F., *Multidrug Resistant Tuberculosis (MDR-TB): An Attempt to Link Biosocial Determinants.* The Foundation for Research in Community Health (Unpublished).
7. Pendse, V., *Maternal Deaths in an Indian Hospital: A Decade of No Change?,* In: Safe Motherhood Initiatives: Critical Issues, edited by Marge Berer and T.K. Sundari Ravindran, Oxford, England, Blackwell Science (Reproductive Health Matters), 1999, pp. 119-26.
8. Kirti and Sharad Iyengar, "Elective Abortion as a Primary Health Service in Rural India: Experience with MVA", *Reproduction Health Matters,* 2002, Vol. 10, No. 19, pp. 54-63.
9. Mavalankar, D.V. "Study of Technical Top Management Capacity for Safe Motherhood Programme in India", Study Commissioned by the World Bank, New Delhi (Unpublished Monograph).
10. Mohan, P., Iyengar, S., Mohan, S.B., Sen, K. "Daily Up-Down". Why would an Auxiliary Nurse-Midwife (ANM) of Rajasthan Prefer to Reside within her Work-Area? *Action Research and Training for Health,* Udaipur, India, 2003.

11. Rifkin, S.B., Gill W., "Why Health Improves: Defining the Issues Concerning Comprehensive Primary Health Care and Selective Primary Health Care", *Social Science and Medicine*, Volume 23, Issue 6, 1986, pp. 559-566.
12. *Ibid.*
13. Kutty, Raman, Panikar, "Impact of Fiscal Crisis on the Public Sector Health Care System in Kerala", A Research Project, Achutha Menon, *Centre for Health Science Studies*, Thiruvananthapuram, 1995.
14. Ranga, Rao, A.P., Report on Role and Efficiency of ANM and Male Worker: In Primary Health Care, Andhra Pradesh: A Qualitative Study Funded by DFID, Unpublished—Paper Commissioned by DFID, New Delhi, India, 2003.
15. *Ibid.*
16. Misra, R., Chatterjee R. and Rao S., "India Health Report", Oxford University Press, New Delhi, 2003.
17. *Rural Health Bulletin*, Ministry of Health and Family Welfare, Government of India, 2004.
18. Vijayanand, S., *Decentralization of Health Planning and Implementation—the Kerala Experience on the Role of Local Government Institutions in Population*, Presented at NIHFW Workshop, 17-23rd. February, 2003.
19. Sethi, G., *Fiscal Decentralization to Rural Governments in India*, World Bank, Oxford University Press, New Delhi, 2004.
20. Bakshi, P.M., "The Constitution of India", Universal Law Publishing Co. Pvt. Ltd., New Delhi, 2003.
21. Justice, R.K., Abichandani, "High Court of Gujarat Report", Ahmedabad, 2004.
22. AIR 1978 SC 597.
23. AIR 1989 SC 2039.
24. Commentary cited from: Arun Thiruvengadam, "The Global Dialogue Among Courts: Social Rights Jurisprudence of The Supreme Court of India from a Comparative Perspective" in C. Raj Kumar and K. Chockalingam (eds.), *Human Rights, Justice and Constitutional Empowerment*, Oxford University Press, New Delhi, 2007, p. 283.
25. AIR 1996 SC 550.
26. AIR 1996 SC 2426.
27. AIR 1993 SC 1960.
28. Bakshi, P.M., *Right to Life and Personal Liberty*, "The Constitution of India", Universal Law Publishing Co. Pvt. Ltd., New Delhi, 2003.
29. AIR 1992 SC 2213.
30. *Op.cit.*
31. *The Samaj*, Daily Oriya Newspaper, Bhubaneswar, 25th June, 2007.

5

Health Care Delivery in Orissa
A Look at Standards

The thrust of the chapter is to explain how health care delivery system works at different levels in the state of Orissa. To go into the details about health care delivery mechanism, before that one has to explain the background of the state and health sector reforms and also context of rights issues which is the major focus of the chapter. One of the prime objectives of any health system is to provide quality health care to its citizens. This is primarily done by strengthening the service delivery mechanism and improving systems and processes. In spite of this, the quality of the state health care varies widely across geographic areas, populations, and levels of care. The Health Policy 1983 and 2002 has emphasized on improving the health status of the people by creating efficient and effective public provisioning of health care in the country. Many studies, particularly, the RCH-facility surveys have revealed the inadequacies of public health facilities and how the public health system has become inaccessible to majority of its citizens. Among many other factors the inadequacies at the facilities affect the outputs and these are policy induced and states with improved output indicates sound and organized transmission mechanism than others.

Given the backdrop, this chapter examines the nature and quality of health care delivery facilities in Orissa. It also discusses the governance process and transmission mechanism of service delivery in the state. It looks into the infrastructure, tools and equipments and manpower in the health care facilities and how this functions to improve the service delivery at the primary and secondary level. The other side of the issues has been discussed in the light of organizational structure and institutional arrangements made to strengthen the service delivery system.

This is based on review of primary data collected from sample health care institutions in one district of Orissa. The two hospitals have been selected on the basis of Human Development Index (HDI) and one hospital with highest HDI and other lower HDI have been selected. Among the hospitals two blocks have been chosen on the basis of distance as criteria because Bhore Committee report suggests that every village where 10,000 to 20,000 people are living that village should have at least PHC with a doctor for that reason distance has been taken as a parameter. From each block, headquarters institution and 50 per cent of the PHCs and 30 per cent of the subcenters have been selected. Informations were collected through a structured questionnaire on different aspects of functioning of health care institutions, constraints faced and steps taken to fill the gap. In order to find out the changes in the system and processes, a series of discussion were held with the key officials and chief district medical officers and other functionaries in the district. It is significant to note that the state of Orissa's brief background and location is relevant to the present study.

Despite gradual improvement in health status over many years, preventable mortality and morbidity in Orissa are high. The root causes of poor health continue to be poverty, social deprivation, low levels of literacy and inefficient health systems and infrastructure for health care and control of diseases, particularly communicable diseases. Socio-cultural inequities and barriers, insufficient assertion and demand for health care, inadequate geographic spread of service outlets and poor quality health care reduce access to and effectiveness of public services.

Organization of Health Services and Health Programmes in Orissa

The Government of Orissa through numerous programmes in the health sector claims that it is providing adequate, qualitative, preventive and curative health care to the people of the State as well as to ensure health care services to all, particularly to the disadvantaged groups like Scheduled Tribes, Scheduled Castes and the Backward Classes. It also aims at providing affordable quality health care to the people of the State not only through the Allopathic system of medicine but also through the Homeopathic and Ayurvedic systems; to ensure greater access to primary health care by bringing medical institutions as close to the people as possible or through mobile health units.

Genesis of Health Sector Reforms in Orissa

Interest in health sector reform in Orissa began in the mid-1990s. Earlier phase of health sector in Orissa through a planned process since 1947, there has been an expansion in infrastructure and systems for providing health care services throughout Orissa. Orissa has adopted Central Government norms, guidelines, policies and programmes for this development. Since the year 1947, there has been a gradual improvement in the health status of the population due to several factors including developmental and educational interventions, economic improvement and better health care services. While the Infant Mortality Rate (IMR) has declined from 135 in 1981 to 97 in 1989, it is still one of the highest in India – much above the national average of 70. Indicators of nutritional status among women and children and burden of diseases indicate a substantial higher proportion of morbidity and mortality. The people of Orissa experience a large number of disasters – about 40 major disasters in 50 years – that adversely affect health and development and health care services.[1]

This was propelled by the occurrence of two events, (1) the formation of a Committee of the Orissa Legislature chaired by the Health Minister (called the House Committee) which looked into three important aspects of health care and in 1995-96 recommended, cost recovery through user charges in hospitals, granting of autonomy to be given to district and tertiary hospitals and abolition of private practice by doctors. These recommendations coincided with the evaluation by DFID, which stated, that in order to ensure effective health care delivery, the Government of Orissa needs to:

- Make funds available for maintenance of buildings and equipment.
- Make funds available for medicine (i.e. drugs and consumables).
- Make funds available for transport (i.e. mobility)—especially for health care delivery and supervision.

These reports served as an impetus for health sector reforms in Orissa. In the five years or so following these two events, a number of reforms, both large and small, have been introduced in the health sector in Orissa. Some of them relate to changes in administrative and operational systems, some to changes in personnel policies including skill development for better service delivery, and some were aimed at giving a minimum health guarantee to the people.

Orissa Health and Family Welfare Reform

After Phases I and II of the DFID supported study, Phase III (1997-2001) was implemented with a project outlay of Rs. 14.55 crore. This study sought to fill the gaps in terms of maintenance of buildings, mobility and medicines with a view to providing quality primary health care at the village level in two demonstration districts of Balasore and Bhadrak. It also aimed to identify areas and mechanisms to ensure community participation and to address the health needs of the disadvantaged population, particularly, the needs of women. Under the reforms, petty maintenance has been made the responsibility of Medical Officers and Waste Management in Primary Health Institutions has been introduced. The Zilla

Swasthya Samitis (ZSS) or District Health Societies have been made functional and the project activities are implemented through the ZSS. Repair and maintenance of health institutions and assets is also taken up through the ZSS. Provision of adequate quantities of quality drugs in primary health care institutions is being ensured.

Orissa Health Systems Development

The Orissa Health Systems Development (OHSD) is under implementation since September 1998 with the assistance of the World Bank. It seeks to improve health care delivery in selected primary and secondary hospitals in the State; increase efficiency in the allocation and use of health resources and address systemic, broad-based problems faced at the first referral and community levels. Furthermore, it seeks to strengthen systems including overall management, procurement of drugs and equipment, referral, Health Management Information System (HMIS), surveillance of major communicable diseases, health care waste management and equipment management system. A Policy and Strategic Planning Unit (PSPU) has been established to provide strategic planning support to the study and to push the health sector reform agenda.

(I) Public-Private Partnership

A. Handing over PHCs to Private or Non-state Actors

The handing over of PHCs to non-state actors was experimentally tried out in two tribal districts as the government was finding it difficult to provide health personnel in single doctor PHCs in remote locations. The Government of Orissa entered into partnership with a view to ensure provision of better health care to the people in remote areas. Under the agreement, the PHCs were to be managed and run by private parties. This experiment did not run for very long and the private parties handed the PHCs back to the government after some time. An evaluation of the initiative revealed that the terms of reference and modalities of transfer were inadequate and the private parties did not have the resources and ability to run the institutions.

The evaluation report recommended trying out the experiment in more places with suitable modifications. Presently, public-private partnerships are being implemented for safe abortion services and social marketing of Disposable Delivery Kit (DDK). Parivar Seva Sangh and Population Services International are being taken as agencies of implementation under the Sector Investment Programme. Also, facilities for 24-hour drug counter have been established by private agencies inside the hospital campus. Presently, discussions are being held between representatives of non-state actors and government and terms of reference are being developed with a view to initiate such public-private partnerships.

It is significant to bring out the argument relating to the process of globalization and its impact on health sector. Globalisation has evolved out of a gradual progress of progressive integration of the world economies through falling trade barriers, greater exchange and mobility of capital and labour. The process further facilitated by a number of developments in international cooperation, emergence of international institutions and the continued advances in information and communication technologies also paved the way for global governance. The new globalisation environment has driven several developing countries with a sizeable public sector to adopt policy reforms including macro-economic and financial stabilization policies, creation of market-oriented environment and more space for the private sector. This goes hand in hand with increasing internationalization of goods, services, labour and capital, and exchange and exposure of human beings for development oriented programmes. However, such a process is likely to have far reaching effect on health sector both direct and indirect particularly in developing countries, where health attainments are low and majority of population lack resources to finance their health care needs.

B. Outsourcing of Cleaning in Hospitals

Given the lack of cleanliness in government hospitals, in July 1997, an experiment was carried out wherein the cleaning work of District Headquarters Hospital, a major hospital, was contracted out to a private agency – viz., Sulabh International at a negotiated price. It was agreed that the existing cleaning staff (i.e. the government employees) would be engaged in other work in the hospital. The State Government's finance department required that while no retrenchment need take place, existing vacancies of cleaning staff be abolished and any new vacancies occurring as a result of retirement or death not be filled up. Initially, there were some protests from the Class IV employees union, but since no retrenchment of staff was involved, the protests did not gather momentum. The contracting-out of select services has led to proper maintenance of hospitals, proper management of waste and better care for patients and their attendants. Some of the challenges faced included resentment from the regular cleaning staff, non-utilization of existing staff and problems in ensuring timely payment to the agency.

Thereafter, other hospitals also sought to contract out the cleaning services in their institutions. Since funds were a constraint, this could not be done, at once, in a large number of hospitals. However, in September 1998, further contracts were signed with Sulabh International for the cleaning of one ward of the SCB Medical College, Cuttack, and six wards of the MKCG Medical College, Berhampur. Subsequently, this was extended to four district hospitals. Presently, contracting out is being carried out on an experimental basis in some of the districts. In addition to this, security services in Capital Hospital, Bhubaneshwar and other such larger hospitals have also been contracted out in the state.

Following a recent State Government decision, the costs of cleaning and sanitation are to be made out of the user fees generated through the ZSS. In case of disputes and controversies in selection of the contractors, the matter is to be referred to State Director and Government for final decision.

The hospital cleaning and sanitation is supervised by the Hospital Superintendent and the payments are passed through the ZSS. It is proposed that catering and laundry services are also contracted out.

In contracting out of cleaning and sanitation of hospital, the selection of the contractor is made through a tender procedure. Experiences in hospital cleaning and sanitation, solvency of the contractor, availability of assets, location of contractor's office, tax clearance certification, registration number, etc. are taken into consideration by the tender committee. This committee is headed by the District Collector (Chairman) and the CDMO or Addl. CDMO or ADMO (PH) as members. Tender notices are published in the newspapers and the Collector of the district is the final authority in selecting the contractor.

(II) Decentralization

A. Initiatives in Decentralization

In the state of Orissa, there has been a move towards decentralization, wherein the districts and the health institutions have been granted the authority to plan, budget and implement its own health programmes. They are also able to generate their own resources, within the purview of the broad government guidelines. Moreover, financial and administrative powers have been delegated to the district administration and the block health administration. The programme officials opine that in terms of success, lessons and challenges, delegation of financial and administrative power has led to improvement of quality of services to staff like timely payment of entitlements, positioning the right person in right place, better control on subordinate and minimization of workload in the Directorate. However, some challenges remain. The delegation of power to block level has not been supplemented with training of MOs in administrative and financial matters. There is no provision made for attached support staff. Another area, which requires strengthening is establishment of interdepartmental harmony. Another development in the realm of decentralization has been the formation of ZSS.

(i) Formation of Zilla Swasthya Samitis

With the increasing emphasis on decentralization, ZSS were developed as an important district level functionary for implementation of health related programmes and activities. The ZSS was initially formed in 1993 as registered societies in five districts of Orissa, with a view to implement the DFID assisted Area Development Project, Phase II. Subsequently, such societies were formed in all districts to implement the various Government of India supported health programmes. Earlier, separate district level societies were established for malaria, tuberculosis, blindness, leprosy and AIDS, wherein each society was operating and implementing specific health programmes under the chairmanship of the District Collector. With a view to reduce the multiplicity of committees and societies at district level, the government issued an order leading to merger of all existing societies into one society—the ZSS and the subsequent modification of by-law of ZSS to this effect. Subsequently, all the CDMOs were asked to dissolve the existing societies in the district and merge them with the ZSS. Also, on merger, the existing assets and liabilities of the merged societies devolved on the ZSS. Autonomy has been given to all hospitals under the jurisdiction of the ZSS/DHH in particular. For large hospitals, the hospital society has been constituted with powers and functions like the ZSS.

The primary objective of ZSS is to provide the Health and Family Welfare Department, with increasing support for effective implementation of its ongoing programme such as population control, reproductive and child health, immunization, school health programme, control of diarrhoeal diseases, control of TB, leprosy, etc. The ZSS acts as a nodal forum for all health and family welfare activities to be undertaken in the district. Over the years, the range of activities to be undertaken by the ZSS has increased to include development and maintenance of health infrastructure, planning and implementation of effective IEC programmes, collection and utilization of user fees for various hospital services, operation of ambulances, procurement and distribution of drugs, delivery of various non-clinical services, provision of training to medical, paramedical and non-medical personnel, volunteers amongst others, ensuring community participation through the PRIs, publication of literature relating to health and family welfare programmes, undertaking research on issues related to health and family welfare, amongst others.

The ZSS is a society at the district level registered under the Society Registration Act, 1860. As per the recently amended MOU 9 of the ZSS, the District Collector is the co-Chairperson, while the CDMO is the Chief Executive *cum* Vice-Chairperson. The members of the general body include government officials like the Executive Engineer (R&B)/PWD, ADMO, ADMO (PH)/(Med)/(FW), PD (DRDA), amongst others as well as NGOs, representatives of donor agencies working in the district, etc. Additionally, there are patron members, ex-officio members, nominated and co-opted members. Any individual or institution with an interest in health activities and an aptitude for social work can become a member of the ZSS on request and by application, subject to the approval of the Executive Committee.

A case study on ZSS was conducted. This study covered one sample districts of Balasore. It mainly involved discussion with the members of the ZSS, review and verification of relevant documents, collection of available data on achievement and performance of the ZSS. The study recommended a set of strategic measures for functional improvement of the ZSS. These include *inter alia,* the essentiality of developing and providing comprehensive operational guidelines for streamlining of bye-laws, consolidation of financial and accounting systems, especially in light of the need for amalgamation of all district level societies; sanctioning of maximum administrative authority to the CDMO as the ZSS activities pertain essentially to health related programmes and projects; need for appointment of full time senior officer to manage the ZSS activities; appropriate orientation and training to the staff, formation of performance monitoring indicators of ZSS, periodic review of the ZSS and need for better inter-sectoral and interdepartmental co-ordination so as to improve its service delivery performance.

(ii) Amalgamation of Zilla Swasthya Samitis

ZSS have been established to manage health care delivery system in the district in a co-ordinated way through involving government, private sectors and community. Earlier, besides a Zilla Swasthya Samiti (District Health Society) which had a variety of functions, a number of individual societies had been set up in the districts for each Central or donor funded programme. There were societies for Blindness, Leprosy, TB, Malaria, etc. The composition of almost all the societies was the same with the District Collector as Chairman, and the Chief District Medical Officer as Member-Secretary. Hence, it was felt that such multiple societies should be amalgamated to form a single district health society. This was done in 1998 across the whole of Orissa and the amalgamated societies went by the earlier name of the Zilla Swasthya Samitis.

(iii) Reforms related to Human Resources

In 1996, as part of a strategic review of the health sector, undertaken by the Government of Orissa in partnership with the DFID, 'in-service training of personnel' was identified as one of the lacunae. Hence, reforms to strengthen and improve the capacity of health personnel were introduced. These included:

B. Mandatory pre-PG Rural Service

In face of the large number of vacancies of doctors in tribal and 'difficult' areas, the lack of adequate success in ensuring the presence of doctors in such areas, absence of rural orientation to the young doctors, an attempt was made to ensure that young doctors were posted to such areas and institutions. Under this scheme, which was introduced in 1998, all-over the state of Orissa, eleven districts, to which doctors are generally unwilling to go to and which have consistently had a large number of vacancies, were selected, and health institutions were identified. The entrance examination for the medical Post Graduate (PG) courses was held one year ahead of the date of admission. Those who qualified were advised about the medical college and the discipline they would get, and thereafter assigned to one of the institutions in the 11 districts. Those who are not already in government employment were given contract appointments and assigned to these districts. Amendments were also made in the Orissa Medical Service Rules so as to make the first posting to rural areas mandatory. The doctors are required to work in these institutions for one whole year, and only after obtaining a certificate regarding completion of the period, are allowed admission into the PG course. Doctors were not willing to go to tribal areas and difficult area earlier, now government has taken the initiative that every newly appointed doctor has to go to difficult and remote areas. It is a part of the agreement while they are appointed.

C. *Internship Training Programme for Better Community Health Orientation*

In the past, medical interns were given community health training in three training centres (under the control of medical college) and their attached health institutions. They were trained in large groups of 25 or more, got hardly any exposure to real community health problems and the quality of the training was poor with little, or no, hands-on training. Further, the supervision was done entirely by the medical college teachers, who are themselves not very much in touch with community health conditions and developments. So, with an objective of improving the quality of community health training of medical interns, a new scheme was introduced in 2000 across the state of Orissa. Under the new scheme, the interns are sent in groups of two and three to community health centres under the control of the CDMOs for a period of three months to be trained in public health activities. They are exposed to real community health situations and get 'hands on' training. They are supervised both by the medical officers in charge of the institutions as well as the medical college teachers.

D. Multi-Skilled Health Personnel

Given the lack of adequate skilled personnel like laboratory technicians, an attempt was made to utilize the existing personnel like the pharmacists, health workers, ANMs for different activities. Pharmacists and health workers have been trained in microscopy for sputum and blood examination, and deployed in the implementation of the Revised National Tuberculosis Control Programme (RNTCP) and the malaria programmes. ANMs have been trained as Directly Observed Treatment, Short-course (DOTS) providers and deployed in the RNTCP in addition to their own duties. This is being done since 1998 and is applicable to the entire state of Orissa.

E. Short-Course Training in Anaesthesia Administration

Because of shortage of anaesthesia specialists, short course training in anaesthesia administration was introduced in 1999, as a pilot programme with a view to enable doctors in CHCs to administer anaesthesia in emergency care. Doctors from the field were given three months training in anaesthesia administration. However, the numbers trained are, so far, very small. The scheme, which was discontinued, is proposed to be restarted.

F. Appointment of Staff on a Contractual Basis

In fact, lack of adequate personnel, Medical Officers (MOs) have been appointed on a contract basis in the vacant posts. These appointments are made after conducting walk in interviews at the district level with due concurrence of the

Director of Health Services. Similar appointments are being made for health worker (female), staff nurse and pharmacist as also for support staff like clerks and drivers against the existing vacant posts.

G. Formation of District Cadres for Paramedics

Prior to the formation of district cadres, most paramedics such as ANMs, nurses, pharmacists, laboratory technicians were employees of the state and were expected to work in any part of the state. They were also subject to transfers from one place to another. As paramedics are mainly low-paid government workers, mostly women, these conditions of service caused considerable hardship and expense. Besides, the workers, who were from the more developed coastal districts were reluctant to go to the remote and unpopular districts and remained on leave on some pretext. Consequently, many posts in these areas remained vacant. Hence, in 1998, a decision was taken to form district cadres for the paramedics. The existing personnel in the state cadre was divided and allotted to different district cadres. Currently, the districts are responsible for all the new recruitments made. During such recruitment, preference is given to candidates belonging to the same district. It was envisaged that this measure would result in better availability of paramedics in difficult areas, less hardship for personnel due to transfers, and consequently better service to the public.

(iv) Changes in Financing Methods

a. User Fees

The system of user fees was in existence in Orissa in the government hospitals prior to 1997 for certain items such as accommodation in cabins, use of ambulance, X-ray and few other investigations. The fee was extremely low and only a fraction of the cost or market prices of the corresponding service. Moreover, the amount paid went to the government coffers and not to the hospital, hence there was little motivation to collect it. However, following the recommendations of a committee constituted by the Orissa Legislative Assembly to review the health system in three medical colleges, the user fees were revised. In keeping with the recommendations of the committee and with a view to generate additional resources to supplement the budgetary allocation, improve and extend the scope of the medical facilities, the Government of Orissa (Government of Orissa) passed an order dated 24th June, 1997, revising the existing user fees and including more items under the purview of user fees such as transportation, accommodation, diagnosis and medical investigations. Initially, these rates were applicable to the three medical colleges, the district headquarters hospitals, the Capital Hospital Bhubaneshwar and the Government Hospital, Rourkela. For the purpose of collection, the State was divided into A, B and C categories, depending on the levels of development and differential rates were levied with lower rates being levied in the less developed and tribal districts. User fees were initially levied for diagnostics, special accommodation and for use of transport (e.g. ambulance, hearse, etc). The user fees were deposited into the accounts of the Zilla Swasthya Samiti (District Health Society) in the case of district hospitals and into the accounts of specially constituted hospital societies in the case of the medical colleges. From this beginning, the user fees initiative has grown and spread.

Presently, user fees are levied in all medical colleges, headquarters and subdivisional hospitals and some area hospitals for diagnostic purposes like pathology, biochemical, radiological, ultra-sonography, colour doppler, CT scan and other such investigations. In addition to this, some designated hospitals have pay cabins or clinics. Pay clinics have been established on an experimental basis at dental college, Cuttack wherein the treating doctor also gets a percentage of the benefit shared by the government. Further, in medical colleges, facilities for Intensive Care Unit (ICU) are available on payment as also the ambulance services. User fees are collected from IPD and OPD patients in some headquarters hospitals, so as to involve the community in the development process. In all cases, the money collected as user fees is spent at the point of collection for improvement of the particular institution. The collection of user fees is limited to families Above the Poverty Line (APL). Families Below Poverty Line (BPL), national health programmes, emergencies and medico-legal cases are exempted from user fees. Furthermore, if necessary, the cost of treatment for the diseases enlisted in the Panchabyadhi Chikitsa Scheme is reimbursed from a fund placed with the ZSS for the patients.

At the point of initiation of user fees, the government had also decided to form hospital level societies to collect and utilize the collected funds. In 1993, District Health Societies known as ZSS were formed and registered as societies under the Societies Registration Act, 1860. These societies were responsible for management of the health care delivery system in a district and in a coordinated manner. Collection and utilization of user fees for all institutions in the district is one of the responsibilities of the ZSS. The ZSS is also free to decide the method of collection and its subsequent utilization, except for spending on employment of personnel. The funds collected are utilized essentially for the maintenance and improvement of respective hospitals/institutions.

In this context this user fee has been brought to the scene in the process of globalization and World Bank and World Trade Organization play key role to introduce in the Third World Countries. Critical evaluation is needed to substantiate the above argument. Is it an ominous development that the government is in posing over the citizens an increase in user fees at public hospitals? Government has been keeping away from crucial free health services and raising the prices of an array of tests and services that users already pay for.

Across the world there is more or less a policy consensus that health care is a common good and not a market commodity and that state expenditure in public health care has far-reaching redistributive effects. According to the World Health Organisation, more than 100 million people slide into ever deeper poverty every year. The out-of-pocket expenditures on health care for a family member causes undue burden. Given this reality, providing free universal health care in a state like Orissa could have a tremendous positive impact of preventing tens of thousands of families from sliding deeper into poverty and debt as a result of a single disease or accident. What this also implies is that when families demarcated by their income level and some other indicators to be exempted from user fee, one has to analyze with lens of equity and more of human rights particularly right to health.

The public sector health care is indeed in shambles. It is being argued that it is rife with corruption and neglect. This cannot be good enough argument to corporatise health care. On the contrary it should institutionalize reforms which ensure more accountability and better services. We see it fit to oppose, in the harshest possible terms, what can only be the government's first step to abdicate its central responsibility in providing universal free health care to its citizens by introducing the concept of user fees in health care, which typically precedes a gradual retreat from provision of such services. Such a move is immoral in that it accentuates the deep-seated inequities that already characterise in the society, and will likely exacerbate poverty, undoing considerable good achieved by government and non-state actors-run anti-poverty programmes of the past decades.

b. Establishment of a State Health and Family Welfare Society

In light of the problems faced with routing of all funds through the budget (i.e. the government system) such as cumbersome withdrawal and accounting procedures, unavailability of funds on time, a method was devised to ensure availability of funding for health care activities as and when required through the establishment of a State Health and Family Welfare Society in 1998, throughout the state of Orissa. With the establishment of the State Society, all non-budgeted funds were received, channelized, and utilized through the Society. To facilitate accounting and to meet the reporting requirements of donors, separate accounts are maintained for each programme. The benefits of having a State Society (and a single society for all the extra-budgetary funds received) were several. Funds could be easily accessed and were available for specific purposes at the time of need; there was flexibility of use; and the funds could be accessed to manage any sudden crisis or contingency. This is well devised system in the state.

c. *Development of a Pancha Byadhi Chikitsa Scheme (Five Diseases Treatment Scheme)*

In face of lack of any clear policy specifying the type and quantum of drugs which would be made available to every person visiting a public health institution, lack of uniformity in dispensing of drugs in public health institutions, patient being asked to purchase drugs from the open market in spite of availability of drugs at the institution, tendency towards overprescription, high cost of medical care borne by the poor, a need was felt to ensure that every patient approaching a public hospital was guaranteed treatment free for certain major diseases. Hence, a scheme called, 'Pancha Byadhi Chikitsa' (Five Diseases Treatment) was developed in 1999, to cover the whole state of Orissa. As a first step, an attempt was made to identify the major diseases prevalent in the population, especially amongst the poor. Using indicators of incidence, hospital attendance, cost and ease of treatment, five diseases were identified. These were malaria, leprosy, diarrhoea, acute respiratory infection, and scabies. Thereafter, treatment protocols were developed, estimation was arrived at for the quantum of drugs required, medication was ordered and distributed to all the public health care institutions, with instructions to the medical personnel for free provision of the same. A media campaign was also carried out to inform the public about the scheme. The benefits of the scheme were that it created a health entitlement and risk protection guarantee for the poor; it curbed the tendency of doctors to prescribe medicines unthinkingly. It addressed the commonest diseases that affect the largest number of people.

The scheme was started initially for six months, and was to be evaluated thereafter. However, it came to a halt after six months because of the super cyclone which occurred a few months later and the preoccupation with cyclone restoration work. It is proposed to be re-started shortly. It was clarified that in case any patient was required to purchase medication from the market, the cost of the same would be reimbursed. These prescriptions in turn would be examined during the clinical audit and action would be taken on erring doctors. The scheme created a health entitlement and risk protection guarantee for the poor; it addressed the commonest diseases that affect the largest number of people; and curbed the tendency of doctors to prescribe unthinkingly. The scheme was first started in 1999 experimentally for 6 months. With the super cyclone striking Orissa in late 1999, attention got diverted and the scheme did not get extended. Subsequently, it was re-started as a major state-wide programme in mid-2001.

Human Rights Standards: Search for Justice

Medical profession is one of the oldest professions of the world and is the most humanitarian one. Inherent in the concept of any profession is a code of conduct, containing the basic ethics that underline the moral values that govern professional practice and is aimed at upholding its dignity. Medical Ethics underpins the values at the heart of the practitioner-client relationship. Medical negligence and malpractices by doctors were the grey areas in health care where legal issues operated. Some of the cases have been selected on the basis of random sampling particularly patients chart and also some cases chosen to strengthen the argument which have been drawn from the National Human Rights Commission, Supreme Court cases and also relevant patients profile. During the field study, the researcher met different types of patients on the basis of their diseases and experiences in hospital and outside to analyse the individual cases in the scope of health and human rights. The following cases are representing the health scenario of the state and nation. Given the health scenario, some of the cases went to the judiciary. The constitutional and judicial processes highlight the crisis of standards and struggle for enforcement standards. In a way this is the search for justice.

Case-I

The National Human Rights Commission has recommended a monitory relief of Rs. 5,00,000 to Mrs. Binapani Khatua of Orissa in a case of medical negligence due to which she suffered physical pain for four years and now cannot bear children. The Commission started the proceeding on 15.6.2007 in the matter on the complaint of Director, Collective Initiation for Social Solidarity (CISS).

The complainant said, Mrs. Binapani Khatua w/o Mr. Pratap Khatùa of Radharamur Village under Athagarh Police limit in the District of Cuttack (Orissa) was admitted in Athagarh Hospital four years ago for safe delivery of her first issue. After gynaecological operation a male child was born but died after four days. The complainant alleged that a surgical scissor was left inside the abdomen of Mrs. Khatua by the concerned surgeon during the operation period. Since that day, the victim suffered medical negligence causing terrible pain on the right side of the abdomen. She consulted several doctors, but none diagnosed the cause of her pain properly except prescribing irremedial medicines. In the meantime, Mrs. Khatua gave birth to a girl child who is alive. But during post delivery, severe bleeding started and her abdominal pain increased. The unbearable pain landed the couple in a private hospital in Cuttack, where Mrs. Khatua again underwent a surgical operation following which her uterus was amputed. She could no more bear a child now. However, even after this surgery she did not get relief from the pain. The couple spent a lot of money on the treatment leading them to a stage of bankruptcy. In the course the couple came in contact with Dr. P.C. Sahoo, who suggested for an X-ray of the belly of the patient. It was found from the X-ray that a surgical scissor was lodged in the belly which was removed by an operation at General Nursing Home (Private Clinic) in District Headquarters. The complainant prayed for inquiry, justice to the victim and action against surgeon responsible for the lapse.

The NHRC taking it as a serious case of professional negligence issued notice to the Chief Medical Officer, Cuttack.

Pursuant to the directions of the Commission the Chief District Medical Officer, Cuttack submitted a report dated 9.7.2007. On perusal of record the Commission observed that the case appeared to be a matter of serious professional negligence and violation of human rights due to negligence of Doctors which was confirmed in an inquiry caused by Chief Medical Officer, Cuttack.

The NHRC issued notice to the Chief Secretary, Orissa asking to show cause as to why monitory relief to the victim should not be recommended by the Commission. It also requested him to conduct an inquiry and take action against the negligent Doctors and take necessary steps to stop recurrence of such incidents.

Pursuant to the directions of the Commission, Commissioner-cum-Secretary, Government of Orissa, Health and Family Welfare Department furnished his response (dated 16.8.2008). His report stated that a specialist team was set up to inquire into the incident. The departmental proceedings were drawn up against the two Doctors*, namely, it also stated that the Government had taken steps to stop recurrence of such incidents but no direct responsibility could be laid on anyone for the alleged lapse and pleaded that the proceedings be dropped.

The Commission on the basis of this reply observed and directed in its proceedings (dated 16.9.2008) that the reply to the show cause notice was silent about grant of monetary relief to the victim and the copy of the specialists' team which conducted an inquiry into the case was not received in the Commission.

The NHRC sent a reminder to the Chief Secretary, Government of Orissa and the Commissioner-cum-Secretary, Government of Orissa, Health and Family Welfare Department in this regard. The Commission also asked for a status of departmental proceedings drawn up against the two Doctors. When no response was received within the stipulated four weeks on the issues from the concerned State Authorities, the Commission recommended a monetary relief of Rs. 5,00,000 to the victim of medical negligence with the instructions for submitting a report on the action taken.

Case-II

Saroj Kumar Tarai and his family sought help from Orissa Government because his life landed in a pathetic condition. He has been suffering from a dreaded disease called 'Rheumatoid Arthritis' since 16 years and in the absence of proper medical attention he is bed-ridden. Now, with all money spent on his treatment and no financial support coming from anywhere, this *dalit* family from Damodarpur in Balasore town sought permission for a mercy death.

"My parents tried whatever they could; we don't have enough money to avail better treatment. I don't want to be a burden on my old-aged father, who is also a paralytic patient. With nobody to extend a helping hand, probably death is a wise option", stated 40-year-old Saroj.

Saroj, once a good badminton player, fell victim to the disease when he was only 24-year old. After finishing graduation he joined three-year law course. But while he was appearing for the final examination he fell victim to Rheumatoid Arthritis. He said "Despite continuous treatment in different hospitals, he didn't get any relief", he narrated this episode with tears rolling down his cheeks.

Being the eldest son of the six-member family Saroj's first option was to search for a job but he is now a burden to 72-year-old father, old mother and two grown up sisters.

"He can't do his own work as his legs are not functioning. His father Siba Charan Tarai and mother Satyabati said "we have to attend to his works even though our health condition doesn't permit". In fact they failed to marry off their daughters due to their poor financial conditions.

Even though the district administration is aware of Saroj's health condition, no help reached him yet. There are various government schemes for the upliftment of poor and *dalits*, but nothing has happened for this family.

"Not even pension for disable persons has been sanctioned, although he gave an application to the Collector three years back. He also told that "I am exhausted physically, financially and mentally, and now I am in total indigence".

One of the letters sent to Collector he urged him to kindly arrange for treatment through the benevolence at the earliest. Otherwise they should be allowed to end our lives in front of the District Collectorate.

Case-III

Shila Jana, a 35-year-old resident of Gobara village under the Ramnagar police station, was admitted in the clinic after suffering from severe infection in her uterus. The Balasore based city clinic and its owner Pratima Pradhan could not properly diagnose the problem but suggested to arrange some money for operation. The doctor operated on her and removed her uterus. The complaint was that the doctor has operated wrongly. Shila was taken to Vellore Hospital in Tamil Nadu for treatment where it was found that during the operation a small hole developed in the urine bladder due to the carelessness of the surgeon.

Since, the complainant suffered due to the doctor's negligence, she filed a case against the doctor in the district consumer redressal forum which fined the Balasore-based City Clinic and its owner Pratima Pradhan for wrongly operating on the uterus. The consumer forum slapped a fine of Rs.1,10,000 on the private hospital which, however, cannot bring back her health.

Case-IV

A woman delivers child under a tree, a *dalit* woman of Jhimani village under Gopalpur police station in Balasore district gave birth to a child under a tree near Srijung Hospital due to indifference of doctors and other medical staff. Shocked over the incident the State Government asked the Chief District Medical Officer (CDMO) to investigate and submit a report on the incident.

As per direction CDMO Sukdev Sethy inquired about the incident and confirmed that this incident occurred due to negligence of Dr. Abhay Das and Nurse Sukanti Panda. "He recommended disciplinary action against the doctor and nurse". The report said that the *dalit* woman Ranju Sethy went to Srijung Hospital to enquire about her delivery due date. Gynaecologist Dr. Abhya Das, on duty, examined and advised her for ultrasound test to ascertain the condition of child in the womb. He also prescribed a pain killer when she felt severe pain during the examination. After getting an ultrasound report Rahama Bajar, 12 km away from the hospital, connecting by a passenger bus, the doctor advised her to take admission in the hospital as the ultrasound report said she had completed 7 months of pregnancy and 1.5 kg weight child was in her womb.

As the woman came out from the hospital and when she was unable to take the pain gave birth to a child under a tree in front of the medical hospital. When asked Dr. Abhay Das clarified that he gave pain killer medicine to avoid her premature delivery but she did not take medicine. The matter of fact is that she gave birth to a baby under the tree.

Case-V

Hakim Seikh fell off a train at Bhadrak station in Orissa on 8-7-2008 at 7.45 p.m. and suffered severe head injuries. When brought to the Primary Health Centre Bhadrak, he was referred to the sub-divisional Hospital or any other State hospital, as necessary facilities for treatment were not available at the Primary Health Centre. Then he was taken to as many as seven State hospitals, but was not given treatment on the ground of non-availability of bed though it was an emergency case. Ultimately he was admitted in a private hospital on 9-7-2008 and was treated till 22-7-2008. Feeling aggrieved by the indifferent and callous attitude of the medical authorities at the various State run hospitals in Orissa in providing treatment for the serious injuries sustained by Hakim Seikh, a petition was filed in the Supreme Court for compensation and appropriate directions. The Court held that failure to provide medical treatment to Hakim Seikh by the government hospitals had resulted in violation of his right under Article 21 to get adequate and timely medical treatment. Article 21 imposes an obligation on the State to safeguard the right to life of every person. It was held that in such cases adequate compensation can be awarded by the Supreme Court under Article 32 and the High Courts under Article 226, of the Constitution. The Court awarded compensation of Rs. 25,000 to the injured from the government.

Case-VI

Brunda, an 11 (eleven) years old girl whose parents work in paddy field was bitten by a stray dog. Immediately she reported it to her parents. Her parents wanted her to wait for some time and take her to *Gunia* (sorcerer or enchanter). Her parents were not serious about dog biting as they are illiterate and also ignorant. The *gunia* (sorcerer) gave the local treatment by giving her banana and assured that it would be cured and advised not to worry. After one and half months Brunda fell sick again and suffered from headache and joint pain. Her parents did not take it seriously.

For almost two months passed nobody in her village had advised the parents to go to hospital. Brunda became thin, weak and was unable to walk. One of her relatives got to know about the dog bite. He advised her father to take her to hospital and consult a doctor. Doctor checked her and demanded some money to give her admission. This was the place where the researcher met her. She was waiting for another doctor. They were advised to buy two injections. Finally Brunda got some treatment.

This is a case where the patient and her father and mother are all illiterate. Instead of she being brought to hospital, she was taken to sorcerer (Gunia). She stated that she should have had access to the doctor so that she could have been saved from all the pain and trouble. She complained that doctor had taken Rs. 200, for giving just the hospital bed. The case suggests that the basic rights of Brunda have been violated. It is significant to note that her father who is old and poor labourer had to pay money which they could hardly afford. The doctor has taken money literally from a pauper without any qualm. When researcher asked about the case she replied in anger "no body cares for the poor people".

Case-VII

Lakshmi who is 45 years old, illiterate and married has been suffering from TB, for seven months. Her husband Nidhiya is a casual labourer. They have four daughters. Lakshmi, although knew of her internal pain, she did not care about it. After three months when the pain further aggravated she informed her husband. The helpless husband who did not have money advised her to go to her parents which she did. Her father is a woodcutter and their family condition was no better. Her father took her to a primary health centre. In the first visit they could not meet the doctor and medical staff did not know where he was. Lakshmi visited the next day again but was unable to walk and not able to get a single cycle rickshaw. When the researcher enquired about her health, she was with full of emotions and tears. She finally met the doctor who advised her to go to district hospital and informed her that this disease was harmful and contagious and advised that she should stay in the hospital. But Lakshmi's father did not have money. Then they went back home and sold some trees at thrown away price. Lakshmi reached district hospital with some money and overcame a lot of hurdles. The chest specialist checked her and demanded five hundred rupees on the plea that it was not his working hours and suggested that she may go to his clinic with money, she was helpless at that moment. She remarked "I heard from my mother doctor is a second image of God, but what kind of God he is?" Here the point is that Lakshmi instead of getting free bed in the government hospital, she got it after six days only after bribing the doctors.

This case highlights the poverty and deprivation of the patient at one level and the casualness and callousness with which the patients are treated in public hospitals.

Case-VIII

Banamali is 70 years old man suffering from joint pain and also muscle pain. He belongs to a poor family. During his ailments, he came to hospital walking eight km. on bare foot. After check up the Doctor prescribed medicine and was advised to buy the medicine. But Banamali had no money to buy the medicine which he informed the doctor. The doctor said, "We cannot do anything". Banamali had no way out as nobody was ready to listen to him. He says, "I do not have a son, if I have one, I would not have come to this hospital, I would have gone to a private hospital". He adds, "I cannot afford the fee. At this point he broke down. One of his friends requested the doctor for some help. The doctor instead of responding to the plea remarked that "We do not have free medicine because government is not supplying, if you are a leader of these people then go to the Ministers and ask them why they are not providing funds for free medicine to the poor".

Banamali was helpless because he does not have son and also money. After five days, he attempted suicide by hanging on the tree near a cow grazing field. At the moment he prepared to hang himself, one of the villagers saw him and shouted then Banamali got disturbed and sat on the ground. This incident reveals the hapless condition of poor and underprivileged people, who cannot afford medical facility which is technically supposed to be free of cost. This is not an isolated case.

Case-IX

Asha Behera is a 65 years old woman struggling hard to eke out a living for herself in an helpless condition. Asha Behera of Tina village of Barunasigh gram panchayat under Balasore Assembly Constituency was forced to work in a motel at the age of 60 after the death of her husband. She had no other option. She knew she had to work for survival. On August 14, 2007 everything changed for her. On that day, when Behera and the motel owner Pravakar Sahoo of Redhua Bazar under

Nilagir police limits were working, a gas cylinder exploded. Two persons sustained serious burn injuries. They were admitted to the Sri Ramchandra Bhanja Medical, Cuttack. After a few days of treatment, Pravakar succumbed to injuries on August 23. His family members brought his body to the village for cremation and Behera, who had till then not recovered from her injuries, was also brought back to the village. However, considering her critical condition, the villagers admitted her to Redha Public Health Centre, where there was no facility for treatment of burn injuries. With nobody to take care of her, the half-burnt Behera is waiting for slow death, lying over a mat on the floor of Redhua PHC. While government-supplied medicines are not available, she is surviving on food provided by the attendants in the PHC. The villagers have drawn the attention of the authorities concerned to initiate necessary steps for her treatment but nobody came forward to help.

Case-X

During the field study, researcher met Aruna Nath Mishra, who has been working on rehabilitation of AID's patients. His experiences with patients may be relevant to the present study. He narrated a case of Basanti Jena who wished that she had died immediately after testing positive for HIV/AIDS rather than undergoing such disgrace, pain and trauma. This is much worse than death, laments Basanti Jena recalling her ordeal at the hands of her family and community members.

When 33-years old Jena, who lives in a village near Rasalpur in Balasore district of Orissa, tested HIV-Positive she was driven out of the house, locked up in the family goat shed, denied adequate food and basic amenities. She was finally rescued by a local NGO working with HIV/AIDS. By then, she was delirious and infested with ticks and worms.

Case-XI

When plumber Maheshware Behera travelled to Surat from his native village Balasore district in search of better employment opportunities, he contracted HIV/AIDS from a local sex worker and returned to his village fearing ostracism from his fellow workers. Later, following AIDS Related Complications (ARC), Behera sought medical help at hospitals in Balasore. But he was repeatedly turned away. Ill-treatment from his family and exclusion from the community finally pushed him to suicide. Ostracism, humiliation and mistreatment at the hands of family members, community and the medical fraternity pressure and absence of organization care and support to people suffering from AIDS (PLWHAs) in the state are driven to despair resulting in suicide.

Case-XII

Shimla Devi, from Kashpa village underwent sterilization on 12th of February, 2004. After the operation, she vomited continuously and no health worker came to assist her. Later she developed more complications and also hernia. On the 26th of June, 2004, she underwent another operation and ended up spending Rs. 5,000. Sulochana, from Balicharia village, was married as early as 13, gave birth at 14 was sterilized at 18 years and soon lost her husband. She has not received the family planning benefits that she was promised but continues to suffer from chronic ill-health.

There were many similar accounts. Kangali Das from Srijang, broke down recounting the story of how his daughter Sudha died after the doctors injured her intestines while doing her family planning operation. Stories from all parts of the district, pointed to how hundreds of family planning operations were being conducted on women with very little care for quality. This was done under the pressure to achieve family planning targets, which were not a part of the National Population Policy.

Doctors often completed an operation in less than five minutes, throwing all norms to the wind. This meant that there were infection, complications, failures and even death, and there were no provisions within the programme guidelines to deal with these.

Conclusion

Quality of care provided by the health care delivery system has become the focus of this chapter. Since quality is a crucial factor in health care, initiatives to address quality of health care have become state-wide phenomena. Many districts are exploring various means to methods to improve the quality of health care services. In Orissa, the quality of services provided to the population by both public and private sectors is questionable. The current structure of the health care delivery system does not provide enough incentives for improvement in efficiency. Mechanisms used in other states to produce greater efficiency compared to Orissa, accountability, and more responsible governance in hospitals are not yet deployed in Orissa. The for-profit private sector accounts for a substantial proportion of health care in Orissa (50 per cent of inpatient care and 60 per cent to 70 per cent of outpatient care), but has received relatively less attention from the policy-makers as compared to the public sector. Thus the private sector health care delivery system in Orissa has remained largely fragmented and uncontrolled, and there is a clear evidence of serious quality of care deficiencies in their practices we have already discussed it above. Problems range from inadequate and inappropriate treatments, excessive use of higher technologies, and wasting of scarce resources, to serious problems of medical malpractice and negligence. Current policies and standards setting process for health are inadequate or not responsive to ensure health services of acceptable quality and prevent negligence.

In the present situation there is a need to establish bodies and systems to set standards for clinical and non-clinical effectiveness of the services offered in the public and private facilities. It concerns about how to improve health care quality which have been frequently raised by the general public and a wide variety of stakeholders, including government, professional associations, private providers and financing health care agencies. They attempt to establish systems and process of standards setting that would ensure quality of health care.

The present study also makes a contribution to the wider literature regarding health care decision-making, in supporting the role of three major factors in influencing utilization of services: reputation, cost and physical accessibility. Reputation—in terms of perceived quality—has been found to be one of the main determinants of utilization of a particular health care provider, and 'recovery' is one of the most important criteria that patients use in order to judge the quality of services and choice of health service provision.[2] Accordingly, non-utilization of a particular type of health provider is often related to a perceived lack of quality. It is found over three-quarters of the women utilizing private practitioners (rather than more generally proximal government practitioners) cited faith in the efficacy of their treatment as the basis for incurring the additional costs of travel and consultation. Despite this last effect, the impact on utilization rates of a particular provider due to cost—indicated in this chapter—has also been widely documented: either through cost of medicines, consultation fees, travel or opportunity cost.

Health as a basic human right has come to be not only accepted but its scope is enlarged through judicial instruments. Now the standards set are quite high. The right to equality encompasses within itself the right of a poor to get adequate treatment and medicines from the State irrespective of their costs. The duties of the State and Municipal authorities can be enforced through the Courts whenever a breach occurs. It is in the enforcement of these obligations of the State and local authorities that the Courts play an effective role in safeguarding the rights of the citizens to prevent and cure diseases. The maintenance of sterile aseptic conditions in hospitals to prevent cross-infections should be ordinary, routine and minimal incidents of maintenance of hospitals. Purity of the drugs and medicines intended for human-use would have to be ensured by prior tests and inspection. However, "owing to a general air of cynical irreverence towards values that has, unfortunately developed and to the mood of complacence with the continuing deterioration of standards, the very concept of standards and the imperatives of their observations tend to be impaired", laments the Apex Court. The remedy lies in the awareness and enforcement of the Health rights of the citizens through Courts, but it more lies in the cure of improper and corrupt approaches in the seemingly healthy ones whose obligation is to provide for adequate health care.

The twelve cases of varied forms of negligence and court verdicts present the evidence that how health as a human right and standard is violated. One has to revisit the concept of standards and norms of the society and draw a line between existing standards and even enlarging legal and constitutional standards in India.

END NOTES

1. Orissa Health Report, Published by Governement of Orissa, Bhubaneswar, 2007.
   * Dr. Sarojini Sarangi, Professor, O&G and Dr. Kirtirekha Mohapatra, Assistant Professor, O&G, SCB Medical College & Hospital, Cuttack for alleged lapses.
2. Haddad S., Fournier P., Machouf N., Yatara F., "What does Quality Mean to Lay People? Community Perceptions of Primary Health Care Services in Guinea", *Social Science and Medicine*, Vol. 47, 1998, pp. 381-94.

6

Health Scenario in Orissa

A Micro Level Survey

This chapter is dealing with the problem of access to health facility and awareness of the district. One has to discuss about the health profile of the district. Considering that good health is an important asset of livelihood and illness a major cause of impoverishment. The health and allied sector in the district has made noticeable improvements compared to past, in Leprosy control, Polio eradication, Infant Mortality Rate (IMR), Maternal Mortality Ratio (MMR), Malaria, Crude Birth Rate, Crude Death Rate, Life Expectancy at Birth, Nutritional Status, Literacy, drinking water supply and sanitation. Yet district administration and other agencies those involved in health delivery system need miles to go. Hence, the health indicators are the parameter to discuss below.

Blood Bank Services

The Blood Bank Service is available at DHH, Balasore. The five mandatory tests being done at the blood bank regularly are H.I.V.1 and 2, H.C.V, H.B.S.Ag, V.D.R.L and Malaria parasite. The Red Cross has constructed the blood bank building which is functioning in the district since 1960. The blood bank has two MOs deputed from DHH, eleven LTs (out of which four are on contractual basis and seven are on deputation from DHH), two Attendants and one Generator operator deputed from DHH, one Clerk-cum-Accountant, one Night watchman and two Attendants on contractual basis.

The district blood bank covers four other adjacent districts like Mayurbhanj, Bhadrak, Keonjhar and Medinapur (Border district of West Bengal). In 2005-06, 7400 blood bottles were collected. In the same year six blocks of Balasore i.e Jaleswar, Remuna, Bhograi, Basta, Nilagiri and Soro had organised blood bank camps.

Table 6.1 : Information on Blood Bank (2005-06)

Total Blood collected	7419
Total Blood collected in camp (Voluntary)	3751=50.50%
Total blood replacement	3668
Sero positive cases detected	HIV=5, Hbs Ags=14 & Hcv=1
Total no. blood issued (Exchange)	4518
Total no. blood issued (Free without exchange)	2901
Thalassaemia and Sickle Cell anaemia	866
Total no. of camp conducted	37

Source: CDMO Office, Balasore.

X-Ray

X-Ray facilities are available in the following Health institutions in the Balasore district—

Table 6.2 : Availability of X-Ray

Name of the Health Institution	*Existing*	*Working*
DHH, Balasore	Y	Y
Khaira, CHC	Y	Y
Pratappur, PHC	Y	N
UGPHC, Basta	Y	Y
Jaleswarpur, CHC	Y	Y
Soro, CHC	Y	Y
Baliapal, CHC	Y	Y
SDH, Nilagiri	Y	Y
G.K. Bhatter Hospital	Y	Y
Area Hospital, Khantapada	Y	Y

Note: Y= Yes, N= No.
Source: CDMO Office, Balasore.

Ambulance Services

Ambulance service is available at the following health units. At Khaira CHC though the ambulance is present but the post of the driver is lying vacant. All ambulances are managed by Zilla Swasthya Samiti.

Table 6.3 : Availability of Ambulances

Block and district health institutions	*No. of ambulances in functional condition*
DHH, Balasore	4
Khaira, CHC	1 (Driver not in position)
Rupsa, CHC-II	1
UGPHC, Basta	1
Jaleswarpur, CHC	1
Simulia, CHC-II	1
SDH, Nilagiri	1
Area Hospital, Khantapada	1

Source: CDMO Office, Balasore.

Medical Services

The Medical Wing in the district is functioning since 1994 in the district and is headed by ADMO (Medical). It deals with medicines provided by Government and also the treatment of indoor and outdoor patient of DHH, Balasore. The OPD services in the DHH Balasore are available at an outdoor ticket of Re. 1 only. The DHH have the specialist facility from the following faculties from Medicine, Surgery, Obs & Gynae, Pediatric, Anaesthesia, Eye, Orthopaedics, Pathology, Dental Surgeon, Radiologist, Skin & VD, ENT and TB & Chest. A well equipped pathology laboratory is available at the DHH. The indoor facility is available for O & G, Surgery, Paediatric, Eye, Contagious disease, TB & Chest and Medicine. A scheme called five diseases treatment scheme (Panchabyadhi) started in 1999 to cover five most common diseases namely ARI, Malaria, Scabies, Leprosy and Diarrhoea. All medicines required for treatment of these diseases are provided free of cost at government health institutions.

Zilla Swasthya Samiti (ZSS) has been formed and registered since 13th February, 1993 under the Chairmanship of President, Zilla Parishad and Collector of the district, for management and development of the Medical Wing and also to oversee the implementation of the National Health Programmes. It regularly meets for the review of hospital activities and all the important activities are conducted with the due approval from the ZSS of the district. The DHH Headquarters Hospital has also leased out some portion of the hospital land for commercial shopping purpose whose rent is being deposited in the ZSS account and the user fees collected is also deposited in the ZSS account which is utilized for the maintenance of the DHH equipments and infrastructures. The expenditures are made with the due approval of the ZSS body.

Family Welfare Wing

The Family Welfare Wing is headed by ADMO (FW & Immunization) which is implementing the Reproductive & Child Health (RCH) Programme in this District since 1994. To carry out the Family Welfare activities at the grass roots level there is subcentre with one ANM who execute the activities in the field. Along with the family welfare activities immunization at the community level is the responsibility of the ANM. In addition to Immunization, registration of pregnancy, care of pregnant women, promotion of family welfare measures, antenatal/post-natal care and measures for reduction of infant mortality and maternal mortality are some of the key activities of Family Welfare Wing. All these services are provided through health subcentre. Registration of birth is done at PHC level. Apart from routine Immunization activities, pulse polio Immunization is being done in a campaign mode on National Immunization Days since 1995. Vitamin "A" supplementation campaign is being done since November 2003. Measles immunization is also done by this Wing.

Public Health Wing

The Public Health Wing deals with prevention of epidemic diseases in the district. Malaria, blindness, leprosy, tuberculosis are major public health problems of the district. Many National Health Programmes such as National Anti Malaria Programme (NAMP), Enhanced Malaria Control Programme (EMCP), AIDS Control Programme, National Leprosy Eradication Programme (NLEP), District Blindness Control Scheme (DBCS) and National Vector Borne Disease Control Programme (NVBDCP) are being implemented in the district.

The Malaria control programme was launched in the district in 1964 and Enhanced Malaria Control Programme was undertaken in the district in 1998. The focus on distribution of Chloroquine tablets are through DDCs (All the 2287 DDCs are functioning in the district). Chloroquine and Chemopropolyxis are provided for pregnant mother and during post-natal period i.e., from 3 months to 1 month after delivery. Also to control the mosquito vector through promotion of Gambusia fish hatchery and the distribution of impregnated bed nets are ensured through the health institutions of the district. Under NVBDCP (National Vector Borne Disease Control Programme), the diseases like Malaria, Filaria, Kalaazar, Dengue and Japanese Encephalitis are addressed. For the prevention of STDs/RTIs Family Health Awareness Campaign (FHAC) is being done by the district and block health institutions.

The National Leprosy Eradication Programme (NLEP) aims at reducing prevalence rate of Leprosy cases to 1 or less than 1 per 10,000. The Balasore district has been declared as leprosy eliminated district as the PR of the district is 0.58 by the end of August 2006.

HIV/AIDS

With the support of Orissa State AIDS Control Society, one Voluntary Counselling and Testing Centre (VCCTC) is functioning at DHH Balasore since December 2003 and the

PPTCT (Prevention of Parent to Child Transmission Centre) activities have started since March 2006. The VCCTC have detected 123 positive cases, of which 6 death cases have been reported. The PPCTC have not detected any cases related to HIV/AIDS. It also provides free counselling on HIV/AIDS and diagnosis of HIV status by blood testing through HIV rapid test for those who come voluntarily. It also distributes condoms. Utmost confidentiality is maintained in the process. To deal with this dreadful disease another initiative is the Targeted Intervention Programme through NGOs. At present 3 NGOs are being involved in TI projects for HIV/AIDS; however there is a need to forge linkages with the NGOs working on HIV/AIDS, as their reporting is directly done with Orissa State AIDS Cell, the apex body managing the HIV/AIDS programme in Bhubaneswar.

National Leprosy Eradication Programme (NLEP)

The prevalence rate of the district at present is 0.65 per 10,000 populations as on 2005-06. As per district data of August 2006, the PR has further come down to 0.58 per 10,000 population. In the 2007-08, the PR has again come down to 0.48 per 10,000 population. However, the focus will be now given to the Prevention of Disability aspect in Leprosy. The present Leprosy activities in the district are carried out by LEU Balasore in DHH Balasore.

Table 6.4 : Five Year Trend of PR and ANCDR of the District

Index	*2001-02*	*2002-03*	*2003-04*	*2004-05*	*2005-06*	*2006-07*	*2007-08*
PR/ 10,000	5.4	5.4	1.9	0.95	0.65	0.58	0.48
ANCDR/ 10,000	8.2	7.4	2.7	2.6	1.2	Not Available	1.01

Source: CDMO Office, Balasore.

Epidemiological Indicators for the District as on 31st March, 2006:

Prevalence Rate	:	0.65%
Annual New Case Detection Rate	:	1.20%
M.B. Proportion	:	46.00%
Child Proportion	:	5.70%
Deformity Proportion	:	2.10%
Female Proportion	:	40.70%

District Blindness Control Society (DBCS)

The primary purpose of the District Blindness Control Society (DBCS) is to plan, implement and monitor all the blindness control activities in the district under overall guidance of the state/central organization for the DBCS. Eye wards have been constructed at DHH. Cataract surgery is being done at these institutions. Currently IOL is the preferable method for cataract surgery.

Revised National Tuberculosis Control Programme (RNTCP)

National Tuberculosis Control Programme was implemented in Orissa from 1964. RNTCP in Balasore district was implemented in an emergency basis. The programme is implemented in the entire district through four TUs and 17 Microscopy centres. 1348 DOTS providers are involved in the delivery of DOTS to the patients. The case detection in the district at present is 50 per cent of the target and cure rate is 81 per cent.

Table 6.5 : National Tuberculosis Control Programme

TU		*DMC*	
Jaleswar	Chandaneswar PHC(N) Jaleswarpur CHC	Hatigarh CHC-II	G.K. Bhattar Hospital
Basta	UGPHC Basta Rupsa CHC-II	CHC Bhograi	PHC Pratappur
Balasore	Remuna PHC Dist. TB Centre	Gopalpur PHC Berhampur PHC	SDH Nilagiri
Soro	Khaira CHC Iswarpur PHC	Simulia CHC-II	Soro CHC

Source: CDMO Office, Balasore.

Prevention of Food Adulteration Programme

This programme is managed by Food Inspector. The present post of Food Inspector is vacant and the food inspector in Municipality Balasore is in dual charge and inspects different food establishments from time to time to check food adulteration.

Iodine Deficiency Disorder Programme

The food section besides their food adulteration work also conducts the activities under IDD Programme. General awareness is created among the people in meetings and seminars of the health department and in ICDS meetings to consume Iodized salt to avoid goitre and other diseases related to iodine deficiency. The ICDS workers create awareness among the pregnant women to consume iodized salt. Global iodine day is observed to encourage public to use iodized salt. The Food Inspector is also responsible to prevent the sale of un-iodized salt.

Orissa Health System Development Project (OHSDP, World Bank Assisted)

Orissa Health System Development Project is being implemented since 1994-95. Seven medical institutions i.e. DHH Balasore, CHC Simulia, UGPHC Basta, PHC Remuna, CHC Soro, Area Hospital Khantapara, Sub Divisional Hospital Nilagiri have been taken up for upgradation of existing building and new building to provide more number of beds for patients, supply of equipments and medicines for better treatment. The OPD and IPD constructions, containment area for waste management, construction, repair and renovation of staff quarters, post-mortem centre etc. The Disease Surveillance, Quality Assurance Activities, Hospital waste management is managed by OHSDP.

Health Scenario Situation Analysis

The health service delivery in Balasore is mainly through the government infrastructure in rural areas and a mixed response of government and private is seen in the urban areas.

MMR & IMR

The IMR in the district is 65 per 1000 population while the MMR of the district is 315 per 1 lakh population as per the district data of 2005.

Nutritional Status

The malnutrition status of the district is broadly categorized under four grades as mentioned below. This shows a good number of people are still included in the status of malnutrition even after the intervention of ICDS in this regard.

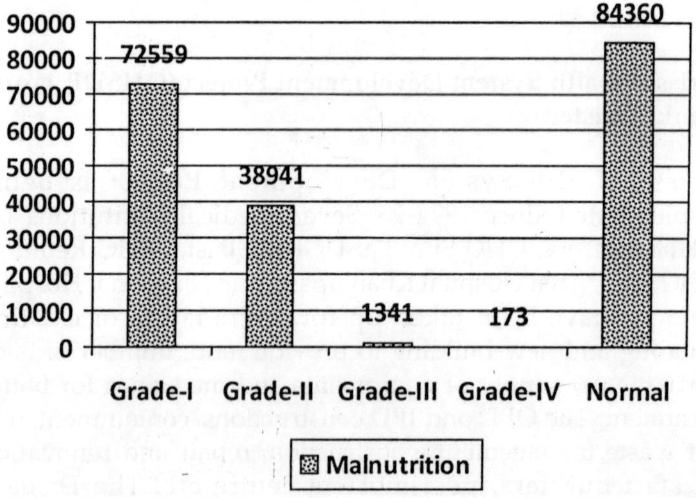

Response Analysis

Malaria Control Programme

To reduce period of sickness and to prevent deaths due to Malaria, the District of Balasore has been successfully implementing the malaria control programme. According to District data from the CDMOs office Table 6.6 reflects the state of Malaria in the district for the past four years.

Table 6.6 : State of Malaria in the District

Year	*BSC/BSE*	*Positive*	*P.F.*	*% P.F.*	*No. of C.M. Death*
2003	147566	2278	2017	72	5
2004	131386	1776	1150	64	4
2005	142291	2687	1898	70	7
2006 (Till July 2006)	67876	1375	1060	77	9

Source: CDMO Office, Balasore.

Leprosy Control Programme

The objective of the programme is to "Eliminate" the disease by detecting all cases of leprosy from the community and treating them with "Multi Drug Therapy" (MDT). "Elimination of Leprosy" refers to reducing the prevalence rate of leprosy below one case per 10,000 population.

Table 6.7 : Vital Health Indicators of Balasore District

	Infant and Child Health	
2005 District Data	Infant Mortality Rate	65
2005 District Data	Crude Birth Rate No. of live b.rths	21
2002-03		36472
2003-04		39069
2004-05		40079
2005-06		40878

District Data/2005-06	Percentage of children fully vaccinated	74 %	
	BCG	97.71 %	(44287)
	DPT	97.22 %	(44065)
	Polio	97.28 %	(44093)
	Measles	94.25 %	(42718)
District Data/2005-06	New born with low birth weight	12.22 %	(4374)
Nutritional status of children, 1-5 yrs age (Gomez Classification), 2005			
Nutrition Profile, Orissa, NIN, Hyderabad, 2000	Grade-I		72559
	Grade-II		38941
	Grade-III		1341
	Grade-IV		173
	Normal		84360
Maternal Health			
District Data/2005	Maternal Mortality Rate		315/1,00,000
	Total no. of Maternal Deaths, (District Data) 2005-06		121
District Data/2005-06	Percentage of women having delivery or post-delivery complication.		12 %
District Data 2005-06	Percentage of Institutional Deliveries.		31.18 %
District Data 2005-06	% of Home delivery by type of assistance:		% of Home delivery by type of assistance:
	ANM		ANM
	Trained TBA		Trained TBA
	Untrained personnel		Untrained personnel
	Percentage of safe deliveries		Percentage of safe deliveries
District Data 2005-06	Birth Order 3 and above		11490
District Data 2005-06	Total No. of Abortions (MTP)		1880
	MTP		3301 (117.52 %)
District Data 2005-06	Percentage of mothers who received full ANC		78.23 %
District Data 2005-06	Percentage of mothers who received any ANC		89.85 %
H & FW Year book (as on 31.3.2004)	Percentage of Eligible Couples protected		34.62 %
SRS-1999	Total Fertility Rate		2.5 per 1 lakh live births
District Data/2003-04	% of couples in the reproductive age group using		
	Any contraceptive method		7.95
	Sterilisation		22.54
	Condoms		4.99

National Disease Control Programme		
District Data 2005-06		Malaria
	No of Cases detected	2687
	No. of deaths	7
2004	No. of Cases detected	1776
	No. of deaths	4
2003	No. of Cases detected	2778
	No. of deaths	5
District Profiles—2005-06	No. of Malaria for 1 Lakh population	128
District Data MDA Programme	FILARIA (MDA Programme 2005)	3981
	Total Blood Slide Collected	44
	No. of Cases detected	
District Data 2005	TUBERCULOSIS	
	New cases detected (Annual)	1316
	Total case detection rate (Annual)	50%
	% of patients under DOTS	99%
2004	New cases detected (Annual)	1749
	Total case detection rate (Annual)	63%
	% of patients under DOTS	98%
District Data 2005-06	LEPROSY	
	Prevalence rate (Per 10,000 Population)	0.65%
	No. of patients under MDT	151
2004-05	Prevalence rate (Per 10,000 Population)	0.95%
	No. of patients under MDT	206
2003-04	Prevalence rate (Per 10,000 Population)	1.9%
	No. of patients under MDT	425
DBCS, CDMO Office, Balasore 2005-06	BLINDNESS	
	No. of Cataract Surgeries done	3295
	Total School children detected with refractive error	1633
District data 2004 & 2005	HIV/AIDS	
	No. of Cases detected	123
	Deaths	6
CDMO Office, Balasore	Iodine Deficiency/Goitre Prevalence Rate	
Up to August 2008		Nil
2007		Nil
August 2006		Nil
2005		Nil
CDMO Office, Balasore	Yaws Prevalence Rate	Nil
District Data Up to Sept. 06	AFP incidence	4 suspect cases

DISABILITY		
District Data (May' 2005-Aug 2006)	No. of cases reported on :	
	Mental illness/Disorder	283
	Orthopaedically handicapped	1196
	Visually handicapped	523
	Hearing Handicapped	480

Orissa Multi Disease Surveillance System (CDMO Office, Balasore)				
Diseases/Syndromes	*Annual incidence Rate*	*Annual mortality Rate*	*Annual incidence Rate*	*Annual mortality Rate*
	< 5	> = 5	< 5	> = 5
Simple Diarrhoea	28999	65860	0	0
Severe Diarrhoea	1536	4542	0	4
Bloody Diarrhoea/Dysentery	4974	28231	0	0
Acute Jaundice Syndrome	4	56	0	2
Neonatal Tetanus	0	0	0	0
Acute Meningitis 2005	0	1	0	1
Measles	15	9	0	0
Heat Stroke	0	29	0	1
SKIN INFECTION, 2005	0	0	0	0
Snake bite, 2005	0	0	0	0

Key RCH Indicators from District Rapid Household Survey (RHS-RCH) 2002-04	
% of Girls marrying below 18 years	24.5
% of births of order 3 and above	33.8
Current use of any modern method	44.8
% of pregnant women with any ANC	85.6
% of pregnant women with full ANC	16.4
% of Institutional Delivery	21.1
% of Safe Delivery	37.1
% of children with complete immunization	67.2
% of children with no immunization	3.9
% of females with symptoms of RTI/STI	10.35
% of males with symptoms of RTI/STI	12.21

Key RCH Indicators from District Rapid Household Survey (RHS-RCH) 1998	
% of females aware of HIV/AIDS	42.1
% of males aware of HIV/AIDS	72.6
% of Rural Population below poverty line 2006-07	13.22

Source: Office of the District Statistical, District at a Glance, Government of Orissa.

Inadequate Health Personnel/Paramedical Staff

There are vacancies in some of the vital posts like MOs in the PHC (N), Clerical hands, Statistical Assistants, MPHW (M), due to which the regular work is also affected. Lack of staff in supervisory level is making the programmes weaker as there is no supervision and feedback to the activities. Not only clerical and paramedical the important posts like MO I/C and specialists are also lying vacant including the PHC (New) doctors. The Medical Officer vacant post are approximately fifteen to twenty in this district.

Lack of Planning, Monitoring and Documentation

Door to Door visits by MPWs are not happening regularly (at least one village to be visited by MPW once in a fortnight). Information system and reporting is very poor at SC/PHC level institutions. While distribution of medicines and instruments were done by OHSDP for different institutions, no prior consultation or planning was undertaken at the district level. Due to absence of awareness among the community people, Malaria cases are not being properly detected and most of the cases are dealt by Quack. Timely submission of U.C. and Vouchers are not made which is affecting the fund flow to the district.

Some of the Priority Needs of the District

Training and capacity building of all staffs on programme management and National Rural Health Mission, Logistic and managerial support is needed. Incentive/Remuneration to personnels who are handling the RCH accounts at the district and block level need to be considered. Infrastructural up-gradation of health institutions at district and block level.

Civil Society Activities

The involvement of the civil societies in the NRHM is a strategic approach to get more effective result to the outcomes. In this regard, the district authorities have given them opportunities to involve in the activities related to Malaria, AIDS, training etc. Moreover, they have also been prominently supporting in RCH activities and providing service in the unserved and underserved areas with poor RCH indicators. Besides this, the

PRIs will be involved in the NRHM activities in a greater way. Through NRHM many more efforts will be carried out much more systematically to ensure greater involvement of all especially with promotion of PNDT Act, raising the age of marriage, promoting institutional delivery etc.

Current Institutional Arrangement

The district health system has been envisaged as per the norm set up for the district to achieve the objectives of primary health care, which comprises of preventive, curative and promotive health. The health system based upon the modern medical care has a wide network of health institutions starting from subcentre level to tertiary level of health care institutions. The network of the health system is such that ideally it can provide health care services at the doorsteps of the common people if properly planned and managed. But it is not happening so.

In the district the health mission is headed by Chairperson Zilla Parishad, Collector and District Magistrate as co-chairperson, CDMO as Member Secretary and members from Zilla Parishad standing committees and different government departments. The inputs to the mission are provided by the District Programme Management Unit. Zilla Swasthya Samiti (ZSS) under the chairpersonship of the Collector to oversee the management and development of Medical wing and also oversee implementation of the National Health Programmes.

There is one District Headquarters Hospital (DHH), Balasore, one District Post-mortem Centre, three Block Post-mortem Centres, six CHC, eight – UGPHC & PHC, 67 Single Doctor PHC (N), five FRUs at DHH Balasore, G.K. Bhattar Hospital, UGPHC Basta, SDH Nilagiri and Soro-II. There are also 22 Ayurveda and 30 Homoeopathic dispensaries. The list of PHC, CHC and UGPHC in Balasore district is detailed in the Appendix. It is only in the official record but at the field nothing in concrete has progressed. Everything is a distance dream for the common people.

District Headquarters Hospital

The hospital is situated at the heart of the town. It was established just after the independence of India in 1948. The colonial masters, built it not for the purpose of hospital, but for their residence. It was this building that converted into a district hospital. From that time onwards it has been functioning as the Districts Headquarters Hospital. Now, it is divided into two parts, one part consists of T.B. hospital and Staff quarters, the other part includes Chief Medical District Office, Additional District Medical Office, general patients ward, women ward, children ward, eye ward, leprosy ward, outdoor patients check room, polio drop branch, blood bank, developmental section, administrative branch and hospital canteen.

It is a referral hospital (secondary level) for primary health centres. The administrative head of the hospital is ADMO (Medical) a senior class-1 Medical officer. Both outdoor and indoor services with diagnostic facilities are available.

In 2007-2008, the total number of OPD patients treated is 2,15,230 and the total number of IPD patients treated 28,231. Total bed strength of this hospital is 239. There is a functional post-mortem centre. Besides the Administrative head, there are 12 specialists (Medicine, Surgery, Obs. & Gynae, Pediatric, Anaesthesia, Eye, Orthopaedics, Pathology, Dental Surgeon, Radiologist, Skin & VD, ENT and TB & Chest).

Table 6.8 : Balasore Hospital Budget: Salary

Unit	*Actual of 2001-02*	*Per cent*	*Requirement for 2002-03*	*Per cent*	*Budget for 2003-04*	*Per cent*
Pay	11217121	66.14	13607750	65.77	13921560	66.73
D.A.	4966088	29.28	5645146	27.28	5707839	27.35
H.R.A.	616506	3.63	1238736	5.98	1032550	4.94
O.A.	130393	0.76	146687	0.70	146890	0.70
RCM	27875	0.16	50000	0.24	53500	0.25
Total salary	16957983	100	20688319	100	20862339	100

Sources: Data collected from Office of the Chief District Medical Officer, Balasore.

Table 6.9 : Balasore Hospital Budget: Physical Facilities

Unit	*Actual of 2001-02*	*Per cent*	*Requirement for 2002-03*	*Per cent*	*Budget for 2003-04*	*Per cent*
TE	27004	2.96	31500	2.29	35500	1.90
Electricity	–	–	535	0.03	570	0.03
Water charges	200	0.02	865	0.06	720	0.03
Telephone	7000	0.76	10000	0.72	11000	0.58
MV	9471	1.03	13000	0.94	16000	0.85
OC	(1) 26000	(1) 2.85	(1) 45	(1) 0.00	(1) 50000	(1) 2.67
	(2) 162500	(2) 17.82	(2) 675	(2) 0.04	(2) 600000	(2)32.15
RR	–	–	30000	2.18	33000	1.76
Diet	399687	43.84	926350	67.61	726350	38.92
Equipment	213998	23.47	230000	16.78	260000	13.93
Medicine	55713	6.11	85000	6.20	85000	4.55
BCW	10000	1.09	42000	3.06	48000	2.57
Total Expenditure	911573	100	1369970	100	1866140	100
Total non-plan salary	1643873		3487850		3154850	
Grand total	18601955		24176169		24019189	

Note: Statement showing the revised estimates for the year 2002-03 and budget estimate for 2003-04, DDO—Name ADMO (MED/TB) Balasore.

As far as the hospital budget and the physical facilities are concerned, they are presented in Tables 6.8 and 6.9. The analysis of the above tables show that payment of total salary in an actual year of 2001-2002 was an amount of Rs. 1,69,57,983, but required amount of the total salary was Rs. 2,06,88,319 for the year of 2002-2004. The deficit amount was to the tune of Rs. 37,30,336, which gets reflected in the deteriorating working condition. The Doctors are not coming in time to hospital and practice privately. Observation reveals that they are treating government hospital job like part-time job. This kind of practice has affected the system of the service to such an extent that the extremely poor people and those who could not afford fee for the doctor have not been attended properly.

Non-plan budget includes: electricity, water-charge, telephone, motor vehicles, diet, equipment, medicine, bed cloth and building maintenance. The total non-plan expenditure in the year of 2001-2002, was Rs. 16,43,873 and for the year 2002-2003 it was Rs. 34,87,850. The deficit is to the tune of Rs. 28,43,977; it has resulted in scarcity of water, electricity, beds, and ambulances. It reflects that the basic requirements of a hospital to function properly have not been fulfilled.

Table 6.9 not only includes the details of doctors but also of patients. Through observation method, we can get the real picture. Electricity, water, ambulances, diet and medicines are the minimum requirements of a hospital, without which we cannot conceive healthy and good sanitation within the hospital. During field study, it is observed that the Balasore district hospital does not have sufficient beds. As a result, patients have to struggle to get even a bed; some of them lie on the floor and for such persons there is not even a sheet available. With regard to water, this hospital has no water facility; patients' relatives have to go half a kilometer to fetch water. Government has not provided sufficient fund for water facility. It also shows that the people are not provided even drinking water, electricity and free medicines. It is too difficult to get a drop of clean water in the hospital. Here, an interesting thing is that the hospital has sixteen ambulances maintained by the hospital itself, three of which are in good condition while the other thirteen are not functioning. For this reason critical patients have been facing acute problems. When patients need ambulance, the standard reply has been 'we do not have vehicles', it is clearly understandable that this district does not have sufficient hospitals and that they still are providing traditional type of treatment as modern technology has become a distance dream for the hospitals here. Only a very few infrastructural and technological support systems such as a piece of X-Ray machine, one operational theatre and one ultrasound machine are available. Given even such scanty facilities, people do keep coming, as they have no other alternatives. The frequency of visits of the patients, in terms of both indoor and outdoor service have been conveyed and shown in Table 6.10 and Table 6.11.

Table 6.10: District Headquarters Hospital: Yearly Patients Chart (2002-03)*

Types of patient	*Number of patients*	*Total patients*	*Daily average*
OPD Male	68756	153042	420
OPD Female	51690		
OPD Children	32596		
IPD Male	7809	22758	62
IPD Female	7478		
IPD Children	7471		
Total OPD & IPD patients	175800	175800	482

Sources: Data collected from Office of the Chief District Medical Officer, Balasore.

Table 6.11 : District Headquarters Hospital: Yearly Patients Chart for 2003-04

Types of patient	*Number of patients*	*Total patients*	*Daily average*
OPD Male	17716	89625	409
OPD Female	45717		
OPD Children	26192		
IPD Male	7669	24898	68
IPD Female	9608		
IPD Children	7621		
Total OPD & IPD patients	114523	114523	477

Sources: Data collected from Office of the Chief District Medical Officer, Balasore.

Tables 6.10 and 6.11 show the frequency of visits of both outdoor (OPD) and indoor patients (IPD). One is different from the other. In the year 2002-2003, the number of OPD male patients that had been registered was 68756 in contrast to the number of OPD, which were 17716 in 2003-2004. It shows that the number of OPD male patients has gradually declined. When the researcher seek help from district health information officer regarding data, she narrated that there is no data at all because it is newly constituted office, so we are settling it down and ask the higher authority to provide document which one can refer in future. Therefore, the data for last four years is not available.

---

* In this section the data has been collected up to the year 2004 because after 2004 there is no systematic data available in the hospital.

The number of OPD female in the year of 2002-03 had reached 57690 in contrast to the year 2003-04, when number of OPD female patient was only 45717. It also shows that both OPD male and OPD female visiting hospital has not been impressive. More or less, in the year 2002-03, the number of patients was relatively high. Gradually, there was a decline in the number of patients coming to the hospital.

The number of OPD children registered in the year 2002-03 was 32596 in contrast to the year 2003-04, when the number registered was 26192, between the two years that the OPD child patients brought to hospital, the difference is 6404. It can be ascertained from the data that the public sector health care system particularly government hospitals are on the verge of collapse. The patient registration file of the hospital reflects a gloomy picture showing a gradual decline of patients in terms of their number. It is significant to note that lack of modern technology, lack of communication (ambulance), bed strength and proper sanitation facility within the hospital are some of the causes for the decline of number of patients.

Profile of the Primary Health Centre

It is significant to note that primary health centre is the cutting edge to meet the basic minimum health requirements of the people. Primary Health Centre in Orissa is the focus of the study. One PHC has been taken as a sample of this study located at Bedipur village of the Kuligan Panchayat. The Bedipur hospital was established in 1977 as a part of Fifth Five-Year Plan development. Even after twenty-seven years of its establishment, this hospital has seen rarely any modern medical facilities, equipment, vehicles or ambulance. There is no drinking water facility available for the patients. Sanitation and unhygienic condition contribute to aggravation of the patients' pain. In the Bedipur hospital where one Medical Officer (doctor), two nurses, two assistants are posted but staff quarters are not provided. According to a doctor of the local peoples' needs and communication facilities were ignored. In fact this hospital was established at a particular area as an influential person of the area took the initiative to establish it. He was the

Deputy Collector of Puri district at that time; this position had given him which he manoeuvred for establishing primary hospital at a particular place. Though the hospital was built, no attention was given to see to it that it is convenient and useful to the common people. At the time of establishing hospital, he gave assurance that "he would provide a room for the doctor's residence" which did not happen. He passed away and his son and relatives did not allow the doctor to stay with them. And they say "what father promised you, we are not bothered about that, so now we have family and need peaceful life", therefore, they asked the doctor to stay outside their house. Government and concerned citizens of the locality expressed helplessness. There is no government land to extend the hospital and build the doctor's quarter. Those who have land in that area are not willing to donate a plot. If we analyse critically one can find the answer to the question as to how can people who are so poor will be able to donate land. They are wage labourers and depend on agricultural sector for their livelihood. Agricultural land is the major source of their income. The land that each possesses is not sufficient to maintain their family.

Again, the doctor explained, "we have fund but do not have government land for construction of quarters". To a question how they manage emergency service; the doctor said "we are not responsible for emergency service". "The Chief District Medical Officer has given a letter permitting the medical staff not to stay within fifteen kilometres radious from the hospital". It is also a fact that there is no modern English medium school where the children of doctor and medical staff can study. They, therefore, prefer to stay in the town which is twenty-five kilometers away from the hospital. Apart from it, there is a frequent shutting down of power. Due to this problem doctors and other supporting staff are not willing to stay there. Added to it, the approaching road is a road block both for medical staff and patients and also for the local people. There is only one road connecting the national highway to Bedipur hospital, which is in a sorry state, especially in the rainy season. For this reason serious patients cannot reach the hospital on time.

Table 6.12 : Primary Health Centre Budget: Salary

Unit	*Actual of 2001-02*	*Per cent*	*Requirement for 2002-03*	*Per cent*	*Budget for 2003-04*	*Per cent*
Pay	780203	65.15	901503	62.08	1192389	62.69
D.A.	387626	32.37	444558	30.61	589651	31.00
H.R.A.	21000	1.75	51695	3.56	65271	3.43
O.A.	6300	0.52	7240	0.49	8560	0.45
RCM	2345	0.19	46951	3.23	45999	2.41
Total salary	1197474	100	1451947	100	1901870	100

Sources: Data collected from Office of the Chief District Medical Officer, Balasore.

The data of the Table 6.12 shows that payment of total salary in the year of 2001-02 was an amount of Rs. 11,97,474, but required amount for the total salary was Rs. 14,51,947. The deficit amount was Rs. 2,54,473, which led to the deteriorating working condition of the medical staff. As a result medical staffs as in the case of district hospital are not coming in time to hospital and practice privately. They are treating government job like a part-time job, which is reflected in their lack of commitment and professionalism. This kind of practice has affected the system and many poor people cannot afford doctor's fee.

Other than salary there are no facilities like water, electricity, telephone, ambulance, equipment, medicine, and bed cloth.

Table 6.13 : Primary Health Centre Yearly Patients Chart

Types of patient	*Number of patient*	*Total patient*	*Daily average*
OPD Male	24648	45074	124
OPD Female	15358		
OPD Children	5068		
IPD Male	1653	5441	14
IPD Female	2032		
IPD Children	1756		
Total OPD & IPD patient	50515	50515	138

Sources: Data collected from Office of the Chief District Medical Officer, Balasore.

Table 6.13 presents the number of visits of both outdoor (OPD) and indoor patients (IPD) in PHC. One is different from the other. The number of OPD male patients registered was 24,648, the number of female patients was 15,358 and the number of children being registered was 5,068. The total number of patients belonging to OPD categories was 45,074 and daily average work out to 124. The number of IPD male patients registered was 1,653, female being 2,032, children being 1,756 and total patients of IPD being 5,441. The daily average of IPD patients works out to 14 in the same year. On the other hand, total IPD patients chart shows a figure of 50,515 in terms of number of patients with the daily average number of patients registered being 138.

Table 6.14 : Primary Health Centre Yearly Patients Chart

Types of patient	*Number of patient*	*Total patient*	*Daily average*
OPD Male	22302	43633	119
OPD Female	16068		
OPD Children	5263		
IPD Male	1956	5614	15
IPD Female	2326		
IPD Children	1332		
Total OPD & IPD patient	49247	49247	134

Sources: Data collected from Office of the Chief District Medical Officer, Balasore.

The yearly PHC patients chart presents the types of patient in terms of OPD and IPD. (See Table 6.14). Both the categories namely OPD and IPD consist of male, female and children. Here, the number of OPD male patients registered was 22,302, of female patients it was 16,068 and the child patients 5,263. Similarly, the IPD male patients registered is 1,956, female 2,326 and of child patients it was 1,332. Total number of OPD patients is 43,633. The daily average of the patients 119 and IPD total number of patients registered in the same year 5,614, daily average works out to 15. The total number of patients belonging to both OPD and IPD category was 49,247, daily average come around 134.

Tables 6.13 and 6.14 have shown the total number of OPD patients as 45,074 and total OPD patients' number was 43,633. It seems that the number of patients coming to government hospitals is decreasing. To know the causes of it one has to examine why people are not interested to come to government hospital. There are certain causes which are more relevant and need to be analyzed with case study.

Field Findings

The researcher as mentioned earlier collected the data from 238 patients visiting the primary health centre during the field study. The response of these patients provides an insight into the working of the primary health system in Orissa which is given below.

Table 6.15 : Patients Visiting: Sex-wise

Sex	*Respondents*	*Percentage*
Male	142	59.66
Female	96	40.33

From the total respondents of 238, 142 (59.66 per cent) respondents belong to the male category and 96 (40.33 per cent) belong to the female category in different segment of the society.

Table 6.16 : Patients Visiting: Caste-wise

Caste	*Respondents*	*Percentage*
General Caste	103	43.27
Scheduled Caste	96	40.33
Scheduled Tribe	39	16.38

The study shows that patients from different social strata come to hospital. It shows that 103 (43.27 per cent) respondents belong to general or open category, it was also noticed by the researcher that Other Backward Caste (OBC) patients have hesitated to reveal their caste so they claim that we belong from open category, when we analyse the data, we club both categories in single column, 96 (40.33 per cent) are from the Scheduled Caste and 39 (16.38 per cent) respondents belongs to tribal group. Though, more respondents are from the upper strata and less from the lower strata in a place where the Scheduled Caste population is fairly high. The reason is that the Scheduled Caste people normally do not turn up to hospital unless they face severe diseases or injuries. For normal fever or small diseases they prefer to go to local unregistered medical practitioner which is dangerous sometimes because without scientific medical knowledge some persons treat the people, in the name of traditional medicine. This kind of practice could be seen in tribal villages normally.

Table 6.17 : Satisfaction of Patients

	Respondents	*Percentage*
Useful	117	49.15
Average	96	40.33
Not Useful	25	10.50

About the usefulness of the hospital Table 6.17 indicates that 117 respondents said useful and 96 respondents feel it is average and 25 persons feel primary health centre is not useful. It clearly reveals that only 10.50 per cent people are dissatisfied with primary health centre and 40.33 per cent respondents are not satisfied. They evaluated this PHC as an average health delivery institute. However, this centre does not have modern medical equipments and lack of well trained doctors. Therefore, they rate it as an average one. Here, the field investigator noticed that those who reported that the PHC is useful to them, but some are less aware and less educated about hospital facility. It is also noticed that those who responded as 'average' and 'not useful' are well informed and educated. There are certain people who never come to hospital when they get any health problem. They prefer to go for traditional herbal medicine available in their locality.

Table 6.18 : Opinion on Free Medicines in Government Hospital

	Respondents	Percentage
Yes	88	36.97
No	150	63.02

About the availability of the medicines Table 6.18 reveals that 88 (36.97 per cent) respondents are availing the facility of free medicines while 150 (63.02 per cent) respondents say that medicines are not available in the government hospital. A number of patients are going to private treatment, the reason being that they would spend anyway for medicine whether it is government hospital or private. They feel private service is better compared to government hospital.

Table 6.19 : Stages of Patients that go to Hospital

	Respondents	Percentage
Immediately	126	52.94
After some days of disease	112	47.05

Table 6.19 deals about the stage that they come to hospital. This indicates that 126 (52.94 per cent) respondents visit the hospital immediately whenever they suffer, whereas 112 (47.05 per cent) respondents decide to go only after it becomes unmanageable.

Table 6.20 : Opinion on Consult of CHW/CHV

	Respondents	Percentage
Yes	13	05.46
No	225	94.53

Table 6.20 reveals that before coming to the hospital, only 13 (5.46 per cent) respondents had consulted community health worker/volunteer (CHV) whereas a majority of the respondents (94.53 per cent) are not even aware of such a facility. This also reveals that community health worker/volunteers are not in contact with the village on a regular basis,

which is a part of their responsibility. Community health workers are supposed to create awareness among the villagers about different health related programmes.

Table 6.21 : Opinion on Medical Test

	Respondents	Percentage
Yes	8	03.36
No	230	96.63

Table 6.21 indicates that only 8 (3.36 per cent) respondents said they conduct medical test, but 230 (96.63 per cent) respondents said that PHC does not conduct any medical test, which has not yet been reasoned out either by government servants or by people at large.

Table 6.22 : About the Medicine Prescription

	Respondents	Percentage
Yes	70	29.41
No	168	70.58

Table 6.22 shows that only 70 (29.41 per cent) respondents feel that the doctor prescribes and give the medicine free. In contrast, 168 (70.58 per cent) respondents held that the doctor prescribes the medicines, but are not available in the hospital. This compels them to buy them from the medical store.

Table 6.23 : Opinion on Health Condition

	Respondents	Percentage
Fine	27	11.34
Not good	25	10.50
Under treatment	186	78.15

Table 23 reflects that 27 (11.34 per cent) respondents felt that 'their health condition is fine' whereas 25 (10.50 per cent) respondents do not feel the same due to various ailments and 186 (78.15 per cent) respondents are 'under treatment'.

Table 6.24 : Opinion on Doctors' Efficiency

	Respondents	*Percentage*
Efficient	156	65.54
Not Efficient	82	34.45

Table 6.24 indicates that 156 (65.54 per cent) respondents are quite positive about the efficiency of the doctor whereas 82 (34.45 per cent) respondents think that doctor is not prescribing proper medicine. Out of 82 respondents 15 respondents said that when doctor check them up in his private chamber, he prescribes proper medicine because he gets money for that. Therefore, 34.45 per cent patients are dissatisfied on doctor's performance in government hospital. Some of the patients prefer to have a check up in doctor's private chamber particularly pregnant women and serious patients.

Table 6.25 : Behaviour of Doctors/Paramedical Staff

	Respondents	*Percentage*
Good	34	14.28
Not good	204	85.71

Table 6.25 represents that the behaviour of doctors and paramedical staff towards patients is not satisfactory, as 204 (85.71 per cent) patients are not comfortable with the behaviour of the doctor because the level of treatment is not up to the mark, which they expect from the paramedical staff and doctor. Only 34 (14.28 per cent) patients are comfortable with the behaviour and attitude of the doctor and paramedical staff.

Table 6.26 : Opinion on Community Health Centre

	Respondents	*Percentage*
Preference	234	98.31
No Preference	04	1.68

The above question is substantiated by the findings of the study. It shows that 234 (98.31 per cent) patients prefer community health centre whereas only four (1.68 per cent) respondents depend on primary health centre.

Table 6.27 : Money paid for Medical Service

	Respondents	Percentage
Paid	86	36.13
Not Paid	152	63.86

Table 6.27 shows whether the doctors and other staff ask for money to render their services, out of 238 respondents, 86 (36.13 per cent) respondents said that the doctor and staff ask for money in government hospital whereas 152 (63.86 per cent) respondents stated that they have not been asked for money.

Table 6.28 : Treatment Provided by the Government Hospital

	Respondents	Percentage
Provided	117	49.15
Not Provided	121	50.84

Table 6.28 shows whether patients are satisfied with the treatment provided by the government hospital, 117 (49.15 per cent) respondents are satisfied with the treatment provided by the government hospital whereas 121 (50.84 per cent) respondents are not satisfied. The reasons for the later response include lack of required trained manpower, less number of bed strength in the hospital, no ambulance arrangement, and prescribed medicines are not available which compel them to go to urban based clinic than government hospital where he/she can get medicine readily.

Table 6.29 : Opinion on Need for New Hospitals

	Respondents	Percentage
Yes	213	89.49
No	25	10.50

Table 6.28 reveals that 213 (89.49 per cent) respondents felt the need for more hospitals in their locality whereas 25 (10.50 per cent) respondents are not aware of the need of any hospital at all. They are skeptical and think that nothing will happen in this locality as local politics are not people centric. It is interesting to note that these 10.50 per cent respondents are of economically sound condition. That could be the reason for their opinion formation. They say that whenever they feel sick they prefer to go to urban hospital or private clinic and sometimes to district headquarters hospital as they can afford the medical expenses. It is the socio-economic profile of the people that determines where to get treatment and where not to get.

Table 6.30 : Opinion on Kind of Hospitals Require

	Respondents	*Percentage*
Permanent	197	82.77
Big with modern medical periphery	09	3.78
Mobile unit	21	8.82
Availability of good facilities with less or no money	11	4.62

In relation to Table 6.30, this table draws our attention where 197 (82.77 per cent) respondents need hospital, but they differ so far as the socio-economic and politico-commercial culture of hospitals is concerned. Here, the study reveals that 197 (82.77 per cent) respondents feel the need of permanent hospitals, 9 (3.78 per cent) respondents prefer hospital with modern medical equipment, 21 (8.82 per cent) respondents prefer mobile unit and only 11 (4.62 per cent) respondents felt the need of hospitals with good facilities with lesser or no money to be charged from patients.

Table 6.31 : Opinion on Private and Public Hospital

	Respondents	*Percentage*
Yes	204	85.71
No	34	14.28

The response to Table 6.31 about private and public hospitals evoked a mixed response. 204 (41.46 per cent) respondents are not in favour of the services of private hospital whereas 34 (14.28 per cent) respondents are in favour of private hospital rather than government hospitals in today's context. They want public hospitals but not with the existing hospital condition in that area. They prefer public hospitals where every possible modern equipment and trained medical personnel are available.

It is to be noted that some of the respondents are women. To a question 'Which place do they prefer for their delivery?' The following were responses (Table 6.32).

Table 6.32 : Place of Child Delivery

	Respondents	*Percentage*
Home	156	65.54
Primary Health Centre	76	31.93
Community Health Centre	06	2.52
Any other	00	00.00

Table 6.32 speaks of the ignorance and illiteracy of the vast majority of the populace of this district. As a consequence of which bulk of the respondents (65.54 per cent) prefer their child to be born at their respective homes as they are not in a position to make their both ends meet. On the other hand, 76 (31.93 per cent) respondents prefer PHC and 6 (2.52 per cent) respondents prefer CHC whereas one respondent is strikingly enough indifferent to it.

Table 6.33 : Awareness of Government Health Policy

	Respondents	*Percentage*
Yes	111	46.63
No	122	53.36

Table 6.33 reflects that the wider propaganda of the Government Health Policy is in a very bad shape in this district, as 111 (46.63 per cent) of the respondents that is less than

50 per cent are aware of the facilities. But 122 (53.36 per cent) respondents are not aware about the health policy of the State and the Centre. It is also noticed that half of the respondents do not know where this policy is coming from. They merely know that government is doing something for them. There are certain health schemes provided by the Government of Orissa and also Government of India which people are not aware of. So it is the responsibility of the government to create awareness among people about their health policy. The government has had set up different line department to make awareness like water and sanitation department, health department etc. These departments are not active enough to raise the awareness of the scheme among the people.

Table 6.34 : Opinion on the Institution Responsible for Health Problem

	Respondents	*Percentage*
Government	48	20.16
Employer	4	1.68
Family	22	9.24
Personal	127	53.36
Any other	37	15.54

To the question who is responsible for the health problem, the respondents, in a large number (53.36 per cent), thought they themselves are responsible for their own health reflecting their indifference to the Government Health Policy. Forty eight (20.16 per cent) patients seem to think that the Government Health Policy is responsible. Only four (1.68 per cent) respondents think that the problem of their health is the responsibility of the employer. 24 (9.24 per cent) respondents feel that family to be the cause, whereas 37 (15.54 per cent) respondents are unaware of the specific reason amounting the problems of their health.

Table 6.35 : Availability of Financial Support to the Respondents

	Respondents	*Percentage*
Yes	11	4.62
No	227	95.37

Table 6.35 deals with resources mobilization and indicates that only 11 (4.62 per cent) respondents received some financial aid from either their salaries or pensions whereas an overwhelming 227 (95.37 per cent) respondents are still in the grip of low income needing support. This is the situation in a world where the State is retreating from its own responsibilities by not rendering any financial aid or proper medical support to majority of the populace of the society.

Conclusion

Overall assessment of working of the health system is that the extent of coordination across sectors has been different at different levels. This analysis throws the light on people's response and their perception on health issue. One common question one may ask where is the problem lying in implementing the government policy, it is simple to get the answer of this question because policy implementing agencies need to re-look their responsibility and accountability. Professional commitment has to be realized by professional body like doctors and staff of the hospital. Generally speaking, coordination at the lower levels in the field has not been good, particularly between the Health Department and the Women and Child Development Department (the ANM and the AWW). The implementation of the ICDS programme and health campaigns such as leprosy and TB are evidence of this. Collection of vital statistics has also improved due to the interaction between the Anganwadi Worker in the villages and the MPHW (F) [Multi-Purpose Health Worker (Female)] in the subcentres. However, at higher levels, the intersectoral coordination is low and needs to be improved. In some cases coordination is high because of individual initiatives and motivation.

The Government of India has been unable to fulfil its commitment of 'Health for All by 2000 A.D.' till now. In fact, primary health care services are becoming more and more difficult to obtain especially for people living in urban slums, villages and remote tribal regions. The condition of government hospitals is worsening day by day. Nowadays, in most of the government hospitals there is inadequate staff, the supply of medicines is insufficient and the infrastructure is also inadequate. The facilities for safe deliveries or abortions are also very inadequate. Given the fact that women do not even get adequate treatment for minor illnesses such as anaemia, services for problems such as the health effects of domestic violence remain almost completely unavailable. At the village level, there is no resident health care provider to treat illnesses or implement preventive measures. All hospitals are located in cities, and here too public hospitals are increasingly starved of funds and facilities. Thus there is lack of availability of government health care services on one hand and the exorbitant cost of private health services on the other. This often leaves common people in rural areas with no other option but to resort to treatment from quacks who often practice irrationally. Thus most of the population is being deprived of the basic Right to Health, which is essential for healthy living.

The Indian Constitution has granted the 'Right to Life' as a basic human right to every citizen of India under Article 21. In Article 47 of the Directive Principles of the Indian Constitution, the Government's responsibility concerning public health has also been laid down. Yet the Government is backtracking from fulfilling this responsibility. This is obvious from the fact that the Government's proportion of expenditure on public health services has been declining with every successive year.

In the background of standard setting of human rights and right to health, the study asks three primary sets of questions. The first set of questions asks: by what formal and informal processes have recent standards been established? What have been the strengths and weaknesses of those processes in different cases? The second sets of questions are: What lessons can be drawn? Which benchmarks are useful? Is there, as some have suggested, a proliferation of standards? What strategic options should private agency consider as they plan ahead? What new approaches should be explored in relation to standard setting? Should some of the resources that currently go into standard setting be focused elsewhere? If so, on what? The final set of questions asks: Which new standards are necessary and which are not, and why? Can organizations cooperate to agree on priorities and criteria? What constraints and opportunities need to be considered?

Specific Gaps Pertaining to District Health System

- Inadequate Infrastructure and Transportation facilities.
- The district has 264 subcentres and of which 87 are running in own building and 40 per cent of them require major repair. Due to non-availability of proper stay facility the ANMs are not staying and S/C headquarters and finally it is leading to compromise in quality service to the people in the community.
- There is no constant support of mobility to all Block MOs-I/C either by providing vehicle and fuel or by having alternative transport arrangement. This is affecting the supervision of the health activities in the blocks.
- The infrastructure of the PHCs and CHCs are not adequate to meet the 24 × 7 delivery service.
- The Medicine in the Kits which is provided to the HW (F) at subcentre level is not available which is interrupting service delivery.
- OHSDP has provided infrastructure and equipments, but due to non-availability of technical hands and suitable place, the facilities are not properly utilized.

7

Conclusion

Reclaiming Health: An Unfolding Struggle for Health Rights

Even with historic conceptual and institutional breakthroughs, a lot remains to be done to secure human dignity. Although human rights standards have been set in virtually all areas that touch on human dignity, normative gaps and weaknesses still exist in many areas. New normative frameworks are needed in some areas, while in others they must be elaborated and strengthened. Standard setting is a dynamic process that must respond to a rapidly changing globe and challenges that come with the emergence of new problems and conditions.

The setting of human rights standards is not a static process. The conditions of humanity that human rights standards seek to safeguard and promote are evolving concepts. New conditions of oppression and powerlessness are forever being discovered, and new challenges are constantly emerging. For example, the gay rights movement and the campaign for the rights of people with disabilities were unthinkable just a few decades ago. The current war on terror has similarly thrown up new obstacles to established norms. There is no doubt that these and many other issues require a normative response.

The struggle for and definition of human freedom and development is a continuous and evolutionary process. These issues require unceasing vigilance, revision, re-evaluation, deepening, and re-definition. Broad norms and standards must be unpacked, broken down, elucidated, revised, and may even need to be rejected and replaced by new and different standards.

The scope, reach, and content of norms must be comprehensible to their beneficiaries, as well as to those who bear the responsibility for their implementation. Vacuous, rhetorical, and vague standards accomplish little. To be effective, standards must have a clear path for their implementation and enforcement. This is an area of weakness. Institutions are responsible for the promotion and protection of human rights standards.

Given the global standard setting process, one has to critically examine weather the standards are attainable, if not at least are they reflected in the process of implementation. India, is looked as a case study, the standard setting process has a global influence. It has also set quite high standards to itself, but the realities on the ground are far from satisfactory. For research this gap between the promise and performance is an area to examine. The conclusion and cases for it from Indian experience constitute the focus of this last part of the study.

Any attempt to conform to the standards must necessarily be involved administrative measures of such magnitude as may well seem to be out of all proportion to what has been conceived and accomplished in the past. This seems to us inevitable, especially because health administration has so far received from governments but a fraction of the attention that it deserves in comparison with other branches of governmental activity. States have provided for the establishment of a health organisation which will bring remedial and preventive services to the people. But particularly the vast section of the community which lies scattered over the rural areas and which has, in the past, been largely neglected from the point of view of health protection on modern lines.

There is no gainsaying the fact that the morbidity and mortality levels in the country are still unacceptably high. These unsatisfactory health indices are, in turn, an indication of the limited success of the public health system in meeting the preventive and curative requirements of the general population. It would detract from the quality of the exercise if, while framing a new policy, it was not acknowledged that the existing public health infrastructure is far from satisfactory. For the outdoor medical facilities in existence, funding is generally insufficient; the presence of medical and paramedical personnel is often much less than that required by prescribed norms; the availability of consumables is frequently negligible; the equipment in many public hospitals is often obsolescent and unusable; and, the buildings are in a dilapidated state of condition. In the indoor treatment facilities, again, the equipment is often obsolescent; the availability of essential drugs is minimal; the capacity of the facilities is grossly inadequate, which leads to overcrowding, and consequentially to a steep deterioration in the quality of the services.

These excerpts from the field study and two major official documents like Bhore Committee Report and National Health Policy 2002, separated by fifty-six years of 'development' of public health in India, give us some idea of how health sector has fared in half a century of post-Independence India, and where it stands today. It is in such a setting that this has critically analysed, from a pro-people perspective, and from different angles and in various contexts, the state of health care in India.

One theme that emerges clearly is that the objective of universal access to quality health care, envisaged over half a century ago at the dawn of Independence, remains unrealized at the grass roots level. Health sector has effectively remained a low priority for the Indian state in terms of financing and political attention. Consequently, there has been a major and growing divergence between the policy rhetoric (Bhore Committee, Alma Ata Declaration) and actual implementation. This has contributed to the slow and inadequate improvement in health of the population, in the period of over half a century of development of health systems in India. Closely related to this, and compounding this situation has been a Techno-managerial model of health care inspired by the West, with an inability to evolve effective indigenous models and appropriate technologies, or to effectively integrate modern and indigenous systems of medicine. The system of Health planning and decision making has been highly centralized and top-down with minimal accountability, little decentralized planning or scope for genuine community initiatives; the failure of most State supported community health worker schemes being one of the most striking consequences of this study. The family planning programme has been the most dominant amongst various externally imposed priorities, attempting to reduce the poor as a substitute to reducing poverty, drawing scarce resources away from health sector, distorting the health system and alienating it from the people.

In this situation of inadequate and top-down development of public health, the impact of globalisation-liberalisation has led to an ultimate denouncement; there has been a retreat from even the nominal universal health care access objectives. Guided by prescriptions from agencies such as the World Bank, public health care is being further constricted to certain 'cost effective' preventive-promotive services and selective interventions such as Family Planning, paralleled by spiralling and unregulated expansion of the private medical sector.

This phase has witnessed staggering health inequities, resurgence of communicable diseases and an even more unregulated drug industry with spiralling drug prices, adding up to the current crisis in health sector in India in general and Orissa in particular. Along with the retreat from the goal of universal access, special health needs of women and children have become further sidelined or inadequately addressed, while important concerns like violence as a health issue remain effectively unrecognised and unaddressed.

This situation of crisis seems to be an appropriate time to place the goal of universal access to appropriate health care on the agenda, and to rebuild a social consensus on the high priority that must be given to health sector. While developing such initiatives, we can draw upon the legal and constitutional provisions for the Right to Health Care, the declared yet never fulfilled health entitlements of the people of this country. The time has come to demand closing of the gaps between entitlements and reality, while simultaneously redefining and expanding the horizon of entitlements; and to reclaim health as an essential, universal good in the framework of Human rights. Therefore, standard setting is necessary to realise health as human right.

The Medium Term Future Goal

Reclaiming health rights, demanding a system for universal access to appropriate health care, in rights based framework. Given the context which we described in detail in the study, today we face a situation that presents both a historic crisis and a unique opportunity. On the one hand, the health sector is in a crisis; on the other hand, the new National Government is forced to accept certain measures to strengthen health sector, in order to alleviate the situation. This opens certain spaces for pro-people civil society organizations to intervene in shaping of national health policy at various levels.

A contention between two paradigms as we attempt such intervention, we may keep in mind that while the health system is usually an instrument of maintaining the hegemony of the dominant social order, it can also be an arena for asserting people's claims for services and accountability, and hence people's power. In this context, in the area of health care, today two competing paradigms confront each other. The ruling paradigm may be characterised as 'Health care as commodity/ health care as safety net'. In this paradigm, citizens should generally purchase health care as a commodity (mostly from the private medical system) and the role of the state is to only provide rudimentary preventive services, and some elementary health care to the poorest sections of the population, who may not be able to afford health care in the market.

It may be noted that within this paradigm the dominant mode is the commodification of health care, and the safety net relates only to the exceptions, to certain 'non-marketisable' preventive services (e.g. immunization, surveillance) and concerning the most indigent section of the population, who would be completely incapable of accessing services in the market. Profit driven, often exploitative and irrational marketised care is the 'real face' while the safety net is the mask, which we are supposed to be gullible enough to perceive as a 'human face'; this, in a nutshell, is 'Liberalisation with a human face' in the health sector. Of course, this is somewhat idealized description of the ruling paradigm, which in practice today is unable to provide the 'safety net' even for the poorest, whom it is nominally concerned about. Therefore, right to health is still distance dream for the people, to realise this right, it requires a strong movement from the ground and that movement has to articulate the problem to the respective government.

Another part of the argument that the dominant paradigm is imposed with impressive 'technical' arguments such as cost-efficiency and macro-economic considerations, which are presented with an air of 'neutrality', though their effects in the health sector, in terms of suffering and lost lives, have been devastating in scale and depth. The technocrats claim the privilege of irresponsibility: "We are neutral" they say.—This ruling paradigm is the emergent, people's paradigm of 'Health care as a Human Right'. The human rights approach to health is of course not novel, since it had been implicit in various community-based and alternative approaches to health care during the last few decades. But with the debilitation and 'internal demolition' of the health sector, and wholesale 'takeover' by the private medical sector especially in the 'last two decades of liberalisation' of the 1990s, the need to assert the undeniable responsibility and public accountability of the state for health care, it has become imperative and urgent, leading to the current relevance of an explicit human rights approach to health. Given the deepening crisis in health sector, the coming period is likely to see a growing public contention between these two paradigms. These two paradigms cannot comfortably coexist with each other, and they will have to be publicly debated and widely discussed.

Following on this, it may be submitted that a task before health sector academics, pro-people health professionals, health activists, people's movements and developmental organisations is to strongly and unequivocally assert the position, that health care is a Human Right in all public platforms and through all means of mobilization available. As in other social sectors, such assertion can lead to widening popular support for this position, providing the basis for a people's countervision to emerge, challenging the dominant paradigm. Some policy objectives to work towards this perspective, it may be suggested that a policy goal which can work towards is establishment of a system for universal access to appropriate, quality health care as a right. Concretising this goal will of course require considerable debate within the health movement, and documents such as the Constitution of India and some international health instruments which are providing a broad framework for such discussions. A complex and difficult process of social mobilisation, policy debate and shaping of political will would be required to make such a situation even partly a reality. As mentioned above, it would not be just a narrow 'demanding of existing entitlements' but would also require a broader interpretation of health rights, with a progressive redefining of entitlements. It may be suggested that one has to work for some of the following objectives (a demonstrative, not exhaustive list), in order to move towards achieving this larger goal.

First and foremost, considerably strengthened, accountable and reoriented health sector. Such a rejuvenation of the health sector would require changes at levels of policy, structure, programmes, and processes; several of such changes that are required have been pointed out in various chapters of the thesis. Such strengthening should ensure adequate infrastructure, human power, services and supplies at various levels, restoring the basic functionality of the system and rebuilding public confidence. However, such rejuvenation would not be possible without bringing the public to the centre of the health sector. Mechanisms for public accountability would need to be put in place, along with reorientation of staff at various levels to rebuild their motivation and responsiveness.

The base of strengthened health sector would need to be a framework of comprehensive Primary Health Care including Community health workers in every habitation, much more functional and accountable Primary health centres and First referral units, combined with a range of appropriate preventive and promotive activities. The need for strong community anchoring, flexibility and local evolution of diverse models, emphasis on empowering women, role of community representation and demand generation by the CHW, and hence a strong, equitable (not top-down) linkage with the health administration system need to be considered while developing these programmes. This would need to be accompanied by a significant degree of genuine decentralisation of planning (which presupposes decentralisation of finances and power, not just responsibility), and evolving options relevant to various local situations, while adhering to the broad principle of universal and equitable access. This would be important factor to consider and before make health policy one has to give careful attention to address this problem.

To institutionalize accountability would require a legal and constitutional framework to assure health services as a right. The definition of 'essential services' i.e., the range of services that would be ensured for all citizens as a legal entitlement, has been an issue of severe political contention in all countries wherever the 'universal access package' has been defined. Once a legal right to health care is considered, the same tussle may be expected to take place in India, and the task of the health movement would be to make sure that the range of services is as comprehensive as possible and to ensure that the services required by various marginalized sections and groups with special needs are definitely included.

Progressively bringing the private medical sector under social regulation would be essential for realization of health rights in any meaningful manner. A first step in this direction would consist of legally and organizationally ensuring that this sector meets minimum standards, follows standard treatment guidelines, and observes ceilings on prices of essential health services. While such measures would be resisted by much of the private medical profession, there may be sections of rational doctors who could participate in the formulation of standards and guidelines, and could promote self-regulation. However, paradoxically, two extreme ends of the spectrum in private medical care—the luxury tertiary medical sector at one end, and the low-cost, completely unqualified rural practitioners (often termed 'quacks') at the other end, may both try to totally escape the net of regulation. The former, because it would never agree to observe ceilings on costs and the latter it may not be able to meet minimum quality criteria. However, the former may be heavily taxed and restricted to catering to a very narrow, high income clientele, while the latter could be replaced in rural areas over a period of time, by well-trained and equipped community health workers linked to the public health system. As a next step, private medical facilities that have demonstrated that they follow minimum standards and treatment guidelines may be progressively brought under the umbrella of a Universal access system and to be contracted by this publicly regulated system to provide services, while the recipient of care is not required to pay while receiving these services.

Much more effective public health support to indigenous healing systems is required, including active research on areas such as community based evaluation of indigenous healing methods and synergistic combination with modern medicine. The level of public funding for Indian System of Medicine institutions, both for care and research would need to be substantially increased to make this possible. The present paradoxical situation where a large proportion of non-allopathic doctors routinely and mainly practice allopathic which needs to be addressed, with a view to ensuring rational and accessible care to all. One option is to offer additional training in rational use of modern medicine for Primary health care to non-allopathic practitioners who want to practice allopathic at the primary level; similarly allopathic doctors may be encouraged to opt for additional training such as in Basic Ayurveda/Basic herbal medicine, to practice certain basic elements of these healing systems. The emphasis would need to be on integration of systems and creation of 'Basic doctors' who can provide a range of appropriate care especially at the primary level.

Ensuring access to essential drugs in a rights based framework, both in form of ensuring availability of the range of essential drugs free of cost in public health facilities, and stringent price control by inclusion of all essential drugs in the DPCO, are objectives to work towards in the immediate future. Promotion of generics, effective drug quality control and elimination of irrational formulations and combinations are issues already on the agenda. With India moving towards becoming WTO compliant, the demand to keep essential drugs and drugs related major health problems outside the purview of TRIPS regulations can attract broad popular support, with the potential of becoming a snapshot issue to oppose the current framework of hegemonic globalisation.

Operationalising accountability and redressal mechanisms to ensure regular civil society monitoring and inputs at various levels (village/block/district/state/national), which would be the concrete form of the public re-entering and reclaiming the health rights. Panchayati Raj Institutions, complemented by various community based organisations including women's groups could play a key role in ensuring accountability of the health system. If a community anchored village worker programme is developed, the health worker supported by a village health group could play a role in ensuring improved utilization and accountability of services. At the same time, an effective redressal system would be required to deal with complaints and denial of health care in various forms through responsive, time bound mechanisms. A genuine concern may be raised, as to whether it is realistic to expect all these, and other similar changes to materialize in the present larger socio-political scenario. There is no guarantee that the state and the political system will respond to demands and assertions of health rights, howsoever justified and popularly supported they may be. Each of the changes mentioned above would require protracted, sustained efforts. Given this scenario, what can be, and should be attempted, is to strongly assert people's Right to health care, while presenting a powerful alternative vision of a pro-people health system, through various forms of mobilisation and political action. If this gains broad and sustained popular support, the system is likely to respond and to yield health rights in certain form. Even if partial, these can become the basis for extension of rights, by further mobilisation and struggle, since rights naturally lend themselves to extension and expansion. A large, long-term vision can guide small, yet definite advances in the short-term; the Rights approach allows us to link the two. However, at some point of time the system may reach its limits of responsiveness, and may stonewall further demands. Such a scenario is likely, relating not to health rights alone, but regarding an entire range of social and economic rights, due to the congealing of powerful vested interests at national and transnational levels. By the time such a juncture is reached, the large majority of social opinion is in favour of a radical restructuring of society in order to enable popular aspirations to be met, and these popular forces are organized in a coherent form, then the stage may be set for larger transformation of the society.

Finally there are issues pertaining to acceptability and quality of health. Here, the Indian state fails totally. There is a clear rural-urban dichotomy in health policy and provision of care; urban areas have been provided comprehensive health care services through public hospitals and dispensaries and now even a strengthened preventive input through health posts for those residing in slums. In contrast rural areas have largely been provided preventive and promotive health care alone. This violates the principle of non-discrimination and equity and hence is a major ethical concern to be addressed.

Medical practice, especially private, suffers from a complete absence of ethics. The medical associations have as yet not paid heed to this issue at all and over the years malpractices within medical practice have gone from bad to worse. In this malpractice game the pharmaceutical industry is a major contributor as it induces doctors and hospitals to prescribe irrational and/or unnecessary drugs. All, this impacts drastically on quality of care. In clinical practice and hospital care in India there exist no standard protocols and hence monitoring quality becomes very difficult. For hospitals, the Bureau of Indian Standards have developed guidelines, and often public hospitals do follow these guidelines. (BIS, 1989; Nandraj and Duggal, 1997) But in the case of private hospitals they are generally ignored. Recently efforts at developing accreditation systems has been started in Mumbai (Nandraj, *et al.*, 2000), and on the basis of that the Central Government is considering doing something at the national level on this front so that it can promote quality of care.

The Long-Term and Larger Vision

Can the goal of 'Health for All' be achieved in the present socio-economic system, in the context of systemic exploitation responsible for massive poverty and structural inequities, in the broader setting of large scale global expropriation, mediated by trade and facilitated by global financial institutions? One answer would be, 'Health for All', in its fullest and most humane sense – requiring, among other conditions, comprehensive nutritional and food security (linked to livelihood security), universal access to safe drinking water and sanitation, provision of healthy housing and local environments, universal healthy working conditions and a safe general environment, access to health related education and information for all, and an equitable, gender—just social milieu, free from violence—should remain our larger vision.

While definite progress can be made towards achieving these goals in the present socio-economic situation, this is unlikely to be achieved in entirely within the globally defined, economic and social framework prevailing in India today. The achievement of a strengthened health sector, which is more accountable to ordinary citizens, is a potentially achievable goal to fight for within the existing system. Similarly, the health movement must lend its strength and voice to movements for improving health related entitlements such as nutritional services and food security, clean drinking water, sanitation and safer environmental and working conditions, which may be achieved to certain extent. Such struggles can lead to some concrete improvement in the situation of the working people, and of various deprived and marginalized sections of society. It can also be one channel for people to assert their strength, by demanding that public institutions work for them effectively. This can become one of many arenas of public organization and mobilisation, of assertion of people's power.

In this broader context, the 'Right to Health' and certain other health related rights are potentially at least partially achievable in the current human rights framework.

However, achievement of the 'Right to Health' for all, in its fullest comprehensive sense, which constitutes our larger vision, is inextricably linked with larger social transformations. Hence, the struggle for health rights, in its deepest sense as envisaged and necessitates that health activists also engage with such a larger vision and also broader struggles.

Keeping this in mind, the struggle for health rights standards must move on to link with several other struggles for the rights to food, water, education, housing, livelihood and social justice in various forms, not only because these rights are extremely germane to the improvement of health, but also because the struggle for health rights must form one strand of a much larger struggle to challenge the dominant social order. Establishing Right to health, even in a partial form, may be one of the platforms for developing people's awareness and strength, and for beginning to shape certain incipient models of the future within the present. But moving further, a broader movement needs to take shape, to present coherent alternatives in myriad spheres of life, to give people capacity and hope, to challenge the dominant system, and to nurture the tender saplings of the future, even in the harsh world of today. Only such a movement can also dream of replacing the current unhealthy and inequitable socio-economic system, by one that is far more just, humane and healthy, in the world of tomorrow.

Some of these conclusions and suggestions are made more to see the gap and bridge the gulf between high standards the international community and Indian society has built over a period of time. What is strikingly clear is that standards are emanating from the human concerns and practices are conditioned by compulsions. In such a paradox concerns have to be concretised and concrete should shape the concerns. If this is not realised the standard setting exercise will be reduced to a mere rhetoric and have no relevance to the real world and everyday life. The essence of the matter is that standard setting exercise has reached its unbelievable limits and what is needed is collective and concerted human action.

APPENDIX-I

Name of the Hospitals and Area Name in Balasore District

Name of the Block	*Name of PHC/ CHC/UGPHC*	*Name of the PHC (N)*	*Name of the Sub-Centres Under Each PHC*
1. SORO	1. Anantapur, CHC	1. Pakhar 2. Manipur 3. Dandapalasa 4. Kesharipur 5. Bagudi	Anantapur Gud Tentei Pokhar Dahisada Ghasua Kedarpur Sajanpur Sabira Madhusudanpur Manipur Wada Kudei Sarsankha Bagudi Mangalpur Mantri Singakhunta Jaleswarpur
2. BHOGRAI	2. Jaleswarpur, CHC	6. Bhogarai 7. Kakhada 8. Deula 9. Sradhapur 10. Dahamunda 11. Kamarda 12. Chande-neswar 13. Nimatpur	Dehunda Katisahi Alalbindha Deula Kalehi Mandar Sahi Kamarda Mahagab Putina Naharh Dheenda

Name of the Block	*Name of PHC/ CHC/UGPHC*	*Name of the PHC (N)*	*Name of the Sub-Centres Under Each PHC*
			Dahamunda
			Aruhabruti
			Kusuda
			Bhograi
			Rasalpur
			Sultanpur
			Jayrampur
			Sardhapur
			Fulbani
			Ranikatha
			Sanakahari
			Hoogli
			Naskarpur
			Dekakhada
			Kakhada
			Sundardihi
			Chaumi S.C.
			Sardabandh
3. JALESWAR	3. Hatigarh CHC	14. Jamalapur	Olmara
		15. Chhamouza	Hatigarh
		16. Lakhananatha	Raibania
		17. Olmara	K.M. Sahi
		18. Salabani	D.P. Pur
		19. Khuarda	Khuard
		20. Jaleswar	Shyamnagar
		21. Nampao	Baradiha
		22. Sikharpur	Teghari
		23. Paschimbad	Chafla
			Sikharpur
			Jaleswar
			Nachimpur
			Laxmannath
			Padhanpura
			M.N. Patna
			Sugo
			Kamarsalia
			Nampo
			Ikda
			R.R. Pur
			Paikauda
			Paschimbad
			G.M. Pur
			Bartana

Name of the Block	Name of PHC/ CHC/UGPHC	Name of the PHC (N)	Name of the Sub-Centres Under Each PHC
			Baiganbadia
			Gopalpur
4. BAHANAGA	4. Gopalpur PHC	24. Bishnupur	Kalyani
		25. Bahanaga	Apitira
		26. Kharasapur	Dwarika
		27. Soud	Aruhabad
			Maharudrapur
			Bishnupur
			Avana
			Ramdha
			Podadiha
			Saud
			Bajana
			Bahanaga
			Betagadia
			Sibapura
			Kasbajaypur
			Khantapada
			Naranpur
5. OUPADA	5. Iswarpur, PHC	28. Oupada	Fatepur
		29. Santragadia	Oupada
		30. Fatepur	Gadasahi
			Pratappur
			Badapokhari
			Iswarpur
			Mareigaon
			Kandagaradi
			Santaragadia
			Patapur
			Chasakhanad
			Kahalia
			Kalasuni
6. SIMULIA	6. Simulia, CHC-II	31. Balikhanda	Ada
		32. Adda	Sahigaon
		33. Kanheibindha	Khirkina
		34. Khirkona	Sungada
		35. Jamujhadi	Bari
			Kanheibindha
			Maitapur
			Purastampur
			Kanchapada
			R.K.Pur
			Andrai

Name of the Block	*Name of PHC/ CHC/UGPHC*	*Name of the PHC (N)*	*Name of the Sub-Centres Under Each PHC*
			Simulia Main
			Jamjhadi
			Anadapur
			Head Qtrs.
7. REMUNA	7. Remuna,	36. Tikirapal	Rasalpur
	PHC	37. Srijanga	Nuaparhi
		38. Inchudi	Patripal
		39. Palasia	Dharaganj
		40. Betdipur	Durogadei
		41. Sergada	Kuruda
			Bhuinpada
			Dahapada
			Chillapada
			Somnathpur
			Balia
			Makanda
			Medinpur
			Gandarada
			Kasimpur
			Kanarali
			Mandarpur
			Srijang
			Inchudi
			Patra
			Kuligan
			Mukhura
			Khaira
8. KHAIRA	8. Khaira, CHC	42. Tudigadia	Mahatipur
		43. Gandibed	Sarugaon
		44. Garsanga	Palasa
		45. Antara	Kaithagadia
		46. Kupari	Kupari
		47. Dungura	Bartana
			Haripur
			Dungura
			Garsang
			Antara
			Jalana Gandibed
			Gandibed
			Kurunta
			Sardang
			Palaspur
			Tudigadia

Name of the Block	Name of PHC/ CHC/UGPHC	Name of the PHC (N)	Name of the Sub-Centres Under Each PHC
			Dagarpada
			Makhanpur
			Sampli
			Sardhapur
			Berhampur
9. NILAGIRI	9. Berhampur, PHC	48. Sajanagaraha	Arabandhi
		49. Kansa	Tentulia
		50. Kalakada	Matiali
		51. Betakasta	Chatrapur
		52. Ajodhya	Kaduani
			Darkholi
			Asoknal
			Kalakad
			Gohira
			Bankisahi
			Naranpur
			Kansha
			Tindesh
			Radhakishorepur
			Domagandira
			Machua
			Begunia
			Ajodhya
			Maisapata
			Jadibali
			Chandipur
			Dhobsila
			Banabhuin
			Sajanagarh
			Tenda
			Jamudihi
			Podasol
			Siadiamal
			Jamudihi
			Basta
10. BASTA	10. UGPHC, Basta	53. Paunasakali	Barunagadia
		54. Singala	Kusudiha
		55. Irda	Paujsapada
		56. Santosapur	Amarda
		57. Amarda	Mathaui
			Baharda
			Nuagan
			Routpada

Name of the Block	*Name of PHC/ CHC/UGPHC*	*Name of the PHC (N)*	*Name of the Sub-Centres Under Each PHC*
			Irda
			Sahada
			Naikudi
			Mukulisi
			Singla
			Putura
			Nabara
			Raghunathpur
			Churmara
			Santoshpur
			Gudikhal
			Paunskuli
			Ambakurdi
			Pratappur
11. BALIAPAL	11. Pratappur,	58. Ghantua	Chowmukh
	PHC	59. Jamkunda	Dagara
		60. Langaleswar	B.Gadia
		61. Srirampur	Bhikagadia
			Nuagaon
			Badas
			Jamkhunda
			Baliapal
			Madhupura
			Asti
			Katisahi
			Ghantua
			Nikhira
			Srirampur
			Nepura
			Tapundia
			L. Swar
			Sankhua
			Bolang
			Panchupali
			Ratei
			Balikoti
			Kasafal
12. RUPSA	12. Rupsa,	62. Sindhia	Sartha
	CHC-II	63. Palasapur	Chak Sartha
		64. Kasafala	Dubulagadi
		65. Rasalapur	Nuasahi
		66. Parikhi	Silada
			Srirampur

Name of the Block	Name of PHC/ CHC/UGPHC	Name of the PHC (N)	Name of the Sub-Centres Under Each PHC
			Machadia Kasipada Rupsa-Hq. Haldipada Fuladi Ol-Saranga Sindhia Baincha Gopinathpur Parakhi Palaspur Gabagaon Ranasahi Hidigaon Rasalpur-S.C. Jayadev Kasba Sargaon Sasang Gudu

Source: CDMO Office, Balasore.

The following medical professionals are responsible for the following health related programme:

CHIEF DISTRICT MEDICAL OFFICER

• Overall Administration Blindness control Programme	Disability Cell Public Information Officer	NRHM Initiatives
ASST. DISTRICT MEDICAL OFFICER (FAMILY WELFARE & IMMUNIZATION)		
• Reproductive & Child Health Care	Immunization pulse polio programme	Acute Flaccid Paralysis
• Janani Suraksha Yojana	Infant Mortality Rate	Mass Media Education/ IEC
• Pre-Natal Diagnostic Technique ACT (PNDT)	Mahila Swasthya Sangha	Regional Vaccine/ District Vaccine Store

ASST. DISTRICT MEDICAL OFFICER
(PUBLIC HEALTH/MALARIA/FILARIA)

• Disaster Management/ Natural calamity	Malaria	Filaria
• Yaws	Leprosy	Panchabyadhi Chikitsa
• Vital Statistics (Birth & Death)	Disease Surveillance	Integrated Child Development Scheme
Food Adulteration Act.	HIV/AIDS	Leprosy
Goitre (IDD)	Revised National TB	
Pollution Control	Control Programme (RNTCP)	

ASST. DISTRICT MEDICAL OFFICER (MEDICAL)

• Users Charge	Hospital Superintendent	Hospital Waste Management

Source: District CDMO, Office.

The Table below shows the block-wise distribution of the various health units in the district of Balasore:

Staff Position : Balasore District : Summary of Doctors' Position of Different Categories as on May 2006

Sl. No.	*Category of Doctors*	*Rank*	*No. of Vacancy*	*Place of Vacancy*
1.	Medical Officer, !/C	Class-I-(Junior)	1	Bhograi, CHC
2.	ADMO	Class-I- (Senior)	2	(PH/M & F), Balasore (FW & Immu.), Balasore
3.	Paediatrics Specialist	Class-II	2	Hatigarh, CHC Soro, CHC
4.	Anaesthesist Specialist	Class-II	—	
5.	Pathology Specialist	Class-II		
6.	Assistant Surgeon	Class-II	12	Soro, CHC Iswarpur, PHC Manipur, PHC (N) Pratappur, PHC Saud, PHC (N) Fatepur, PHC (N) G.K. Bhatter Hospital, Jaleswar Gandibed, PHC(N) D.H.H., Balasore. Rupsa, CHC Jaleswarpur, CHC Hatigarh, CHC
		Total	17	

Summary of Staff Position of Different Categories as on May 2006

Sl. No.	*Category of Post*	*Sanctioned Strength*	*In Position*	*Vacant*
1	CDMO-Joint Director II	1	1	0
2	OHSDP (C)	31	28	3
	Staff Nurse	73	72	1
	PH Nurse	5	5	0
	Asst. Matron	1	1	0
	Technical Store Keeper	1	0	1
	Pharmacist	94	92	2
	Nursing Sister	9	9	0
	Sister Tutor	2	2	0
	Ear mould Technician	1	1	0
	Multi-purpose rehabilitation Assistant	1	1	0
	P.A. Technician	1	1	0
	Health Assistant	1	1	0
	Ophthalmic Assistant	5	5	0
	Treatment Organizer	1	0	1
	Mechanic Malaria	1	1	0
	Food Inspector	2	1	1
	Motor Mechanic	1	1	0
	Refrigerator Mechanic	1	1	0
	Projectionist	1	1	0
	Senior Stenographer	1	1	0
	Jr. Stenographer	1	0	1
	Paramedical Worker	47	19	28
	Statistical Investigator	2	2	0
	Paramedical Asst.	2	0	2
	MPHS(M)	65	31	34
	MPHS(F)/LHV	44	43	1
	Foremen	1	1	0
	Supervisor (NMS)	6	6	0
	Artist. Cum Photographer	1	0	1
	HA	1	1	0
	Driver	42	24	18
	Dai	3	3	0
	BEE	12	12	0
	Statistical Assistant	13	3	10
	Head Clerk	2	2	0
	Jr. Clerk	28	12	16
	VS Clerk	16	16	0
	Sr. Clerk	18	18	0
	MPHW(M)	223	154	69
	MPHW(F)	337	333	4
	Health Visitor (TB)	2	1	1

Sl. No.	*Category of Post*	*Sanctioned Strength*	*In Position*	*Vacant*
	LT (Path.)	20	19	1
	LT (Malaria)	13	12	1
	Radiographer (Sr.)	1	1	0
	-do- (Jr.)	6	5	1
	VDI	1	1	0
	Head Clerk	2	2	0
	Sr. Helper	16	14	2
	Stretcher Bearer	2	2	0
	Dresser	4	4	0
	Night watchman/Chaukidar	3	3	0
	Jamadar	1	1	0
	Peon	33	32	1
	Cook	21	17	4
	Gardener	2	2	0
	Attendant	180	158	22
	Sweeper	116	93	23
	SFW	1	0	1
	Kitchen servant	3	3	0
	Utensil cleaner	3	3	0
	Ambulance cleaner	3	3	0
	Dhobi	6	5	1
	Orderly	1	1	0
	Packer	1	1	0

Source: CDMO Office, Balasore.

Protocol of San Salvador

Article 10

1. Everyone shall have the right to health, understood to mean the enjoyment of the highest level of physical, mental and social well-being.
2. In order to ensure the exercise of the right to health, the States Parties agree to recognize health as a public good and, particularly, to adopt the following measures to ensure that right:

   a. Primary health care, that is, essential health care made available to all individuals and families in the community;
   b. Extension of the benefits of health services to all individuals subject to the State's jurisdiction;
   c. Universal immunization against the principal infectious diseases;
   d. Prevention and treatment of endemic, occupational and other diseases;
   e. Education of the population on the prevention and treatment of health problems; and
   f. Satisfaction of the health needs of the highest risk groups and of those whose poverty makes them the most vulnerable.

The Pan-American Health Organization (PAHO), located within WHO, promotes health in the America and implementation of these OAS instruments that recognize an international human right to health.

Bibliography

Abeysekera S., "Activism for Sexual and Reproductive Rights: Progress and Challenges", *Health Human Rights,* 1997; 2(3): pp. 39-43.

Aeberhard P., "A Historical Survey of Humanitarian Action", *Health Human Rights,* 1996; 2 (1): pp. 30-44.

Agarwale, S.N., "Rising the Marriage Age for Women: A Means to Lower the Birth Rate", *Economic and Political Weekly,* Issue 19, 1964, p. 797.

Alleyne G.A., "Health and Human Rights: The Equity Issue", *Health Human Rights,* 1997, 2 (3): pp. 65-70.

Altman D., "HIV, homophobia, and human rights", *Health Human Rights,* 1998; 2(4): pp. 15-22.

Anita, N.H., "An Alternative Strategy for Health Care? The Madwa Project", *Economic and Political Weekly,* Issue 51-52, Vol. XX, 1985, p. 2257.

———, "Health for All: A Reaffirmation", *Economic and Political Weekly,* Issue 33, Vol. XVI, 1981, p. 1363.

———, "Poor Health Services: Who is to Blame?", *Economic and Political Weekly,* Issue 39, Vol. XXIV, 1989, p. 2214.

Annas, G.J., Grodin, M.A., "Reflections on the Fiftieth Anniversary of the Doctors' Trial", *Health Human Rights,* 1996; 2(1): pp. 7-21.

Annigeri, V. B, "District Health Accounts: An Empirical Investigation", *Man in India,* May 17-13, 2003.

Anonymous, "Health-care Ethics in Zimbabwe", Lancet 2002; 359: pp. 791-2.

Archer, Sarah Ellen and Ruth Fleshman, "Community Health Nursing: Pattern and Practice", University of California, San Francisco, Duxbury Press, North Scituate, Massachusetts, 1975.

Attaran, A. "Human Rights and Biomedical Research Funding for the Developing World: Covering State Obligations Under the Right to Health", *Health Human Rights,* 1999; 4(1): pp. 26-58.

Backler, Patricia, "Will the 'Age of Bureaucracy' Silence the Rights Versus Needs Debate?" *Community Mental Health Journal* 31(3), 1995, p. 201.

Bakshi, P.M., "The Constitution of India", Universal Law Publishing Co. Pvt. Ltd., 2003.

Bal, Arun, "Medicines: Doctors and Drug Companies", *Economic and Political Weekly,* Issue 6, Vol. XXII, 1987, p. 120

Balasubhramanyan, Vimal, "Women and the burden of Child health", *Economic and Political Weekly,* Issue 9, Vol. XXII, 1987, p. 363.

Baldwin, L., de Gruchy J., London, L. (eds.), "An Ambulance of the Wrong Colour: Health Professionals", *Human Rights and Ethics in South Africa, Cape Town*: UCT Press, 1999.

Banergi, D., "Class View of Health and Diseases", *Economic and Political Weekly,* Issue 27, Vol. XII, 1978, p. 1103.

———, "Crisis in the Medical Profession in India", *Economic and Political Weekly,* Issue 20, Vol. XXIV, 1989, p. 1091.

———, "Health and Population Control in the Draft Plan", *Economic and Political Weekly,* Issues 31-33, Vol. XIII, 1978, p. 1385.

———, "Health Behaviour of Rural Populations: Impact of Rural Health Services", *Economic and Political Weekly,* Issue 51, Vol. IX, 1974, p. 2261.

———, "Health Policies and Programmes in India in the Eighties", *Economic and Political Weekly,* Issue 12, Vol. XXVII, 1992, p. 599.

———,"Health Service and Population Policies", *Economic and Political Weekly,* Issue, 31-33, Vol. XI, 1976, p. 1247.

———, "National Health Policy and its Implication", *Economic and Political Weekly,* Issue 4, Vol. XVIII, 1983, p. 101.

———, "Political Dimensions of Health and Health Services", *Economic and Political Weekly,* Issue 22, Vol. XIII, 1978, p. 424.

———, "Rural Social Transformation and Changes in Health Behaviour", *Economic and Political Weekly,* Issue 26, Vol. XXIV, 1989, p. 1474.

———, "Simplistic Approach to Health Policy Analysis: World Bank Team on Indian Health Sector", *Economic and Political Weekly,* Issue 24, Vol. XXVIII, 1993, p. 1207.

———, "Social and Cultural Foundations of Health Services System", *Economic and Political Weekly,* Issues 32-34, Vol. IX, 1974, p. 1333.

———, "Techno centric Approach to Health: Western Response to Alma Ata", *Economic and Political Weekly,* Issue 28, Vol. XXI, 1986, p. 1233.

———, "What Next in Family Welfare?", *Economic and Political Weekly,* Issue 20, Vol. XIV, 1979, p. 876.

———, "Health and Family Planning Services in India: An Epidemiological, Socio-Cultural and Political Analysis and a Perspective", New Delhi, Lok Paksh, 1985.

Banerjee, Abhijit, Angus Deaton and Esther Duflo, "Health Care Delivery in Rural Rajasthan", *Economic and Political Weekly,* Feb. 28-March 5, 2004.

Beloqui, J., Chokevivat, V., Collins, C. "HIV Vaccine Research and Human Rights: Examples from Three Countries Planning Efficacy Trials", *Health Human Rights,* 1998; 3(1): 38-58.

Benatar, S. "Human Rights in the Biotechnology era I", *BMC International Health and Human Rights,* 2002; 2(3).

———, "Dying and 'Euthanasia", *South African Medical Journal* 82(1): 35-8, 1992.

Bernier, L. "A Selected Bibliography of Human Rights and the Right to Health", *Health Human Rights,* 1994; 1(1): 110-120.

Beyrer, C. "Burma and Cambodia: Human Rights, Social Disruption, and the Spread of HIV/AIDS", *Health Human Rights,* 1998; 2(4): 84-97.

Bhore, J., "Report of the Health Survey and Development Committee", New Delhi, 1946.

Bianco, M. "Women's Human Rights and Health in Developing Countries", *Health Human Rights,* 1997; 2(3): 83-89.

Boyce, W., Koros, M., Hodgson, J. "Community based rehabilitation: A strategy for peace-building", *BMC International Health and Human Rights*, 2002; 2 (6).

Braveman P., Gruskin, S. "Poverty, equity, human rights and health", *Bulletin of the World Health Organization*, 2003 (July); 81: 439-45.

Brennan, Troyen, "Just Doctoring: Medical Ethics in the Liberal State", 1991.

———, "Human Rights Education in Public Health Graduate Schools : 1996 Survey", *Health Human Rights*, 1996; 2(1): 129-139.

British Medical Association, "The medical profession and human rights: Handbook for a changing agenda", London: Zed Books (in association with the BMA), 2001.

Burris, S., Lazzarini, Z., Gostin, O., "Taking Rights Seriously in Health", *The Journal of Law, Medicine and Ethics*, Boston: Winter 2002, Vol. 30, Issue 4; p. 490.

———, "Introduction: Merging Law, Human Rights, and Social Epidemiology", *The Journal of Law, Medicine and Ethics*, Boston, Winter 2002, Vol. 30, Issue 4; p. 498.

Cameron, E. "The Deafening Silence of AIDS", *Health Human Rights*, 2000; 5 (1): 7-24.

Chafkin, Sol., "Bashing Nutritionists: The Small But Hypothesis", *Economic and Political Weekly*, Issue 20, Vol. XX, 1985, p. 896.

Chen, Marty Dreze, Jean, "Windows and Health in Rural North India", *Economic and Political Weekly*, Issues, 43-44, Vol. XXVII, 1992, p. ws-81.

Chinitz, David, and Joshua Cohen, "Governments and Health Systems Implications of Differing Involvements", John Wiley and Sons Publication, Chichester, 1998.

Claude, R.P., Issel, B.W. "Health, Medicine and Science in the Universal Declaration of Human Rights", *Health Human Rights*, 1998; 3(2): 127-142.

"Concurrent Evaluation of IRDP in Orissa (V Round: August 1995-July 1996)", Nabakrushna Choudhury Centre for Development Studies, Bhubaneswar (mimeo), 1997.

Cook, R.J. "Gender, health, and human rights", *Health Human Rights*, 1995; 1(4): 350-66.

Cosmas, Cheka and Bergis Schmidt-Ehry, "Human Rights and Health in Developing Countries: Barriers to Community Participation in Public Health in Cameroon", *Health and Human Rights* 1(3): 244, 1995.

Curle, A., "Violence and Alienation: An Issue of Public Mental Health Medicine", *Conflict and Survival* 12(1):14-22, 1996.

Dandekar, Kumudin, and Vaizayanti Bhate, "Maharastra's Rural Health Services Scheme: An Evaluation", *Economic and Political Weekly*, Issue 50, Vol. XIV, 1979, p. 2047.

Danis M., Sepinwall A. "Regulation of the Global Marketplace for the Sake of Health", *The Journal of Law, Medicine and Ethics*, Winter 2002. Vol. 30, Issue 4; Boston, p. 667.

Dantwala, M.L., "Block Level Planning Revisited", *Economic and Political Weekly*, Issue 30, Vol. XV, 1980, p. 1279.

Das, Sujit, K., "Left Front's Health Cirens", *Economic and Political Weekly*, Issue 21, Vol. XXIII, 1988, p. 1056.

———, "Public Health: A Question of Entitlements", *Economic and Political Weekly*, Issue 39, Vol. XXVII, 1992, p. 2095.

Das, Gupta, Monica, "Health, Poverty and Development in India", Oxford University Publication House, New Delhi, 1985.

———, "Health Poverty and Development in India", Oxford University Press, New Delhi, 1996.

Dayal, Chand, "Community Financing for Primary Health Care: Report of the study", *Economic and Political Weekly*, Issue 24, Vol. XXII, 1987, p. 951.

Dean, B., Valdeavellano, E.E., McKinley, M., Saul R. "The Amazonian Peoples' Resources Initiative: promoting reproductive rights and community development in the Peruvian Amazon", *Health Human Rights*, 2000; 4(2): 219-26.

Dever, Alan G.E., "Community Health Analysis, Global Awareness at the local Level", An Aspen Publication, 1991.

Dolan C.G., Tollman, S.M., Nkuna, V.G., Gear, J.S. "The Links Between Legal Status and Environmental Health: A Case Study of Mozambican Refugees and Their Hosts in the Mpumalanga (Eastern Transvaal) Lowveld, South Africa", *Health Human Rights*, 1997; 2(2): 62-84.

Doyal, Lesley and Imagen Pennell, "Health Medicine and Underdevelopment", *Economic and Political Weekly,* Issues 31-33, Vol. XI, 1976, p. 1235.

Elahi, M., Kushner A. Doctors with "dirty hands", *Washington Post,* 2003 Aug 6; B7.

"Estimates of State Domestic Products 1950-51 to 1988-89", Directorate of Economics and Statistics, Bhubaneswar, 1991.

"European Network of Scientific Co-operation on Medicine and Human Rights, The Human Rights, Ethical and Moral Dimensions of Health Care: 120 Practical Case Studies", Council of Europe Publishing, Strasbourg, 1998.

Farmer, P., Connors, M., Simmons, J. "Women, Poverty, and AIDS: sex, drugs, and structural violence", Common Courage Press, Monroe, ME, 1996.

———, "A visit to Chiapas", America, 1998; 14-18.

———, "Infections and Inequalities: the Modern Plagues", University of California Press, Berkeley, CA, 1999.

———, "Pathologies of Power: Health, Human Rights, and the New War on the Poor", University of California Press, Berkeley, CA, 2003.

———, "Rethinking Health and Human Rights: Time for a Paradigm Shift", *The Journal of Law, Medicine and Ethics,* Winter, Vol. 30, Issue 4; Boston, 2002, p. 655.

Feachem, R. "Globalisation is Good for your Health, Mostly", *British Journal of Medicine,* 2001; 323: 504-506.

Fein, H. "Genocide by Attrition 1939-1993: The Warsaw Ghetto, Cambodia, and Sudan", *Health Human Rights,* 1997; 2 (2): 10-45.

Fluss, S.S., "A Select Bibliography on Health Aspects of Human Rights: 1984-1999", *Health Human Rights,* 1999; 4(1): 265-76.

Freedman, L.P., "Reflections on Emerging Frameworks of Health and Human Rights", *Health Human Rights,* 1995; 1(4): 314-48.

Fried, M.G. "Abortion in the United States: Barriers to Access", *Health Human Rights,* 2000; 4(2): 174-94.

Gadgil, Dr., "Planning Without a Policy Frame", *Economic and Political Weekly,* Issues 3-5, Vol. II, 1967, p. 253.

Ganesh, S., "Politics of Health in a Colliery Town", *Economic and Political Weekly*, Issue 3, Vol. XXIV, 1989, p. 122.

Geiger, H.J., "Inequity as Violence: Race, Health and Human Rights in the United States", *Health Human Rights*, 1997; 2 (3): 7-13.

George, Thomas, "Distorted Perspective on Health Care", *Economic and Political Weekly*, Issue 30, Vol. XXIX, 1994, p. 1913.

Gillespie, Stuart, "Struggle for Health", Concept Publishing Co. Pvt. Ltd., New Delhi, 1993.

Gopalan, C., "Changes to Public Health Systems", *Economic and Political Weekly*, Issue 20, Vol. XXIX, 1994, p. 1204.

———, "Health Nutrition Technology Transfer", *Economic and Political Weekly*, Issue 4, Vol. XXV, 1990, p. 223.

Gostin, L., Mann, J.M., "Towards the Development of a Human Rights Impact Assessment for the Formulation and Evaluation of Public Health Policies", *Health Human Rights*, 1994 Fall; 1(1): 58-80

Government of India, "First Five-Year Plan (1951-56) to Tenth Five-Year Plan (2002-2007)", Planning Commission of India, New Delhi, 1961.

———, "Health Series and Medical Education: A Programme for Immediate Action: A Report of the Group on Medical Education and Support Manpower", (Chairman: Srivastava), Ministry of Health and Family Planning, New Delhi, 1975.

———, "Initiatives from Nine States", Ministry of Health and Family Welfare, GoI., New Delhi, 2004.

———, "National Health Policy 2002", Ministry of Health and Family Welfare, New Delhi, 2002.

———, "National Sample Survey Organization (NSSO), Morbidity and Utilization of Medical Services", Report No. 364, Department of Statistics, GoI., New Delhi, 42nd Round, July 1986-June 1987.

———, "Report of the Committee of Multipurpose Workers under Health and Family Planning Programme", (Chairman: Kartar Singh), Ministry of Health and Family Planning, New Delhi, 1973.

———, "Report of the Health Survey and Development Committee", Vol. II (Chairman: Bhore), Delhi, Manager of Publications, 1946.

———, "Report of the Health Survey and Planning Committee", (Chairman: Mudaliar), New Delhi, Ministry of Health, 1961.

———, "Statement on National Health Policy", Ministry of Health and Family Welfare, New Delhi, 1983.

———, "Economic Survey 2000-01", Ministry of Finance, New Delhi, 2001.

———, "National Sample Survey Organization (NSSO). Morbidity and Utilization of Medical Services", Department of Statistics, GoI., New Delhi, 52nd Round, July 1995-June 1996.

Government of Orissa, "Economic Survey 1993-94 and 2000-01", Planning and Coordination Department, Bhubaneswar, 1994 and 2001.

Gray, G. "The Centre for Justice and Accountability", *Health Human Rights*, 1999; 4(1): 277-83.

Green, Andrew, "Health Policy and Planning", a Journal of Health in Development, Vol.10, No. 1, Oxford University Press in Association with the London School on Hygiene and Tropical Medicine.

Gruskin, S., Mann, J., Tarantola, D. "Past, Present, and Future: AIDS and Human Rights", *Health Human Rights*, 1998; 2(4):1-3.

Gruskin, S., Studdert D. "A Selected Bibliography of Women's Health and Human Rights", *Health Human Rights*, 1995; 1(4): 477-497.

———, "The Highest Priority: Making Use of Conference Documents to Remind Governments of Their Commitments to HIV/AIDS", *Health Human Rights*, 1998; 3(1): 107-42.

Gulcur, L. "Evaluating the Role of Gender Inequalities and Rights Violations in Women's Mental Health", *Health Human Rights*, 2000; 5(1): 46-66.

Gupta, G.R. "Strengthening Alliances for Sexual Health and Rights", *Health Human Rights*, 1997; 2(3): 55-63.

Gupta, Narendra, Pritam Pal, Madhu Bhargava and Mahesh Daga, "Health of Women and Children in Rajasthan", *Economic and Political Weekly*, Issue 42, Vol. XXVII, 1992, p. 2323.

Hannibal, K., Lawrence, R.S. "The Health Professional as Human Rights Promoter: Ten Years of Physicians for Human Rights (USA)", *Health Human Rights*, 1996; 2(1): 110-127.

Heggenhougen, K. "Are the Marginalized the Slag-heap of Globalization? Disparity, Health, and Human Rights", *Health Human Rights*, 1999; 4(1): 205-13.

Hendriks, A. "Disabled Persons and their Right to Equal Treatment: Allowing Differentiation While Ending Discrimination", *Health Human Rights*, 1995; 1(2): 152-173.

Heredia, Rudolf, E., "Social Medicine for Holistic Health: An Alternative Response for Present Crisis", *Economic and Political Weekly*, Issue 48-49, Vol. XXV, 1990, p. 2673.

Herek, G.M. "Thinking about AIDS and stigma: A psychologist's perspective", *The Journal of Law, Medicine and Ethics*, Boston: Winter 2002, Vol. 30, Issue 4; p. 594.

Heymann, S.J., Sell, R.L., "Mandatory public health programmes: to what standards should they be held?" *Health Human Rights*, 1999; 4(1): 193-203.

Heywood, M., Altman, D. "Confronting AIDS: Human Rights, Law and Social Transformation", *Health Human Rights*, 2000; 5(1): 149-79.

———, "Human Rights and AIDS in South Africa: from Right Margin to Left Margin", *Health Human Rights*, 1998; 2(4): 60-82.

Horton, R., "Violence and Medicine: the Necessary Politics of Public Health", Lancet 2001; 358: 1472-1473.

http://www.cesr.org/text%20files/actors.pdf

Huss, Carol, and Srinivasan, S.P., "Od, Health Care and Social Change", *Economic and Political Weekly*, Issue 48, Vol. XXII, 1987, p. m-161.

Iacopino, V.V., Rasekh, Z. "Education, a Health Imperative: The Case of Afghanistan", *Health Human Rights*, 1998; 3(2): 98-108.

Iles, A.T. "Health and the Environment: A Human Rights Agenda for the Future", *Health Human Rights,* 1997; 2(2): 46-61.

Indian Council of Social Science Research (ICSSR) and Indian Council of Medical Research (ICMR), "Health for All: An alternative strategy", Report of a Study Group, New Delhi, 1980.

Iyengar, Sudarshan and Ashok, Bhargara, "Primary Health Care and Family Welfare Programme in Rural Gujurat", *Economic and Political Weekly,* Issue 27, Vol. XXII, 1987, p. 1087.

Jackson, Walsh and Warren Mandon, "Health and Policy", New York, Routledge, 1979.

Jeffery, Roser, "Allopathic Medicine in India: A Case of De-professionalisation", *Economic and Political Weekly,* Issue 3, Vol. XIII, 1978, p. 101.

———, "Estimates Doctors in Delhi—A Note", *Economic and Political Weekly,* Issue 4, Vol. XII , 1977, p. 132.

———, "Health care delivery system—A comment", *Economic and Political Weekly,* Issue 28, Vol. XI, 1976, p. 1046.

———, "New Pattern of Health Sector Aid", *Economic and Political Weekly,* Issue 7, Vol. XVII, 1982, p. 1495.

Jesanani, Amar, "Repression of Health Professional", *Economic and Political Weekly,* Issue 40, Vol. XXVI, 1991, p. 2290.

———, "Limits of Empowerment: Women in Rural Health Care", *Economic and Political Weekly,* Issue 20, Vol. XXV, 1990, p. 1098.

———, "Medicine at Risk: Health Professional as Abuser and Victim", *Economic and Political Weekly,* Issue 29, Vol. XXIV, 1989, p. 1638.

Jha, Petal. "Improving the Health of the Global Poor, Science", 2002; 295:2036-2039.

Jochnick, C. "The Human Rights Challenge to Global Poverty", *Health and Human Rights,* 2005.

John, Rohde, Meera Chatterjee and David Morley, edited, "Reaching Health for All", Oxford University Press, Delhi, 1993.

Kamat, A.R., "Family Planning Programme: A Reassessment", *Economic and Political Weekly,* Issue 13, Vol. VI, 1971, p. 723.

Kanaaneh, H., McKay, F., Sims, E. "A Human Rights Approach for Access to Clean Drinking Water: A Case Study", *Health Human Rights,* 1995; 1(2): 190-204.

Kapur, Malavika, "Mental Health of Indian Children", Sage Publication, New Delhi, 1995.

Keough, M.E., Kahn, S., Andrejevic, A. "Disclosing the truth: informed participation in the Antemortem Database Project for Survivors of Srebrenica", *Health Human Rights,* 2000; 5(1): 68-87.

Kethineni, Veeranarayan, "Political Economic of State Interpretation in Health Care", *Economic and Political Weekly,* Issue 42, Vol. XXVI, 1991, p. 2427.

Kim, J.Y., Millen, J.V., Irwin A., Gershman, J. "Dying For Growth: Global Inequality and the Health of the Poor", Common Courage Press, Monroe, ME, 2000.

Kirby, M. "The right to health fifty years on: still skeptical?" *Health Human Rights,* 1999; 4(1): 6-25.

Klugman, B. "Sexual Rights in Southern Africa: a Beijing Discourse or a Strategic Necessity?" *Health Human Rights,* 2000; 4(2): 144-73.

Koning, De Korrie, and Marion Martin, "Participatory Research in Health: Issues and Experiences", Sage India and Vistarar Publication, Delhi, 1997.

Kulkarni, Mani, N., "Whose Health—Women's or Mother's?", *Economic and Political Weekly,* Issue 8, Vol. XXIX, 1994, p. 452.

Kumar, Shiva, A.K. Mukherjee, Vanita Nayak, "Health as Development: Implications for Research, Policy and Action", *Economic and Political Weekly,* Issue 16, Vol. XXVIII, 1993, p. 769.

Kumble, N.D. "Rural Health" Ashish Publication House, New Delhi, 1984.

Kunhikannan, T. P., "Family Health Expenditure after Liberalism Kerala Experiences", *Economic and Political Weekly,* Issues 2-3, Vol. XXXI, 1996, p. 85.

Kutty, Raman, "Historical Development of Health Care in Kerala", Health Policy and Planning, 2000.

Leaning, J., "Health and Human Rights: the BMA's Latest Handbook on Human Rights Challenges Us All", *BMJ,* 2001; 322: 1435-6.

Leary, V.A., 'The Right to Health in International Human Rights Law", *Health Human Rights,* 1994 Fall; 1(1): 24-56.

Lehman, Edward, W., Forwarded by Amitai Edzioni, "Coordinating Health Care", Vol. 17, Sage Library of Social Research, Sage Publications, Beverly Hills, London, 1975.

Leichter, Howard, M., "A Comparative Approach to Policy Analysis, Health Care Policy in Four Nations", Cambridge University Press, Cambridge, New York, 1979.

Levy, M.H., Reyes, H., Coninx, R. "Overwhelming consumption in prisons: human rights and tuberculosis control", *Health Human Rights,* 1999; 4(1): 166-91.

Lewis, S. "Promoting Child Health and the Convention on the Rights of the Child", *Health Human Rights,* 1997; 2(3): 77-82.

Listorti, James, A., "Environmental Health Components for Water Supply, Sanitation, and Urban Projects", The World Bank, Washington DC., 1990.

Loff, B., Heywood M. "Patents on Drugs: Manufacturing Scarcity or Advancing Health?" *The Journal of Law, Medicine and Ethics,* Boston: Winter 2002. Vol. 30, Issue 4; p. 621.

Logie, D., Rowson, M. "Poverty and Health: Debt Relief Could Help Achieve Human Rights Objectives", *Health Human Rights,* 1998; 3(2): 82-97.

Maantay, J. Zoning "Law, Health, and Environmental Justice: What's the connection?" *The Journal of Law, Medicine and Ethics,* Boston: Winter 2002. Vol. 30, Issue 4; p. 572.

Mabry, Hunter, J., "Criteria for Denying Medical Termination of Pregnancy—A Comment", *Economic and Political Weekly,* Issue 36, Vol. XIII, 1978, p. 1565.

MacDowell, E.G., "Juridical Action for the Protection of Collective Rights and its Legal Impact: A Case Study", *The Journal of Law, Medicine and Ethics,* Winter, Vol. 30, Issue 4, Boston, 2002, p. 644.

Madan, T.N., "Who Chooses Modern Medicine and Why", *Economic and Political Weekly,* Issue 37, Vol. IV, 1969, p. 1475.

Maddocks I., "Evolution of the Physicians' Peace Movement: a Historical Perspective", *Health Human Rights,* 1996; 2 (1): 89-109.

Mahal, A., Singh, J., Afridi, F., Lamba, V., Gumber, A., "Who Benefits from Public Health Spending in India—Results of a Benefit Incidence Analysis for India", National Council of Applied Economic Research, 2002.

Malini, Karkal, "Health for All: A Reaffirmation", *Economic and Political Weekly,* Issue 7, Vol. XVII, 1982, p. 249.

Mallik, R.M. and R.K. Meher, "Impact of IRDP on KBK Districts of Orissa", Nabakrushna Choudhury Centre for Development Studies, Bhubaneswar (mimeo), 1999.

Mankad, Dhrub, "Health Under Capitalism", *Economic and Political Weekly,* Issue 5, Vol. XXII, 1987, p. 184.

Mann, J., Gruskin, S., Grodin, M., Annas, G. (eds.), "Health and Human Rights", Routledge, New York, NY, 1999.

———, "Dignity and Health: The UDHR's Revolutionary First Article", *Health Human Rights,* 1998; 3(2): 30-38.

———, "Human rights and the new public health", *Health Human Rights,* 1995; 1(3): 229-33.

———, "Health and Human Rights: Broadening the Agenda for Health Professionals", *Health Human Rights,* 1996; 2(1): 1-5.

Mann, J.M., Gostin, L., Gruskin, S., Brennan, T., Lazzarini, Z., Fineberg, H.V. "Health and Human Rights", *Health Human Rights,* 1994 Fall; 1(1): 6-23.

Mann, J.M., "AIDS and Human Rights: Where do we go from here?" *Health Human Rights,* 1998; 3(1): 143-9.

Marc, Rushikesh, M., "Health Manpower Strategies for Rural Health Services: India and China", *Economic and Political Weekly,* Issue 31-33, Vol. XI, 1976, p.1253.

Marks, S., "The Evolving Field of Health and Human Rights: Issues and Methods", *Journal of Law, Medicine and Ethics* 2002; 30: 739-754.

Marks, S., "Common Strategies for Health and Human Rights: From Theory to Practice", *Health Human Rights,* 1997; 2 (3): 95-104.

———, "The Evolving Field of Health and Human Rights: Issues and Methods", *The Journal of Law, Medicine and Ethics,* Boston: Winter 2002, Vol. 30, Issue 4; p. 739.

Meher, R. K., "Development Disparities in a Backward Region—A District Level Analysis", A.P.H. Publishing Corporation, New Delhi, 1999.

Miller, A.M., Rosga, A., Satterthwaite, M. "Health, Human Rights and Lesbian Existence", *Health Human Rights,* 1995; 1(4): 428-448.

———, "Sexual but not Reproductive: Exploring the Junction and Disjunction of Sexual and Reproductive Rights", *Health Human Rights,* 2000; 4(2): 68-109.

Mishra, G., "Development Policy and Planning", *Economic and Political Weekly,* Issue 21, Vol. IV, 1969, p. 879.

Misra, G., Mahal, A., Shah, R. "Protecting the Rights of Sex Workers: the Indian Experience", *Health Human Rights,* 2000; 5(1): 88-115.

Moore, K., Randolph, K., Toubia, N., Kirberger, E. "The Synergistic Relationship Between Health and Human Rights: A Case Study Using Female Genital Mutilation", *Health Human Rights,* 1997; 2(2): 137-46.

Mrs. Swaraj, Sushma, "Memorandum—Independent Commission on Health in India", *Health for the Millions,* June-Sep, Vols. 29 and 30, Nos. 2 and 3, 2003.

Muraleedharan, V. R., "When is Access to Health Equal? Some Public Policy Issues", *Economic and Political Weekly,* Issue 25, Vol. XXVIII, 1993, p. 1291.

N. Chaudhury, Jeffrey Hammer, Halsey Rogers, "Teacher and Health Care Provider Absence: A multi-country study Development Research Group", World Bank, Washington, June 2004.

Nag, Mani, "Political Awareness as a Factor in Accessibility of Health Services", *Economic and Political Weekly,* Issue 8, Vol. XXIV, 1989, p. 417.

Nandraj, Sunil, "Beyond the Law and the Lord: Quality of Private Health Care", *Economic and Political Weekly*, Issue 27, Vol. XXIX, 1994, p. 1680.

Navarro, Vicente, "International Journal of Health", Vol. 33, Number 1, Baywood Publishing Company, Inc, 2003.

Ngwena, C. "The Recognition of Access to Health Care as a Human Right in South Africa: Is it Enough?", *Health Human Rights*, 2000; 5(1): 26-44.

Nitcher, Mark, "Community Health Worker Scheme", *Economic and Political Weekly*, Issue 1, Vol. XV, 1980, p. 37.

Niveau, G., Ummel, M., Harding, T. "Human Rights Aspects of Trans-sexualism", *Health Human Rights*, 1999; 4(1): 134-64.

Norman, Daniels, "Just Health Care", Cambridge University Press, Cambridge, London, 1985.

Pachauri, Saroj, edited., "Non Governmental Approaches to Community Health", Ford Foundation, New Delhi, Sage Publication, 1997.

Padma, Prakash, "New Approach to Women Health: Means to End?", *Economic and Political Weekly*, Issue 51, Vol. XXVIII, 1993, p. 2783.

———, "Changing Priorities in Health Care", *Economic and Political Weekly*, Issue 12, Vol. XXIX, 1994, p. 661.

Padmanabham, V.T., "Health Hazards are at Plants", *Economic and Political Weekly*, Issue 50, Vol. XXII, 1987, p. 2197.

Panikar, P.G.K., "Financial Health Care in China: Implications of Some Recent Development", *Economic and Political Weekly*, Issue 16, Vol. XXI, 1986, p. 706.

———, "Resources not the Constraint on Health Improvement: A case study of Kerala", *Economic and Political Weekly*, Issue 44, Vol. XIV, 1979, p. 1803.

———, "Sexual Rights: Concepts and Action", *Health Human Rights*, 1997; 2(3): 31-37.

Petchesky, R.P. "Rights and Needs: Rethinking the Connections in Debates Over Reproductive and Sexual Rights", *Health Human Rights*, 2000; 4(2): 17-29.

Phukan, Niranjan, "Class Structure and Social Philosophy in Health Care", *Economic and Political Weekly*, Issue 33, Vol. XXVIII, 1993, p. 1688.

Piot, P., Timberlake, S., "HIV/AIDS and human rights: continued commitment in the second decade", *Health Human Rights*, 1998; 3(1): 1-6.

Poitevin, Guy, "Primary Health Care as a Gender Issue", *Economic and Political Weekly*, Issue 44, Vol. XXIII, 1988, p. ws-65.

Prabha, Ramalingaswami, "Women's Access to Health Care", *Economic and Political Weekly*, Issue 27, Vol. XXII, 1987, p. 1075.

Purohit, Brijesh, C. Siddiqui, Tasleem, A., "Utilisation of Health Services of India", *Economic and Political Weekly*, Issue 18, Vol. XXIX, 1994, p. 1071.

Qadeer, Imrana, "Reshaping Health Services: A Note on Draft Plan on Rural Health Services", *Economic and Political Weekly*, Issue 23, Vol. XII, 1977, p. 926.

Rahman, A., Pine R.N. "An International Human Right to Reproductive Health Care: Toward Definition and Accountability", *Health Human Rights*, 1995; 1(4): 400-27.

Rane, Wishvas, "Society and Medicine: Bridging the Unfortunate Gap", *Economic and Political Weekly*, Issue 5, Vol. XXVII, 1992, p. 191.

Rao, Bhasker, N., and Ramesh Kanabargi, "Criteria for Denying Medical Termination of Pregnancy", *Economic and Political Weekly*, Issue 48, Vol. XII, 1977, p. 1985.

Rao, J.V.R., and H.S. Verma, "Secularity Correlates and Health Practices Adoption", *Economic and Political Weekly*, Issue 46-47, Vol. II, 1969, p. 1785.

Rao, Mohan, "Health and Structural Adjustment: Major Shifts at Policy Level", *Economic and Political Weekly*, Issue 20, Vol. XXX, 1995, p. 1156.

Rawls, J. "A theory of justice" (revised edition), Oxford University Press, Oxford, 1999.

Reddy, P.H., "Resources not the Constraint on Health Improvement: A Comment", *Economic and Political Weekly*, Issue 2, Vol. XV, 1980, p. 123.

Robinson, M. "The Universal Declaration of Human Rights: Hope and History", *Health Human Rights*, 1998; 3(2): 27-29.

Rosenthal, E., Bauer, E., Hayden, M.F., Holley, A., "Implementing the right to community integration for children with disabilities in Russia: a human rights framework for international action", *Health Human Rights,* 1999; 4(1): 82-113.

Roy, T.K., Sumati Kulkarni, Y. Vaidehi, "Social Inequalities in Health and Nutrition in Selected States", *Economic and Political Weekly,* Feb. 14-20, 2004.

Sadik, N. "Progress in Protecting Reproductive Rights and Promoting Reproductive Health: Five Years Since Cairo", *Health Human Rights,* 2000; 4(2): 7-15.

Sandor, J. "Reproductive Rights in Hungarian Law: A New Right to Assisted Procreation?" *Health Human Rights,* 2000; 4(2): 196-218.

Sen, Amartya and Sunil Sengupta, "Malnutrition of Rural Children and the Sex Bias", *Economic and Political Weekly,* Issue 21, Vol. XVIII, 1983, p. 855.

Sen, Amartya, "Poverty Inequality and Unemployment", *Economic and Political Weekly,* Issues 31-33, Vol. VIII, 1973, p. 1457.

——— Article: "Objectivity Health and Policy", Health Poverty and Development in India, Oxford University Press, Delhi, 1996.

——— "Inequality re-examined", Oxford University Press, Oxford, 1995.

Shah, Ghanshyam, "Public Health and Urban Development", Sage Publication, New Delhi, 1997.

Shalev, C. "Rights To Sexual And Reproductive Health: the ICPD and the Convention on the Elimination of All Forms of Discrimination Against Women", *Health Human Rights,* 2000; 4(2): 38-66.

Shepard, B. "The "Double Discourse" on Sexual and Reproductive Rights in Latin America: the Chasm Between Public Policy and Private Actions", *Health Human Rights,* 2000; 4(2): 110-43.

Shinn, C. "The Right to the Highest Attainable Standard of Health: Public Health's Opportunity to Reframe a Human Rights Debate in the United States", *Health Human Rights,* 1999; 4(1): 114-33.

Sidel, V.W., "The Right to a Just and Peaceful Social and International Order", *Health Human Rights,* 1998; 3(2): 110-125.

Snow, R. "Operationalizing Cairo and Beijing: a training initiative in gender and reproductive health, The International Coordinating Committee", *Health Human Rights,* 2000; 4(2): 227-34.

Steiner, H, Alston, P. "International Human Rights in Context", Oxford University Press, New York, NY, 2000.

Subramanian, S. and Guhan, S. "India's Development Experiences", Oxford University Press, 1994.

Sukhatme, P.V., "Nutritional Policy: Need for Reorientation", *Economic and Political Weekly,* Issue 26, Vol. XV, 1980, p. 1101.

Sullivan, D.J. "The Nature and Scope of Human Rights Obligations Concerning Women Right to Health", *Health Human Rights,* 1995; 1(4): 368-98.

Tan, D., Upshur, R., Ford, N. "Global Plagues and the Global Fund: Challenges in the Fight against HIV, TB and Malaria", *BMC International Health and Human Rights,* 2003; 3(2).

Tarantola, D. "The Shifting HIV/AIDS Paradigm: Twenty Years and Counting", *Health Human Rights,* 2000; 5(1): 1-6.

Tarantola, D., Gruskin, S. "Children Confronting HIV/AIDS: Charting the Confluence of Rights and Health", *Health Human Rights,* 1998; 3(1): 60-86.

Timberlake, S. "UNAIDS: Human Rights, Ethics, and Law", *Health Human Rights,* 1998; 3(1): 87-106.

Tulasidhar, V. B., "Expenditure Compression and Health Sector Outlays", *Economic and Political Weekly,* Issue 45, Vol. XXVIII, 1993, p. 2473.

Turmen, T. "Reproductive Rights: How to Move Forward?" *Health Human Rights,* 2000; 4(2): 31-6.

Upadhaya, Purna Chandra, "Poverty and Health Condition of the Nats of Mirzapur", *Man In India,* Vol. 83, Nos. 3 and 4, July-Dec, 2003, p. 349.

Vincent, A. "A Selected Bibliography on Current Issues in Humanitarian Action", *Health Human Rights,* 1996; 2(1): 151-157.

Vincent, A. "The French Doctors' Movement and Beyond (An Introductory Editorial)", *Health Human Rights,* 1996; 2(1): 25-29.

Wagstaff, A. "Economics, Health and Development: Some Ethical Dilemmas Facing the World Bank and the International Community", *Journal of Medical Ethics,* 2001; 27: 262-267.

Waldron, J. (ed.), "Theories of Rights", Oxford University Press, Oxford, 1992.

Warren, K.S., "The Evolution of Selective Primary Health Care", *Social Science and Medicine,* 1988.

Warren, B., "Imperialism: Pionner of Capitalism", London: Verso, 1980.

Washbrook, D. A., "The Emergence of Provincial Politics: The Madras Presidency, 1870-1920", Cambridge University Press, 1976.

Watchirs, H., "Review of Methodologies Measuring Human Rights Implementation", *The Journal of Law, Medicine and Ethics,* Boston: Winter 2002, Vol. 30, Issue 4; p. 716.

Welsh J., "Freedom of Expression and the Healthy Society", *Health Human Rights,* 1998; 3 (2): 66-80.

Werner, D. "Questioning the Solution: The Politics of Primary Health Care and Child Survival", *Health Wrights,* Palo Alto, CA, 1997.

———, "Turning Health into an Investment: Assaults on Third World Health Care", *Economic and Political Weekly,* Issue 3, Vol. XXX, 1995, p. 147.

Whelan, D. "Human Rights Approaches to an Expanded Response to Address Women's Vulnerability to HIV/ AIDS", *Health Human Rights,* 1998; 3(1): 20-36.

Winston, M., "The Prevention of Institutionalized Inter Group Violence", *Health Human Rights,* 1997; 2 (3): 15-25.

Witzig, R., Ascencios, M. "The Road to Indigenous Extinction: Case Study of Resource Exportation, Disease Importation and Human Rights Violations Against the Urarina in the Peruvian Amazon", *Health Human Rights,* 1999; 4(1): 60-81.

Wodak, A., "Health, HIV Infection, Human Rights, and Injecting Drug Use", *Health Human Rights,* 1998; 2(4): 24-41.

World Bank, "Implementation Completion Report", Andhra Pradesh First Referral Health System Project, February, 2002.

———, "Implementation Completion Report", State Health Systems Development Projects II, Washington, USA: World Bank; September 2004.

World Conference on Human Rights, "Vienna Declaration and Programme of Action", Vienna, 1993.

World Health Report 2000, World Health Organisation, Geneva, 2000.

———, "Primary Health Care: Report of the International Conference on Primary Health Care", Geneva, WHO, 1978.

Yamin, A.E. "Protecting and promoting the right to health in Latin America: selected experiences from the field", *Health Human Rights,* 2000; 5(1): 116-48.

———, "Ethnic Cleansing and Other Lies: Combining Health and Human Rights in the Search for Truth and Justice in the Former Yugoslavia", *Health Human Rights,* 1996; 2(1): 58-87.

Index